The Whole-Brain
Path to Peace

The Whole-Brain Path to Peace

The Role of Left- and Right-Brain Dominance in the Polarization and Reunification of America

James Olson

ORIGIN PRESS

Origin Press
San Rafael, California

Origin Press
PO Box 151117 • San Rafael, CA 94915
www.originpress.com
888.267.4446

Copyright © 2011 by James Olson

Cover, interior design, and illustrations by Diane Rigoli
www.rigolicreative.com

Cover image by James Olson:
Flying Dutchman Butterfly, Hortus Botanicus (Amsterdam)

Library of Congress Card Catalog Number: 2010936173
ISBN: 978-1-57983-055-7

Publisher's Cataloging-in-Publication
(Provided by Quality Books, Inc.)

Olson, James, 1943-
    The whole-brain path to peace : the role of right-
    and left-brain dominance in the polarization and
    reunification of America / James Olson.
p. cm.
Includes bibliographical references and index.
LCCN 2010936173
ISBN-13: 978-1-57983-055-7
ISBN-10: 1-57983-055-2

1. Cerebral dominance. 2. Cognitive styles.
3. Peace. 4. United States—Politics and government.
I. Title.

QP385.5.O47 2011   612.8′25
QBI10-600184

First printing October 2010
Printed in the United States of America

10 9 8 7 6 5 4 3 2 1

Table of Contents

Preface

O n one level, this book is about the differing perspectives of
the left and right hemispheres of the brain, and the effects
of brain dominance on our lives and creations. But it is also
about personal and cultural transformation, especially that
which leads to peace. Peace, like everything else, is an energy,
and the two brain hemispheres process energy in radically different ways (one unifies, one separates). Because we tend to
direct our energy toward either peace or conflict, depending on
which brain hemisphere is dominant, our choice of one or the
other brain perspective—or both—profoundly conditions our
creative response to life challenges. The crucial role of brain lateralization in decision making will be clearer once we explore
the role of perspective in practical terms, such as in producing
the military-industrial-congressional complex, the drug war, and
the wars against abortion and homosexuality.

In addition to the common practice of supporting ideas by
quoting reputable scientists or scientific evidence, I frequently
turn to works of spiritual insight, some of which have interesting
origins. I refer to these works as *modern revelation*. When I use
this term, I am not referring to some exclusive truth etched in
stone tablets—quite the contrary. I believe that revelation comes
in all times and places, and through every kind of source, from
the apparently mundane to the apparently extraordinary. In this

preface, I am going to explain at some length why I have resorted not only to conventional and solid scientific-based sources, but to modern revelation as well. And I will provide some background on how this book came to be.

As a young man, I was troubled by the confusion and fighting that I saw in the spiritual community as a whole. The people with whom I worshiped were relatively peaceful, loving, and harmonious. And from what I could see, the same was true of the other religious groups in my community, as well as in most communities. But the harmony stopped at each group's front door. There was little harmony *between* the various religious organizations.

From my perspective back then, the problem seemed to originate in *certainty*. Each religious organization was certain that it—and only it—had the truth. Although this certainty held *that organization* together in harmony, it also separated the organization from other groups. From what I could see, disagreement between religions (and even local groups within the various religions) over a variety of things, ranging from what to eat or drink, to when to pray, was *separating* religious followers rather than *uniting* them and making them whole and holy.

It wasn't the differences of opinion as such that bothered me; rather, it was the *responses* to these differences. In some cases, religions were actually waging physical war over misunderstandings that originated in their holy books. The more of this I observed, the more these wars of doctrine and practice appeared absurd. (And this situation has grown worse. Religion-based terrorism has gone global.) Would a merciful, unlimited God confine revelations of divine truth to a few ancient books? Not in my opinion. Nor could I believe that God would intend the interpretation and teaching of these precious revelations to be carried out by a few flawed individuals operating in highly sectarian, warring environments. From my perspective, I saw a merciful God, a loving God, whose children were in trouble.

Yet I was supposed to believe that in the midst of all this chaos, the God who had once apparently spoken to all kinds of people was no longer communicating—no written explanations, no clarifications, no updates, and no press releases! Religious authorities said that we had been told everything we needed to know. I wasn't buying it.

I'm no rocket scientist, but it doesn't take one to figure out that if God used to inspire books, God might still be doing so. It seemed to me that there might be *modern* holy texts out there— books that could help heal religious divisions, books that might better explain what life was about in a way that made sense to us today. And so for years I prayed to be led to a modern equivalent of the Bible, Christian or not. I wanted something that had *not* been translated and retranslated and copied multiple times. Endless squabbles about which books should or should not belong in an official sacred canon held no interest for me.

An answer to my prayers for a source of modern revelation eventually came in the form of a thick (2,097-page) blue book that contained what must be the most incredibly difficult foreword ever written but was quite amazing once one got past that hurdle. I found it at a bookstore appropriately named Peace of Mind. It was called *The Urantia Book*. I was impressed by its extraordinary breadth and depth, and when it discussed topics beyond the knowledge of mortals, the explanations were all harmonious with my sense of reason. The book's stated origin was impressive: it claimed to be a message of outreach to the planet written from the perspectives of various universe personalities. The book's 196 papers covered a wide variety of subjects written by a diverse group of spirit types—angels being a familiar example. Ultimately, though, I realized that its origin was of little consequence. A tree identifies itself by its fruit, and so I set out to see what "fruit" I might find. I read every page of the book at least three times, and many of my longstanding questions were clearly answered.

Having found one such book, I started actively searching for other examples of modern revelation and began encountering people who would ask me if I had ever read A *Course in Miracles*. As promised, once practiced, the Course produced miracles. In contrast with the intellectual gifts of *The Urantia Book*, the Course produced miracles of an emotional/spiritual nature. I also found that many individuals and groups were receiving and sharing celestial transmissions on a regular basis. Some were associated with one or more sources of modern revelation; some were not. I discovered that some of the inspired communications were coming from modern-day teachers, beings who had attained extraordinary wisdom and enlightenment while in a human body, and now taught from the celestial realm. Other sources of revelation bore familiar names from a variety of ancient scriptures, both Eastern and Western.

However, we face a problem in seeking modern revelation: how to know it when we find it. And how does one go about finding it? Where does one begin? Who are the experts one can consult in such an important matter? The keepers of traditional faiths tend to be rather unhelpful; they already have their scriptures and their doctrines, and with a few exceptions they will not acknowledge the validity of other revelations. There are no simple answers to the questions posed here. Ultimately we must decide for ourselves what is, and what is not, a useful and inspired revelation. It is my belief and experience that revelation, like most everything else in this world, comes to us by degree, and will come to us to a greater degree the more sincerely we seek it.

In trying to decide what to believe, I do what most of us do when we are seriously seeking the truth: I check to see how the "revelation" fits into context. In other words, I ask myself, how does the idea or body of ideas fit into what I feel and believe to be true? I look to see how well a book or an idea correlates with what we already know, including the findings of science. Of course, scientists themselves are not always in agreement, but if a purported revelation conflicts with what seems to be sound science, I'll be looking for explanations, always keeping my skepticism close at hand.

But the burden of verification is not exclusively on science, so I also pay attention to what spirit is saying through feeling. In addition, I want to consult the body of spiritual knowledge with which I am familiar, and from which I have received valued insights. Therefore, when reading what might be modern revelation, I search for ideas that integrate with the context of my knowledge of science and my experience with spirit (through feeling)—knowing that agreement coming from a variety of sources is more likely to ensure the harmony I seek. The result of this process is a body of science and spiritual knowledge that is in relative agreement or harmony.

This process of learning is a holistic one, involving an integration of both brain hemispheres with the wisdom of the heart. The focus of this book is on integrating the two sides of the brain, because the left hemisphere needs to be integrated with the right hemisphere in order to have a strong heart connection. This situation is especially acute in our culture, in which the left brain is dominant and the holistic influence of the right brain is often suppressed. In order for our feelings and our most fundamental principles to be more closely aligned, the two hemispheres must be unified in ways that this book will explore.

Revelation tends to be associated with spiritual issues, but scientists and philosophers also experience revelation, so naturally a work of science or philosophy can be a work of revelation. An example is *The Biology of Belief*, by Bruce H. Lipton, whose ideas we will explore in this book. (Lipton, a cell biologist, has revealed a link between life and consciousness that helps us to better understand the effect our thoughts have on our cells.) Similarly, if we look at books (or at discoveries) dealing with such areas of life as health and business (and certainly many others), we can find many insights that might transform our lives and our understanding. As best I can tell, new revelations of truth can come from anyone at any time. God does not have the prejudices that we have and does not always send the messengers (or the messages) we are expecting. Rather than focus on the source when evaluating modern revelation, I focus on the ideas, while looking for truth, beauty, and goodness—qualities we would expect to find in a truly spirit-inspired communication.

And what might the inclusion of modern revelation alongside modern science in this book mean to readers? Modern revelation offers us a second, radically different perspective—a spiritual perspective that complements and enlarges the more traditionally scientific, Earth-based one. Think of how our moon-based view of Earth following the first moon landing altered our view of our own planet. In a similar way, the more mundane perspective of science is given added dimensionality with the addition of a fully elaborated spirit-based perspective. Confirmation from additional trusted sources also instills confidence, which can help power our ideas. Thus, modern revelation can sometimes provide a valuable service by helping us decide what to believe.

In working with ideas, I have two fundamental rules. The first is, *never place limits on God*—meaning, don't place limits on what God might or might not do, or love, or consider beneficial. The second is, *expect to find exceptions.* Exceptions are the rule, but that means there are also exceptions to *that* rule.

Finally, one weekend, a local *Urantia Book* organization of which I was a member held a weekend workshop in which a university professor mapped our brains based on the four-quadrant model pioneered by Ned Herrmann. Once mapped, we were lined up in the form of the letter *U*, ranging from extreme right-brain dominants on the right side of the room to extreme left-brain dominants on the left side. I found myself close to the end on the left-brain side (although my second-strongest quadrant was the right half of my neocortex, which has greatly aided me in the production of this book). This brain-mapping experience whetted my mental appetite for more.

Fascinated by the experience, I started reading about the differences between the two hemispheres and their perspectives. Sages from a variety of traditions have long taught that the greatest knowledge a person can possess is knowledge of self. What better to study, I thought, than my brain? I soon found that we have much to learn about how the two brain hemispheres respond, but that the left hemisphere is much better understood than the often-unappreciated right hemisphere. In essence, this discovery, and the recognition that we need to be using both halves of the brain if we are to achieve our highest and most urgent goals (such as peace), led me to write this book.

For more information on modern revelation,
please visit www.modernrevelation.org.

Part One

Universal Fundamentals:
Who We Are and What We See

 Chapter One

We Are Gods

The best way to know God is to love many things.
—VINCENT VAN GOGH

In this chapter, we will explore the meaning and significance of the assertion that "we are gods." Of course, for most people, the idea that we are gods is either blasphemous (to many believers) or patently absurd (to nearly everybody else). But such an idea is actually consistent with the position taken in both Eastern and Western sacred texts, as well as in the traditions of many native peoples. Both the Tanakh, or Old Testament, and the New Testament support this assertion.

Why start this book with such a radical assertion? It might seem puzzling to include this in a book that is primarily about the differing perspectives of the two brain hemispheres and how brain dominance affects all aspects of our life. But, as we shall see, this statement is a good starting point for understanding the left- and right-brain perspectives, especially since the often-neglected right brain has been acknowledged by Native Americans and others as the "God brain."

Before going further, I should point out that this assertion does *not* require that you believe that we are literally gods, or even that there is a God. Rather, it serves as a starting point for examining our role as creators (or creative managers). Because the right brain is inclusive and holistic, it gives us a vision of wholeness—which is the state we associate with God. To get the full benefit of our right brain's holistic perspective, it is helpful to be open to the idea that we not only are one with the universe but also possess some creative capacities generally associated with God—capacities that are mentioned in our familiar holy books (as well as in many sacred texts that might not be familiar to us), if only we knew where to look.

We perceive all of this and navigate the world of ideas guided by a brain that is split down the middle into a right hemisphere and a left hemisphere. In a sense, these two hemispheres are physically and functionally two brains—and, as we shall see, in many respects it is helpful to consider ourselves as having two brains, one of them dominating our functioning and our self-identification, and the other acting in a complementary or supporting role.

To get a simplistic, fundamental sense of how we navigate our journey through life, recall the image of playing a video game by using an old two-button controller. Press the left button and your screen character moves or turns to the left. Press the right button and your character moves or turns to the right. The two buttons take us in different directions, yet together they enable us to go anywhere. So do the two brains—but remember that in the holistic universe in which we live, when we go far enough in any one direction, we always come back full circle to where we started.

Of course, three-dimensional movement, whether physical or mental, is more complex than two-dimensional movement, but as we shall see, it still contains an element of dualism (or choices between apparent opposites). We face many dualistic choices as a result of having a two-part, or dual, brain and living in a dual-brain culture. One brain takes us in the direction of expansiveness and a broad, constructive, inclusive view; the other brain takes us into a detailed, deconstructive view that tends to exclude other viewpoints. A complementary pair, the two brain halves, or hemispheres, see and interact with different aspects of wholeness, and then integrate their findings.

What is important about all of this is that our perspective is under our control. One brain hemisphere will tend to be dominant—and that probably won't ever change. Nevertheless, we can override our dominant perspective for short periods of time by shifting our attention. This means that at any moment, we can choose our brain perspective. And this is a source of great freedom, because, as we shall see, choosing our brain perspective also means being better able to control our thoughts—the very thoughts that control the reality in which we live and move.

Perspectives (whether physical or mental) change as we move about in our world and take in new information. And as our perspectives change, our perceptions tend to change. Of course, as our perceptions change, our creations change: we create, or attempt to create, that which we perceive to be missing from our lives. Because what we see is often what we get, what we see at any moment—which depends on our perspective— is critically important to us.

Since we are able to choose our perspective to some degree, we naturally want to know our options. What are our choices in terms of navigation, of expanding our access to ideas and opportunities? As creator-gods, we can ultimately create an environment of peace and love and joy within ourselves that spreads out into the world. The power of creativity to transform our inner and outer environments is unlimited.

In this chapter, I'll start to lay a foundation by providing a short overview of our creative potential as "gods," or as beings with godlike powers. In chapter 2, we'll expand our foundation by looking at the subject of *wholeness*, including the four parts of which all wholes are made up. We will also look at how the left and right brain hemispheres process and interact with the four fundamental parts of wholes.

Chapters 3 and 4 provide an in-depth look at the left brain hemisphere and its interaction with the right brain, with emphasis on both the critical role played by the left brain in protecting us and the dangers inherent in our overreliance on its separative point of view.

Chapter 5 brings us into the heart of our inquiry, the right brain, which is sometimes called the feminine brain. We will see how the right brain provides a holistic, "God's-eye" perspective and a sense of oneness that is so often critically missing in our left-brained culture. We will also observe how a true holistic perspective integrates the critical information provided by the left brain into the big picture of the right.

In the remaining chapters, we'll look at how American culture has become polarized and shaped along the lines of perspective. Left-brained cultures such as ours respond to life challenges in one way, right-brained cultures respond in another, and they leave "footprints" that identify them. Starting with chapter 6, we will look at examples of how each perspective affects culture. In chapter 7, we'll focus on the military-industrial-congressional complex, where we see evidence of the left brain's perspective running amok. Chapter 8 continues our tour of the wreckage wrought by our overreliance on left-brain polarized thinking—as epitomized by war in all its forms. We'll give special attention to the drug war, but the lessons gained here apply to all types of polarized thinking. In chapter 9, we'll examine how we can achieve inner and outer peace, and why this is so central and critical to every level of our individual and collective lives.

What Sacred Texts Say about Who We Are

This chapter is designed to help you overcome any doubts about who you are. Although the evidence we explore is powerful, so too will be the resistance of your ego and the collective ego of society. The ego senses correctly that if you change this one belief—the belief that you are not a god—it will change your whole life, and so the ego will tend to act as if your very existence (based on your false self-identity) were at stake.

Let's begin by looking at both traditional and modern revelations, Eastern and Western, and see what they have to say about who we are.

References in Judeo-Christian Scriptures

In a story told in the Gospel of Luke (Luke 17:21–22), some Pharisees ask Jesus when the Kingdom of God will come. The environment where this story takes place is one in which a group of Pharisees, a major sect of Judaism at the time (a Pharisee being "one who *separates* himself"[1]), are presuming that the Holy Spirit comes to us from an outside source and connects us to God—a common belief even today. Jesus's response is that they are wrong, and he answers (in *Today's English Version*), "The Kingdom of God does not come in such a way as to be seen. No one will say, 'Look, here it is' or, 'There it is!'; because the Kingdom of God is within you."[2]

Another such instance in the Gospels appears in the book of John, chapter 10, verses 22–39. It is winter, and the festival of the Dedication is being held in Jerusalem. Jesus is surrounded by men intending to stone him to death. As they begin to pick up stones, Jesus asks which of his works he is about to be stoned for. According to the *New International Version*, the men respond that they are stoning him because of his blasphemy— "because you, a mere man, claim to be a god." Jesus's response is a question: "Is it not written in your Law, 'I have said you are gods'?" (The *Living Bible* translates Jesus's answer to the Pharisees as a statement rather than a question: "In your own Law it says that men are Gods!") In this story, Jesus is about to be stoned for suggesting that we, and he, are gods—and his disarming reply is, *Your own scripture says the same thing.*

The quotation to which Jesus refers in this story from John is found in Psalms 82:6–7. The *New Revised Standard Version* translates this as, "I say, 'You are gods, children of the Most High, all of you; nevertheless, you shall die like mortals, and fall like any prince.'" We see clear acknowledgment here that human beings, whatever their failings, were seen as gods by these biblical writers.

A Sampling of Eastern Viewpoints

In *Living Buddha, Living Christ*, Thich Nhat Hanh writes, "From a Buddhist perspective, who is not the son or daughter of God? . . . *When we are in touch with the highest spirit in ourselves, we too are a Buddha, filled with the Holy Spirit, and we become very tolerant, very open, very deep, and very understanding.*"[3]

Nithyananda, a contemporary teacher from the Hindu tradition, tells us, "I am here to proclaim that *you* are God. When Krishna says he is God and proclaims or proves his divinity, He creates a situation and prepares you to receive His message and realize that you too are divine."[4] Paramahansa Yogananda

(1893–1952), perhaps the most famous Hindu-based teacher to come to the West from India, speaks to the point even more holistically in his references to the oneness of Hindu scriptures with the Bible: "Point by point I have compared the salient message of the Bible and Hindu scriptures, and have found only harmonious unity between them."[5] From Yogananda's perspective, not only do both scriptures say we are gods, but the scriptures *as a whole* are in agreement.

Support from Modern Revelation

As discussed in detail in the preface, throughout this book we reference *modern revelation*. Central to this category are numerous works of recent times (some claiming to be of divine or "higher" origins) that seem to convincingly convey intrinsic spiritual authority. Like traditional scripture or holy books, modern revelation is best judged based on its fruit, and in the case of the works mentioned, the fruit is quite impressive.

Here we will briefly survey what some of these works say about the idea that we are gods. And as we will see, on this subject modern revelation tends to be in accord with both Eastern and Western religious and spiritual traditions.

A Course in Miracles, perhaps the most widely known example of modern revelation, describes us as God's children, returning to God. "You should thank God for what you really are. The children of God are holy and the miracle honors their holiness, which can be hidden but never lost."[6]

In *Journey Beyond Words*, a companion to the workbook of *A Course in Miracles*, we find our relationship to God expressed in this way:

Love is All That Is. God is All That Is.
You are God, and you are All That Is.
Your entire universe, in every detail,

Is just an expression of love,
Put into the dense form of energy you call your physical world.
It is put there by you out of your desire
To experience it at that level.[7]

And also in this way . . .

It is our inheritance to be One with God,
To be co-creators of All That Is.[8]

The Urantia Book describes a God that is diverse beyond our understanding, a God that manifests through many forms, a God that is not content to simply watch creation unfold but wants to participate, a God that samples, that experiences. It describes us as a manifestation of Deity that is focused on the personal experience of evolution. In other words, we are a part of God that evolves and experiences.[9]

God, *The Urantia Book* tells us, manifests through both *ascending* and *descending* parts. *Ascending* parts are imperfect in their incompletion, but evolving into perfection and oneness. *Descending* parts are perfected parts that come to less-perfected realms to help guide spirit (in all of its particular forms, including the human) to eventual perfection.[10] Jesus, for example, was descending—and hit bottom here. We are ascending parts of God. Observe how this structure fits into the flowing circular/elliptical pattern so common in the universe. It's both linear (over relatively short periods of time such as we experience here) and circular. Fundamentally, God, from Total Oneness, moves outward from the center of the universe and downward in consciousness by expanding (or separating) into ever smaller, less knowledgeable, less perfected parts. At the extreme where we currently exist, God (or *God consciousness*) is pure in spirit but lacks an understanding of the universe. From this point in the cycle, God consciousness is a relatively blank slate that through experience ascends back to perfection over eons.

The Human Soul as God

In Neale Donald Walsch's *The New Revelations: A Conversation with God* (a continuation of his *Conversations with God* series), God explains to and through Walsch that our soul is our embryonic spirit body.

> Soul is the individuation of the Divine Spirit, which is All There Is. The soul is the universal life energy, focused and localized and vibrating at a particular frequency in one specific time and space. Energy vibrating in such a highly specific way is a Singular Outflow of Universal Life. You may abbreviate that in English as S.O.U.L. . . . Your soul is who you are. Your body and your mind are what you use to experience who you are in the Realm of the Relative. The home of your soul is the Realm of the Absolute, where Divine Spirit dwells.[11]

Elsewhere, in *Conversations with God: An Uncommon Dialogue, Book 3*, God says to Walsch, "The soul is the part of You which never sleeps; never forgets."

> The soul is everywhere in, through, and around you. It is that which contains you . . . The soul is larger than the body . . . "Aura" . . . is as close as we can come in your language, in your understanding, to giving you a picture of an enormous and complex reality. The soul is that which holds you together.[12]

"The soul *is* freedom personified," God tells Walsch. "God *is* freedom, by definition—for God is limitless and without restriction of *any* kind. The soul is God, miniaturized. Therefore, the soul rebels at any imposition of limitation, and dies a new death each time it accepts boundaries from without."[13]

"Masters," God tells Walsch in *Friendship with God: An Uncommon Dialogue* (another in the *Conversations with God* series), "give themselves the freedom to make any choice they wish—and give those they love the same freedom. Freedom is the basic concept and construct of life everywhere, because freedom is the basic nature of God. All systems which reduce, restrict, impinge upon, or eliminate freedom in any way are systems which work against life itself. Freedom is not the *goal* of the human soul, but its very nature."[14]

Understanding the Creative Process

We are powerful creators. Most of our life is spent engaged in the process of creation in which we seek to bring into our lives positive feelings, thoughts, objects, and other experiences. And typically, once we obtain them, we must continue to create in order to hold on to them. Whether or not we think of ourselves as creators, and whether or not we think of ourselves as managers, life forces us to manage the creative process. Naturally, the better we understand the creative process, the more effective we can be. And what we know of the creative process is in part the result of the perspectives we obtain.

The process of creation involves energy. Energy comes in three fundamental forms: physical energy (molecule-based creations—physical objects), mind energy (thought-based creations, such as beliefs), and spirit energy (such as our feelings, of which happiness is an example). Whether we are trying to create an object, an idea, or a feeling/relationship, we are working with energy. Think of energy as the clay we use in our efforts to create; think of mind as hands that enable us to shape energy;

think of spirit as the manager, the one force that orchestrates all the others. The three energy systems are integrated and function as one. Remember that we are always working with three energies even though we might be focusing on only one of the three.

Rediscovering Our God Nature

For some reason, many of us are willing to accept that we are children of God, even if we resist the idea that we are gods. Interestingly, it might be in children themselves that we most clearly see the connection between God and humans. We often speak of "childlike innocence" (the implication being that we know something they don't), but if we look closely, we are really talking about a certain transparency to life. Children have not yet erected the defenses that adults have. They engage life in the moment. In some ways, they are as we might imagine God to be. They are usually joyful and always creative. And when they are frustrated and demanding, it is often in response to our self-imposed sense of limitation. Their expectation of having all their desires met instantaneously might seem to us just a sign of immaturity, but perhaps it is much more. Perhaps this is partly that their God nature is at the surface of who they are. Before they become "socialized," they are in touch with — even take for granted — the instantaneous nature of creativity and have a view of the universe as a kind of cornucopia of fulfillment.

To those who reside in the "God brain" (the right brain), creation and processing are instantaneous, as we shall see in coming chapters. The cartoon world where everything can happen at once — and nothing ultimately dies — is a world with which they are familiar. Is this just because they don't know better? Or is it perhaps because their identity as gods, for whom the processes of creation and manifestation seem to have no limits, has not yet been hidden by the analytic and deconstructive left half of their brain and by a culture that projects left-brain dominance? It is interesting to note that in right-brain-dominant "primitive" cultures, this magical perception of the world continues in many ways throughout life. Perhaps a fully integrated brain would allow us to be adults but at the same time not lose the qualities we perceive to be childlike—qualities that might be better described as godlike. That is a possibility we will explore in this book.

In our culture, which equates the left brain's analytic perspective with maturity and defines the "real world" on that basis, only young children seem immune from the taboo against believing and expressing our God nature. By the time we get to be teenagers, we are losing most of our conscious connection, but there is still a sense of God in us. One way in which this gets expressed is, oddly enough, through reckless behavior. Because a part of us still remembers that we are powerful and immortal, we take risks that are not acceptable to someone who is more tuned in to the frailty of the human body. As we advance through adulthood, our godlike idealistic visions are increasingly swept aside by the drive for survival and other competitive quests. However, the separation from God that arises in life as a result of cultural teachings such as fear is sometimes resolved during later stages of life. So as we age, we often start to find our way back to God, and consequently we can often see God in the more spiritually advanced elderly.

It is true that by the time we are adults, our God nature is mostly hidden, but when we give people back their love, when we give them back their freedom, when we give them back their peace—and we will look at ways to do that in this book—we see God "come back" into them. It is also true that, although our God nature is always present, it can be invisible to consciousness by being overlooked, ignored, and misunderstood, among other things. God can be invisible to us because of certain beliefs that we hold, including beliefs about the universe (or the "real world") itself. Because of the intensity of our beliefs, if we do catch a glimpse of our godliness, we typically dismiss it as an illusion. We might even see it as a threat (as a sign of insanity, for example) and fear it. Our God nature is also effectively hidden from us by a preoccupation with our daily fight for survival. And when we do get a break from the daily grind, most of us prefer some form of distracting entertainment to getting in tune with our natural capacity for creativity and joy.

Finally, when it comes to discovering our God nature, our very search for God can often be counterproductive. In our attempts to focus on finding God, we typically find that our efforts usually do not meet with success. And no wonder. As we shall see, to focus on God is to put a limit on that which is inherently unlimited. It is like perceiving the whole, or All That Is, by splitting it up into small pieces. God is found in the whole itself, not in the search.

God's All-Inclusiveness also means that we cannot split up the world into parts that are holy and parts that are profane. And that includes people. Jesus's injunction to "love your enemy" is not merely a moral command. It is also a command not to look for God in some separate place and shun God everywhere else.

In Neale Donald Walsch's book *Tomorrow's God: Our Greatest Spiritual Challenge* (a continuation of his dialogues with God that began in his *Conversations with God* series), God says to Walsch:

> Until you see God in the face of your enemy, you cannot see God at all. For, in truth, there is no such thing as an "enemy." There is only that part of you which is in contrast to another part of you. God doesn't exist for you if He exists for you only

in the things and the people you like. God isn't real for you if She is experienced by you only in those things with which you agree.

The real master is one who knows and understands that God exists in, as, and through all things. That God is absent from no one and nothing.

"If that is true," Walsch asks God, "how can some people act the way they act?"

"People act in ways that are not beneficial to themselves or others when they have forgotten Who They Are."

"Why have they forgotten?" Walsch asks.

"Because they have been *taught to*, because they have been *told to*."[15]

Chapter Two

Parts, Wholes, and Holons

Everything you do counts forever. You are an expression of the whole process of creation; you are a cocreator.

— BARBARA MARX HUBBARD, *CONSCIOUS EVOLUTION: AWAKENING THE POWER OF OUR SOCIAL POTENTIAL*

This book—and in particular the seven chapters that follow this one—is fundamentally about how the holistic perspective can lead us (individually and as a society) to both truth and healing. And it is about how the inclusive, integral, and holistic perspective must include and value even its apparent opposite— the analytical, dualistic, deconstructive perspective that is most common in our culture—the left brain's perspective.

To get started, we will introduce several ideas that will help form the basis for the applications in the rest of the book. We will look at how every whole can be divided into four parts, each of which reveals a different aspect of the whole (which means of everything, whether in the physical universe or in our minds or feelings). And we will look at the relationship between wholeness and *incompletion*—what happens when parts of a whole go missing.

We will also look at the relationship between the wholeness we all sense and seek (consciously or subconsciously) and the culture and the environment of duality in which we live our lives. We will look at the analogies between the worlds we inhabit—physical, mental, and spiritual—and how movement and change occur in each world. Having laid this groundwork in the early chapters, we will then (in the later chapters) turn to an in-depth investigation of some of the most intractable problems society faces, and discuss how we can resolve and go beyond them.

The two brain hemispheres provide complementary perspectives. The right brain takes in what is before it as an all-encompassing whole, but in doing this it can miss critical details required for making correct decisions. The left brain selects, contrasts, analyzes, ranks, reduces, and deconstructs what is before it—and, especially in a cultural context, destroys, devalues, and takes reductionistic stances. At its best, the left brain is a superb tool for arriving at what is true by separating the wheat from the chaff, and for making fine (and necessary) distinctions of all kinds. At its worst, the left brain's tendency toward abstraction can result in such total separation from the whole that the whole is either completely devalued or not even acknowledged. Therefore, correct and humane decision making requires the cooperative efforts of both brain hemispheres.

Viewed from the dualistic perspective of the left brain, the two brain perspectives appear to be opposing or contradictory. But when they cooperate in their functions (which actually overlap considerably), they can give us a seamlessly integrated (or integral) picture of reality. Nevertheless, in much of our discussion, we will look at the two hemispheres as if they were in isolation in order to bring their characteristic differences into broad relief. Seeing these differences will help us to better understand both the strengths and the pitfalls of these two perspectives, and how the left-brain-dominant culture we live in (which reflects an unnaturally isolated left-brain perspective) creates distortions that seriously affect our ability to relate to one another and to understand and cope with life's challenges.

Another way of stating these distinctions is to say that the holistic right brain is looking and working for *wholeness* (and happiness, and other things that come with it). This is a process that works to bring us together spiritually. The dualistic left brain complements this perspective by looking and working for a *lack* of wholeness, thus reflecting the whole brain's dual yin/yang structure. The left brain seeks to determine if anything is missing from a whole—obviously an essential function, as it helps to protect us from the deceptions of dishonest people or tricky situations that can be hidden behind a façade of wholeness. Thus, the left brain can assist the right brain in its pursuit of wholeness by helping it to avoid costly traps.

The importance of wholeness in our lives is a common theme in modern revelation. In one of Neale Donald Walsch's "conversations with God," God tells Walsch, "When you are not being whole, you are being less than yourself. *That* is what is meant by 'unholy.'"[1] *The Urantia Book* gives us an example of how wholeness affects our *collective* self by explaining that religion "would rehabilitate itself if, in addition to its moral mandates, it would give equal consideration to the truths of science, philosophy, and spiritual experience, and to the beauties of the physical creation, the charm of intellectual art, and the grandeur of genuine character achievement."[2] In other words, religion as it exists today lacks wholeness. It needs to integrate with science and philosophy, and with itself, if it is to achieve its goal of wholeness (and thus holiness) and escape polarization, including war in all its manifestations.

Parts, Wholes, and Holons

Subatomic particles, cells, symbols, images, concepts: all share a common design element. All are both wholes and parts, or *holons*, as Ken Wilber famously describes them.[3] Whether we shift our perspective inward or outward, toward individuals or collectives, we find a structure in which wholes become parts or vice versa, depending on our focus. But we can also go beyond space-time references, in which case the whole becomes an all-encompassing singularity. A *Course in Miracles* describes the relationship this way: "The whole does define the part, but the part does not define the whole. . . . The idea of part-whole relationships has meaning only at the level of perception, where change is possible. Otherwise, there is no difference between the part and whole."[4]

From our perspective in a universe of relationships, all wholes are parts, and all parts are wholes; that is, everything is a holon. Although we will be using the contrasting (or dualistic) terms *part* and *whole* rather than the holistic term *holon* most of the time, we will be using *part* and *whole* in full knowledge that every whole can be a part, and every part can be a whole. The difference in what we call these fundamental relationship-based structures depends on the relationship being viewed, as well as the perspective of the viewer. The right brain tends to see wholeness, and the left brain tends to see parts (typically, one part at a time)—but in truth, everything functions as a whole made up of parts, and as a part of another whole.

The same kind of relativistic principle applies to the individual and collective realms. For example, we think of ourselves as individuals, but Bruce Lipton points to the fact that each of us can also be viewed as a collective. "As a cell biologist I can tell you that you are in truth a cooperative community of approximately 50 trillion single-celled citizens. . . . As a nation reflects the traits of its citizens, our human-ness must reflect the basic nature of our cellular communities."[5] As we have seen, whether we perceive a particular thing as a whole or a part (or as an individual or a collective) depends on our perspective. As our focus shifts, our perspective shifts, and along with it, our perception of wholeness shifts. When we are focusing on something, the object of our focus tends to become our whole, and the rest of reality becomes a part or context. If the focus is sufficiently strong, context is sometimes completely ignored, a good example being religious followers who, although they seek to understand the same God—and thus share the same goal— nevertheless irrationally divide themselves by arguing whose leader or doctrine is greatest, as if God, or whatever name you prefer to use to describe the universe's organizing principle, were capable of blessing or responding to only one formulation or interpretation.

Because everything is both a part and a whole, confusion can arise when discussing parts and wholes. Families, schools, orchestras, businesses, and the like have both an individual identity and a collective identity. Up close, within them, we perceive them as collectives, but if we shift our focus and move away from them, our perceptions also shift. From a sufficiently distant perspective, when we look at these collectives (the schools, the orchestras, the businesses), we perceive them as individual wholes rather than collectives—in other words, as individual parts of a larger collective. When we remove a car's engine to overhaul it, we see the engine as a whole that has parts. Once the engine is back in the car, it's viewed as a part of the vehicle.

If a part can become a whole simply by our shifting our perspective, how can we understand one another when discussing it? How do we understand which level of wholeness people are referring to when they speak of a whole? Generally, we know from the context of the communication, so this is usually not a problem. The important thing to remember is that everything is both a part and a whole—a holon—and the identity (part or whole) we assign changes as our focus on it changes. Basically, the object of our focus (along with any whole of which it is a part) tends to be identified as a whole. On the other hand, wholes nested within the whole on which we are focused tend to be seen as parts.

Dualistic and Holistic Perspectives

What makes a perspective dualistic or holistic? Put most simply, a holistic perspective perceives reality as a *unity*; it perceives wholeness, the whole—the big picture. On the other hand, the separation of wholeness into two parts produces a dualistic perspective. We see dualism in nature when we observe the cycle of light and darkness, or seasons that bring heat and cold. Pick any quality and it can be seen to be on a continuum—from large to small, from interesting to boring, from bright to dull. Extremes of heat or cold can be life threatening or at least very unpleasant, but heat and cold in moderation are part of the variety that makes life interesting. At times, however, dualism creates such a divide between the two parts that polarization is produced, and conflict (either internal or external to us) results. This is common when the specialized functions of the left brain are allowed to run amok (either individually or culturally)—as can be seen in the extreme polarization that exists around many public issues (local, national, or international), the predatory behavior of large corporations (where corporate interests are sometimes in conflict with public interests), and the emphasis on short-term gains and narrow selfish interests in every level of society.

On the other hand, when the dualistic perspective is embraced by the holistic brain (or by the whole brain), the results can be very different. The dualistic and holistic perspectives, working together through the two brain hemispheres, can give rise to a new level of holistic integration as well as a culture that honors growth and integration. A full understanding of ourselves and our world requires both perspectives. As we proceed through the chapters, we will apply these explorations to the most urgent issues of our time and see what they tell us about ourselves, individually and culturally, and what we need to do to transcend polarized, warring viewpoints and move toward a creative, productive peace.

The Fourth of the Seven Hermetic Principles, included in the *Hermetica*, a set of primarily Greek mystical tracts handed down from ancient times, sums up the polarity of a dualistic system by saying that "everything is dual; everything has poles; everything has its pair of opposites; like and unlike are the same; opposites are identical in nature, but different in degree; extremes meet; all truths are [partial]; all paradoxes may be reconciled."[6]

As pointed out above, a dualistic perspective tends to be a *polarizing* perspective, especially where ideological and cultural issues are concerned. The left brain, by its nature, tends toward a narrow focus and thus does not see the broader wholes of which the parts are limited expressions. Thus, its inherent tendency to dissect and deconstruct is reinforced by its narrow field of vision. In this way, the relationships between parts of a whole may be missed altogether. When broad relationships cannot be seen (whether due to physical distance, cultural differences, or complex interrelationships of mind and ideas), there is less ability to find sympathetic resonance with other realities or points of view. We see cultural polarization all around us—in political parties that seem incapable of bridging the chasm that divides them, in cultural splits between segments of our population, and in our own narrow identifications. We see the effects of polarization in such signals as fear, anger, mistrust, and blame. We also can be internally polarized as individuals, as when we fail to respect one of our perspectives (inevitably, the perspective of the nondominant brain hemisphere). Polarization can provide stimulation or even a certain amount of clarity—such as what we find in a good debate—but it can also be highly draining of our physical, mental, and spiritual energy.

The Building Blocks of Wholeness

Quantum physicists tell us that we live in a universe of multiple possibilities. They have discovered that some very small particles of matter are able to completely disappear and then reappear in another place. They have found that some particles can even be in many places at once![7]

Quantum physicists have also found that the observer has an effect on the reality he or she observes. Our creative minds activate the creative energies of our world and cause matter to shift. In other words, in the process of simply *observing* our physical world, we alter reality at the particle physics level—*we literally change physical reality as we interact with it.* What we perceive depends largely on where we look and what we expect to perceive. This provides scientific support for a point I made in the first chapter: we are powerful creators. Quantum physics is revealing the mechanics of how we create.

When we focus deeply into physical matter, we find waves where we expect to find particles, and we find process where we expect to find structure. That has led some to conclude that there is no such thing as a smallest particle (or a fundamental building block, as we would ordinarily think of it). More and more, it is looking as though energy manifests in the form of a wave. What we have long thought to be particles now appear to be waves of energy that reflect light.[8]

The wholeness that we refer to as "reality" is traditionally thought to be composed of two fundamental parts: *elements* (waves, particles, molecules, plants, people, planets, etc.) and *relationships* ("seen" in connections and spacing—and felt). From the dualistic perspective of the left brain we see these as separate; nevertheless, as two parts of a whole, elements and relationships are integrated. Consequently, when we look closely, we see that elements such as waves or particles *embody* (contain) a relationship component—suggesting that elements and relationships are not as different as they seem. Depending on one's perspective, relationship may be seen as a characteristic of elements (as evidenced by the fact that relationships can be found internally in elements), or elements can be seen as a part of relationships (since elements exist in a complex field of relationship to other elements). Both elements and relationships are holons—both are parts of wholes as well as wholes consisting of parts.

Knowing that relationship is spiritual-energy based, and that spiritual energy is characterized by oneness or wholeness, it follows that relationship closely corresponds with wholeness. (And we see evidence of connection between relationship and wholeness in the fact that there is no place where relationship starts or stops. Relationships just grow closer or more distant.) We might say that relationship is the oneness in which the parts are fit to form the whole. In chapter 5, we will examine relationship in much more detail.

Every Whole Has Four Essential Parts

Every whole has four parts or aspects (two pairs of two). First, every whole is expressed both individually and collectively; that is, every whole (including ourselves) can be viewed either as a single part of a greater whole or as a whole comprising parts. Further, every whole has an interior and an exterior aspect. The *interior* aspect is more or less "hidden" in the sense of being only experientially (subjectively) accessible, or in the sense of needing to be "discovered" through analytical rigor or dissection. The *exterior* aspect presents itself outwardly—as part of the objective, empirical, publicly observable world, or as a part of the big picture in which every whole is in relationship to other wholes.

Our interest in the four-part structure of wholeness is primarily due to the specialized nature of the two brain hemispheres and their perspectives. In the following chapter, we will go into more detail about this relationship and how brain dominance affects our understanding of wholeness, but for now let us simply note that the two hemispheres divide up the task of perceiving wholeness. The holistic right brain perceives *collective* wholeness and is omnidirectional but predominantly *outward looking*. In other words, the right brain takes in the broad view and sees wholes especially in their *outside* aspect, in the context of the field of relationship to other wholes. The dualistic left brain specializes in showing us the *individual* aspect of wholeness and is predominantly *inward looking,* in the sense of being focused on the *insides* (or *parts*) of things—hence its tendency to dissect, to look for what makes things "tick."

Although most of us are unaware of this four-part structure at the conscious level, at the subconscious level we are highly aware of it—as can be seen in our efforts to find a mate. In looking for a mate, we clearly recognize that people have an *inner* and an *outer* persona, a private and a public face. In such a case, their inner persona—their subjectivity, or what they are like "inside"—is discovered only gradually and often indirectly, in how it affects other areas of their life and relationships. We also recognize that when we connect with someone, we are connecting to more than an *individual*—we are also connecting to a *collective*. In this case, it's the family, friends, and even exes. When you enter a relationship with someone, you are entering a complex set of relationships that include family

habits, attitudes, responses, genetics, and a more or less compli-
cated past that affects the present in countless ways.

A whole *always* can be divided into four fundamental parts,
but almost without exception, those parts have parts—and they too
can have parts (and so on)—and some of them can go missing,
leaving the whole incomplete. Missing parts can make the whole
nonfunctional, as when an automobile is missing its engine or
transmission, or be of little consequence, as when it loses a hubcap.

Incompletion

We cannot simply seek wholeness. The complexity of reality
ensures that even critical parts are sometimes missing from
wholes. Therefore, when dealing with important issues, we need
to be aware of the possibility of incompletion—something we
instinctively do, for example, as a result of the experience of having been cheated. The detection of missing or flawed parts is the
responsibility of our detail-oriented left hemisphere, which sees
and seeks incompletion in wholes. To monitor completion, we
have the brain's right hemisphere, with its holistic perspective,
designed to see and seek wholeness.

We care about this subject because an incomplete or frag-
mentary whole can keep us from discovering the truth about it.
We care because through our own activity and choices (our
choice of perspective, for example), we can move toward or away
from greater wholeness. The workbook for *A Course in Miracles*,
referring to the effect that incompletion has on our ability to
find truth, explains: "The aim of all defenses is to keep the truth
from being whole. The parts are seen as if each one were a
whole within itself. . . . Defenses must make facts unrecogniz-
able. . . . Every defense takes fragments of the whole, assembles
them without regard to all their true relationships, and thus constructs illusions of a whole that is not there."[9]

All Wholes Connect Horizontally and Vertically

Whether we call something a part, a whole, or a holon, one thing is certain: movement and change occur everywhere and affect the lives of everyone—and movement introduces *process*.

Any time we consider two wholes, we also need to consider their *relationships*. We cannot consider wholes in isolation: they are interconnected (physically, mentally, and spiritually) in a complex energy system. For that reason, we must consider their various relationships in the context of the whole.

Wholes no doubt connect with one another in many ways, but the nesting structure perhaps describes universe connectivity as well as anything. Wholes can be said to nest in two fundamental ways—*horizontally* and *vertically*. Perhaps a clearer way of explaining this structure is to say that wholes nest both *with* and *within* other wholes. *With* describes horizontal nesting. *Within* describes vertical nesting—but rather than envisioning a traditionally vertical structure, it might be more useful to envision a series of concentric spheres (two-dimensionally depicted in figure 1), each of which includes and envelops the preceding one.

To use a three-dimensional illustration, *vertical* nesting is the structure we are familiar with in Russian nesting dolls, where we find a hollowed-out doll that contains, or nests, a smaller doll *within* it, and that doll nests an even smaller doll, and so on in a sequence. We see this vertical one-within-another pattern in nature. The nucleus of an atom is vertically nested within an atom that is vertically nested within a molecule. We see this same pattern expressed in cultural nesting. Individuals are vertically nested within families, teams, schools, and businesses. These, in turn, are vertically nested within rural or urban communities that are vertically nested within states or provinces, which in turn are vertically nested within

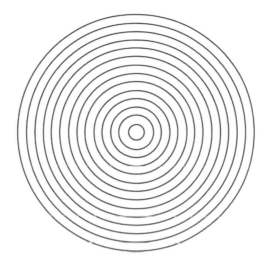

Figure 1. **Collective wholeness.**

nations nested by a planet nested in a solar system, and so on. This structure is sometimes called a *holarchy* (a hierarchy of holons).

Horizontal nesting refers to the relationship in which we see elements connected *with* others having a (more or less) similar purpose, such as the individual members of a team (sports or business) working to support a common greater whole or goal (or sometimes working to interfere with it, as is the case with defective parts, or selfish players, for example). The horizontal elements of nesting dolls are the unpainted wood, the paints of different colors, and the artistry, the beauty of the relationships created by the painter. Notice that teams and other collectives can also take a vertical form in which, for example, a football team might enlist its supporters (which it nests) and the university (in which it nests) for a fund-raising drive.

The nesting activity of wholes takes place in an environment of *interdependent* relationships. Being connected, the various parts depend on one another. From a right-brain perspective of wholeness, what hurts one hurts all to some degree, and what benefits one benefits all to some degree. This contrasts sharply with the left brain's perspective, which is the prevailing viewpoint in our left-brain-dominant culture. From its perspective of separation and winner-take-all competition, what hurts one individual often helps another. Although we often speak of win–win situations (the right brain's point of view), the more common point of view tends to be that if you win, I lose, and vice versa.

In horizontal nesting, the elements of wholeness are relatively *competitive*. Members of a family compete with one another for family resources. Business and governmental departments compete with one another for funding, material resources, or personnel. Animals tend to compete with one another, as do students. Competition usually implies a certain similarity of function between competitors.

Contrast that with *vertical* nesting. There, competition is usually absent. Students do not compete with their schools. Nor do schools compete with the cities in which they nest, except in unusual circumstances, such as cases where a school and a city may both apply for the same grant for funding. In general, students compete with students; cities compete with cities. In vertical nesting, the focus is inherently encompassing and, at least in ideal circumstances, supportive—although in interpersonal, cultural, and institutional contexts there can also be acrimony (such as when a state usurps money intended for a local government).

We find an environment of *domination* in vertical nesting. Whether or not the domination creates problems in interpersonal or institutional situations depends on how it is managed. If the relationship is managed by individuals coming from a harmony-seeking, holistic perspective, the relationship can be very cooperative and mutually beneficial. On the other hand, if management takes on separative characteristics, then the relationship can be bullying and coercive from the dominant side, and rebellious or nonfunctional from the weaker side. Size, we all know, tends to dominate. So, for example, a city, because of its size, has more power and control than the individual families that are nesting within it. Likewise, cultures dominate schools, and schools dominate students (or at least try).

Because every whole is both horizontally and vertically nested, we face, for example, horizontal pressures to cooperate with our friends and associates, and vertical pressures to succumb to more powerful cultural forces such as parents, schools, businesses, and governments. And we must deal with another pressure as well. Sometimes a horizontal element (a brother, coworker, or partner, for example) will try to dominate us. We deal with a complex mix of entangled nesting structures, and what we might predict doesn't always happen.

Due to all of the problems associated with competition, horizontal nesting within a culture or country (not to mention between countries) can present its own problems. Vertical nesting, on the other hand, involves hierarchy and domination, and acceptance of this structure is heavily resisted by many people at relatively high levels of consciousness. As Ken Wilber explains this reaction,

> "When any holon in a natural holarchy [a *vertical* nesting of holons] usurps its position and attempts to dominate the whole, then you get a pathological or dominator hierarchy—a cancerous cell dominates the body, or a fascist dictator dominates the social system, or a repressive ego dominates the organism, and so on. But the cure for these pathological holarchies is not getting rid of the holarchy per se—which isn't possible anyway—but rather in arresting the arrogant holon and integrating it back into the natural holarchy, or putting it in its rightful place, so to speak. The critics of hierarchy—their names are legion—simply confuse these pathological hol-

archies with holarchies in general, and so they toss the baby
with the bathwater. . . . Without holarchy, you simply have
heaps, not wholes."[10]

In other words, you become heapistic, rather than holistic.

Which Way to God?

Religion is divided over whether to go inward or outward in its
search for the divine. Progressive individuals—including those
associated with Eastern religions and new religious movements
in general, and certain others—tend to believe that the search
must be inward, whereas the more traditional and orthodox tend
to search outward for God.

Whether or not we need to go inward to find ourselves
depends on what we mean by going inward, and it depends on
where we think we are. If by "going inward" we mean to transcend our preoccupation with the material world and move
into the spiritual world (by calming the mind, for example),
then we do need to go inward. Spirit is an inward destination
in that sense. But do we really have to look or go inward to
reach our spirit? If we are looking inward to find ourselves, does
this not suggest that we are outside of ourselves (where, ironically, some religious traditions have long taught that God is
found)? Does this perspective not suggest that we have perhaps
become separated from ourselves and need to reunite with our
own essence?

But this line of thinking assumes that we can actually be separate from ourselves. Perhaps that very concept of a self from
which we can be separated is an illusion set up by our cultural
beliefs. The real question is, how can you go to where you already
are? Great masters have asked that question for centuries. The
idea that we need to go somewhere before we can be who we are
sounds dualistic, as if we had to bridge some great divide.

From my perspective, the fact that we *believe* we are separate from ourselves or from God sets up the belief that we must look inward *or* outward to find ourselves or the God who will save us (as if spirit occupied only a small point somewhere within us, or some distant realm outside of us, rather than being everywhere). Perhaps we just need to *be* who we are—we need to act out of our values. Rather than look inward or outward, perhaps we need to look around—look around at the mirrors others hold up for us and recognize who we are. Since there is only one spirit, the same God is in everyone. Therefore, even though we are different from one another in many ways, the very same God that can be found within us and teach us about ourselves can also be found within *others* and teach us about ourselves.

Because the two brain hemispheres are connected, when we choose the holistic perspective, we get the dualistic perspective as well. Since the holistic integrates everything we see, the dualistic perspective is obviously a part of the holistic. But always remember that the dualistic content of the holistic perspective is dependent on the contribution of the brain's left hemisphere, as well as other factors such as cultural programming and brain wiring. If the left brain's dualistic perspective fails to obtain the information that the right brain needs, this limits the right brain's ability to show us the way to wholeness.

In summary, whether a given whole be physical, mental, or spiritual in energy; whether it be a book, house, cat, tree, idea, hero, or villain; whether it be boundlessly large or infinitesimally small—it is connected to other wholes because it has both an individual wholeness and a collective wholeness in which the connections are made. Individual and collective wholes have an interior and an exterior, giving us the four fundamental parts we associate with wholeness.

An essential characteristic of the dualistic, left-brain perspective is a need for control. Control (at least of a particular domain) is more possible when the field of perception is smaller and more intensely focused. To separate a whole into parts and analyze them is to abstract one's field of attention from the seeming chaos that surrounds it. The right brain, on the other hand, takes in everything, and that involves standing back and letting go of limiting perceptions. For one who is not naturally right-brain dominant, letting go of a need for control so that we can "go with the flow" of the universe often has to be a conscious activity; nevertheless, it is one that can lead to growth. But remember, while it is necessary to see the whole picture, it is also necessary to have a sharp focus and be detail oriented. These are means, not ends in themselves, and the specializations of the two brain hemispheres are both necessary for a higher level of integration and functioning.

We have looked at the nesting structures that together reveal the unity of the universe. Every whole, individual or collective, shares a horizontal nest (connection) with a limited number of other wholes—wholes sharing a generally similar purpose such as a sports team, a company, or a country. Every whole—individual and collective; physical, mental, and spiritual—is also connected vertically by virtue of being nested in a series of wholes that are in turn nested in other wholes, ad infinitum—with all wholes ultimately nested in God.

Horizontal and vertical structures combine in a three-dimensional matrix; therefore, both are present in holistic structures and can often be seen in physical structures, especially during the early stages of development (the framework of a building, for example). Whether we see a vertical or a horizontal structure often depends on our perspective. If we look at families from the distant (broad) perspective of the holistic brain, they can be seen to be *vertically* nested if our context is the universe (or the unrestricted, broad view), or *horizontally* nested if our context is the family unit. However, if we zoom in on the whole that is a family, from this closer (narrower) perspective of the left brain, we see that parents vertically nest their children.

All wholes contain both horizontal and vertical nesting structures. What we see depends on our choices of perspective and wholeness. More important for our purposes than the particular nature of the relationship or nesting structure is the sheer primacy of relationship everywhere, at every level in the universe (physical, mental, spiritual). There is nothing that is not nested in multiple relationships and no moment when anything is out of relationship.

Part Two

Theory: How Perspective and Dominance Produce Polarization

Chapter Three

Perspective and Perception

> If the doors of perception were cleansed, everything would appear as it is—infinite.
>
> — WILLIAM BLAKE, *THE MARRIAGE OF HEAVEN AND HELL*

We now turn our focus to the human brain and start to explore its role in the perception of wholes. We will be exploring the split brain's relationship with perspective, perspective's relationship with perception, and perception's impact on our creative efforts. In this chapter, we will explore how both sides of the brain affect our perception, but our primary focus will be on understanding the role of the polarized and polarizing left brain.

Our creative choices derive from a complex brain system that is a whole of many parts, including a reptilian brain with a focus on the body; a more evolved, thinking mammalian brain; and the most recent evolutionary development in the human brain system—the neocortex. These three brains are then laterally divided into a complementary pair made up of right and left halves, or hemispheres. Each half is nested *horizontally*—that is, each works together as a whole with its partner. Each is also nested *vertically*—the three halves on each side (left and right) work together as a whole. However, because the reptilian brain controls involuntary, automatic life functions such as breathing and heart rate, and does not think (whereas the mammalian brain and the neocortex do), when we refer to the left or the right side of the brain as sharing a perspective and processes, we are largely referring to the contribution of the two thinking brains, a distinction that is reflected in brain researcher Ned Herrmann's four-part Whole Brain Model.[1] Herrmann's research found that the brain uses a three-dimensional process that is side to side, front to back, and top down.[2] To simplify a complex subject, we will focus on the best understood of these—side to side.

Most of us are under the impression that we have one perspective (at any given time), a perspective that varies depending on where we are positioned. The fact is, we have *three simultaneous* perspectives. They include two fundamental perspectives—the left brain's dualistic perspective, which zooms in on details, and the right brain's holistic, outward-looking big-picture perspective—as well as a third perspective that is an integration of the two, a perspective that is our personal and cultural creation, a perspective that reflects the mental artistry with which we combine our two fundamental perspectives. And keep in mind that each of the three perspectives takes in the mental and spiritual as well as physical realms.

Each of the two hemispheres has its own unique approach to understanding and interacting with holons, and this distinction is reflected in the differences between their respective perspectives and processes. Although both sides *contribute* to our integrated perspective, one side or the other tends to *dominate* in creating that perspective. Nevertheless, through conscious control of mind and will, it is possible to shift hemispheres and perspectives. Naturally, when we shift our perspective, we experience new vistas and acquire new information inputs, and with that shift we experience a shift in perception. Such shifts can be so small as to be imperceptible or inconsequential, but can also be very meaningful and enrich our lives in countless ways.

Case studies suggest that the cerebral commissures, the connective fibers that link the left and right sides of the brain, "transmit information that is inhibitory in nature. In other words, activity in one hemisphere leads to callosal transmissions that serve to moderate, decrease, or stop certain activities in the other."[3] Once side or the other takes the lead based on the individual's hemispheric dominance, and the other follows, assists, backs off, or shuts down as a way of maintaining relative internal harmony. With the two sides having such opposite values, this functional hierarchy is probably necessary. If the two hemispheres had to come to a harmonious agreement before we were able to act, we might be unable to reach a decision. It seems that one perspective needs to lead.

By being paired and separated, our eyes perceive physical depth. Paired brain perspectives appear to produce a similar effect on our mental depth perception. There is, however, an important difference between physical and mental perspectives. The two eyes show us wholes from two *slightly* different perspectives, perspectives that are essentially parallel and similar. The two brain perspectives, on the other hand, might best be described as opposites (illustrated in figure 2). One way to describe this complementary pair is to say that they give us back-to-back perspectives (in terms of the size of the whole), one zooming *in* to focus on smaller parts, the other spreading *out*, taking in a broad, "fisheye lens" view (actually, a 360-degree omniview).

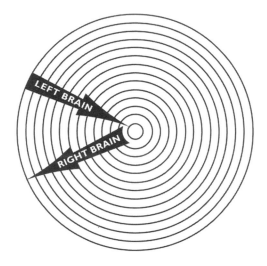

Figure 2. **Perspective directionality.**

In most people, the right hemisphere is the hemisphere that reveals an inclusive perspective of the universe that seeks to understand *collective* wholeness, a perspective that gives us a big-picture view of life. In contrast, the left hemisphere gives us a dualistic perspective that seeks to understand *individual* wholes by probing them to see what they are made of, and in the process it supplies us with a never-ending string of details. Given the unified nature of reality, it should come as no surprise that *brain structure closely resembles the molecular structure from which it is made.*

The Polar Brain and the Nonpolar Brain

For the purpose of our discussion, *dualistic* means just one thing: characterized by having a dual (two-part) nature. Basically, a dualistic structure is one whole consisting of two complementary parts that are often perceived as being polar opposites—such as we have in up/down, black/white, yes/no, and past/future. In dualistic structures, we find a dynamic system (that is, a system involving movement and change) driven by the tension between the energetic charges of the two extremes.

We see another example of this dualistic structure physically revealed in the molecules from which our world is constructed. As cell biologist Bruce Lipton explains, "All the molecules in our Universe can be divided into non-polar and polar categories based on the type of chemical bonds that hold their atoms together. The bonds among polar molecules have positive and/or negative charges, hence their polarity. These molecules' positive and negative charges cause them to behave like magnets, attracting or repelling other charged molecules. Polar molecules include water and things that dissolve in water. Nonpolar molecules include oil and substances that dissolve in oil; there are no positive or negative charges among their atoms."[4]

Because molecules are the building blocks of the universe and come in both polar and nonpolar forms, we should not be surprised to find that this structural element can also be found in the human body. In *The Whole Brain Business Book*, Ned Herrmann refers to our polar nature when he writes, "The human body is seemingly symmetrical but actually significantly asymmetrical. That is, there are differences between paired structures throughout the body system."[5] Look at people's faces and you can see that in almost every case the two sides are slightly different—and often significantly different—reflecting the differences between the brain hemispheres that control them; the left brain controls the right side of the body and vice versa. For example, because of this structure, the left hemisphere controls the right hand, and the right hemisphere controls the left hand.

Molecules come in shapes that are mirror images of one another, resulting in some rather amazing differences. Thanks to Louis Pasteur, we've known this for over a century and a half.

As Robert Ornstein explains in *The Right Mind: Making Sense of the Hemispheres*, "Many organic molecules can form in two different shapes, isomers, that are mirror images of one another, just as a right-handed glove is a mirror image of the left. While they are chemically identical, such molecules are physiologically different. . . . Consider the orange and the lemon, each with its distinctive fragrance. The smells come from the same chemical, limonene. But the limonene of oranges is the mirror image, the 'left-handed' one, of lemons. A reversal in the molecule leads to a distinct smell. The same elements, in the same structure, simply reversed, give off different properties. Lemons turn left into oranges."[6]

We see this pattern exhibited in brain dominance, where we again find that (quoting Ornstein from above) "the same elements, in the same structure, simply reversed, give off different properties." Accordingly, males and females form into two fundamentally different types, depending on whether their dominant hemisphere is the left or the right. Under most circumstances, when the left hemisphere dominates, the individual has perspectives and processes that are predominantly *dualistic*. When the right hemisphere is dominant, the result is a naturally *holistic*-oriented individual. In either case, we find a spectrum of gradations; the predominant perspective may be overwhelmingly favored or only slightly favored in a given individual.

The same mirroring structure that Ornstein discusses is also found in the world of ideas, where the two perspectives can produce apparently opposite takes on a single idea. Consider the contrasting solutions offered by a polar versus a nonpolar approach to problem solving. The belief that "fear and force offer the best solution to problem solving" reflects a mental response derived from polar thinking; the belief that "love and harmony offer the best solution to problem solving" reflects a mental response derived from nonpolar thinking.

We see and feel this structure reflected in spiritual energies as well. The polar (and polarizing) left brain, being dualistic, separates and contrasts our individual and our collective spirit, favoring the individual over the collective. This process unleashes a *feeling* (spirit-energy) of separation, and consequently, selfishness. On the other hand, the holistic right brain perceives spirit in its oneness (its nonpolar state, its true state), and this produces a feeling of fulfillment and a spiritual response that seeks to serve the whole in its collective totality (when you believe that everything is ours/yours, selfishness is meaningless). Thus we have the left brain's polarized us-versus-them mentality, which often tends to exacerbate differences, and the right brain's natural inclination to seek peace and harmony in spite of differences.

Analysis and Synthesis

Now that we have outlined the fundamental structure from which perspective arises, let's begin to look more deeply into how this structure affects the way we perceive reality.

The brain's left hemisphere is polar, or dualistic, in perspective and in action, we have said. As a result, the left brain's response to problems is to focus on certain parts of a whole, rather than to view the whole in its entirety. In a dualistic system, this separation most often takes the form of dissection (or, in the world of ideas, analysis). In attempting to understand wholes (people, things, and ideas, for example), we typically divide them into two polarized parts, and the parts are compared as a way of differentiating them in order to detect problems or flaws. We will explore this process further, but for now simply recognize that the left brain supplies us with a focused perspective that specializes in seeing the details.

In contrast, the typically nonpolar, holistic right brain hemisphere naturally seeks out integrative solutions. This is evident in its fundamental response to problems, which is synthesis, a process that works to harmonize wholes (in other words, attempts to unify people, ideas, and objects as we encounter them). From a purely holistic outlook, there is only oneness, so there is only "us" (as opposed to the dualistic "us and them," for example). And everything is viewed as ultimately good because it serves our experience and understanding in the broader (holistic) view. Thus, for example, a decision or choice that produces an undesired result (such as pain or suffering) helps us to better see or understand the effects of certain choices. Sometimes this point of view is expressed in the notion that the world, taken as a whole, is only good (or even "perfect"), because the parts, however flawed they appear, are integral to helping us understand ourselves.

If we are to understand our world—a world constructed from polar and nonpolar elements—it is essential that we acquire and evaluate both polar and nonpolar information. This information is apparently gathered and delivered to consciousness via polar and nonpolar perspectives. Although each of us has access to, and to some degree uses, both hemispheres and perspectives, one usually dominates the other (we will be looking into dominance on the following pages). To the degree that we identify with either our polar or our nonpolar perspective, and feed our consciousness a steady diet of its data, we can be said to have either polar or nonpolar consciousness.

We have long known of the dual (or dualistic) nature of the left brain, as is implied by the fact that we have long referred to the right brain as the nondual brain. Because the left hemisphere sees dualities—in other words, sees a whole as two or more parts rather than as a unity—it perceives wholes as pairs of polarized opposites: good or bad, light or dark, etc. In an integrated brain where both hemispheres are allowed to function as a complementary pair, this dualistic perspective is then absorbed into the right brain's holistic perspective, and this in turn allows us to see both the details and the big picture.

Wholes do not exist in isolation, but in *relationship*. All wholes, as we have seen in chapter 2, can be viewed as wholes consisting of parts, and as parts of other wholes. (The word *holon* was invented to describe this part-and-whole characteristic.) Whether something is viewed as a part or a whole depends on our perspective. And perspective itself has a dual structure in that it is divided into two fundamental parts (a holistic and a dualistic perspective). In terms of structural relationships (or how the various parts of a whole relate to one another), perspective consists of a dual structure nested within another dual structure. (And this structure might well continue to unfold in ways that we have yet to recognize.)

Holons, then, are simultaneously *wholes* consisting of parts in a horizontal relationship, and *parts* in a vertical, holarchical relationship. When we have two of anything, there are not just two discrete elements to deal with: there are the two elements *in relationship*. The relationship between two holons is an energized space that the two elements combine to create, and that energized space results in a third element—a new holon based on the other two. We see this in the world of spatial relationships, such as *left and right*, which can be viewed from a central (and somewhat more inclusive) perspective; or *ahead and behind*, which have *here* as a central perspective; or *past and future*, which have *now* as a central perspective.

Since any two holons in a relationship create a third, our integration of the two fundamental perspectives effectively produces three functional perspectives: a dualistic (polar), a holistic (nonpolar), and our integrated perspective. Of the three, typically we acknowledge only one or two. The first and most obvious of these is our integrated perspective. The second is the perspective that dominates and thus largely shapes our integrated perspective. When we rely on two perspectives rather than three, we effectively position ourselves to one side or the other of the continuum of perspective (rather than in the middle, as one might expect). This is because our integrated perspective, although including both hemispheres, tends to be weighted much more toward the point of view of our dominant hemisphere. With the addition of a third perspective (the perspective of our *non*dominant hemisphere), we obviously create a broader, more encompassing perspective from which to view our world. In the physical world, we can escape the instability of a two-legged (dualistic/polar) stool simply by adding a third leg. In the world of mind, we obtain similar support by connecting a third perspective through intent and attention. With the information of three perspectives, we are better able to harmonize the seemingly opposite perspectives of our two brain hemispheres into one—and to do so both within ourselves and within our collective being. Working with a set of three perspectives, we are better equipped to understand and communicate with a wider range of people.

In addition to two fundamentally different *perspectives*, the two brain hemispheres supply us with two different sets of *processes* to use in response to our perspective. If we personify the two brain hemispheres, we might say that they have different reactions to what they see, or that they process information in different ways—one synthetically, the other analytically. *One assembles or integrates wholes* (seeking the big picture); *the other disassembles or separates wholes* (probing wholes, seeking details). Although this process unfolds automatically, more or less according to our needs, we can also choose to consciously manage it (such as when we are focused on an important subject or event and want to do our very best). We can always choose to bolster the sometimes-ignored nondominant perspective and its processes in an effort to create a more harmonious integration. As we explore our two fundamental perspectives throughout this book, we will also be looking at the *processes* they employ.

In summary, the division of hemispheres down the middle (sometimes referred to as a *lateralized brain structure*) offers us two fundamental choices with respect to what we *see*—a dualistic and a holistic perspective. And matched with each of the two perspectives is a basic process, giving us two synchronized *responses*—analysis and synthesis. The holistic brain, being inclusive in perspective, not only perceives whole assemblies, but also assembles wholes—albeit in an almost instantaneous fashion. The complementary dualistic brain naturally gives us the opposite perspective and the reverse process—a process that disassembles wholes. Although we come programmed at birth with a default perspective that is either dualistic or holistic to one degree or another (or, in a relatively few cases, a near-balance of the two), nevertheless, we can *choose* our perspective at any moment in time. And when we choose a perspective, *we also tend to choose our creative response*. Our holistic, nonpolar right brain perceives the big picture, which reflects the larger (and typically more valuable) elements of reality. Our dualistic, polar left brain perceives a detailed perspective that, because it probes into wholes as a way of checking them out, is focused on the smaller elements of reality. This process is separation inducing, but also brings detail to the right brain's big picture.

Hemispheric Dominance and Perspective

Our physical perspective changes as we change positions. We also know that physical limitations can somewhat restrict our perspective. Mentally, our experience is similar. Perspective changes as we move about in the dimension of mind and ideas, and in addition, is somewhat restricted by the characteristics of our dominant brain hemisphere, through whose door our perspective is most often accessed.

Brain dominance is simply the tendency to favor one side of the brain over the other. Most men, being left-brain dominant, tend to view reality from a dualistic perspective. Although the numbers are not clear with respect to women and dominance, it appears that most women inherit the right brain's holistic perspective as their dominant perspective; then, as a result of cultural programming, many are shifted into what we might call an artificially (culturally) induced dualistic perspective (dominance results from that which we practice). In effect, many of those who are right-brain dominant have been culturally instructed (programmed) to look to their left brain for guidance when they interact with the world. This is perhaps reflected by studies that show that most women are right-handed, and most people who are right-handed are left-brain dominant. But this data fails to account for the many fundamental characteristics that women, as a whole, obviously share with right-brain perspectives and processes. By the time you finish this book, you will be capable of judging for yourself whether or not most women are right-brain dominant. For simplification, in the rest of this book we will generally refer to women's right-brain dominance without the qualification we have given here, but keep in mind that there is much about brain science, as about other sciences and areas of knowledge, that is subject to some degree of revision.

As Ned Herrmann explains dominance, "One member of the [brain] pair, through increased use due to preference, develops to a higher level than the nondominant one." In other words, initially we might have a preference for only one side or the other, but eventually we become practiced and comfortable with one or the other and it comes to dominate. Herrmann adds that "as dominance of one structure over its partner develops through life's experiences, the degree of that dominance becomes evident from the mental preferences the person exhibits."[7] Some of us end up viewing the world from an extreme position; we are not just dualistic or holistic; we are *extremely* dualistic or holistic. Others, closer to the center, experience lesser degrees of dominance. Because they are farther from the energy of the poles, the energy of the poles has a less extreme influence over their perspective and perception.

Occasionally, individuals are positioned so close to the center of the continuum that they are nearly in balance. On the surface, this might sound great; however, balance alone is not always advantageous. From a central position, our interaction with, and our vision of, the two defining extremes occurs from a relatively great distance. Thus, our view of reality (especially if our life experience is limited) may come at the expense of a fuller understanding of the dualistic and holistic extremes. For example, if we were to be raised in an environment where the temperature of everything was always constant, the ideas of heat and cold would not exist. Similarly, persons who have not experienced the extremes of life may seem rather blank or lacking in depth to those of us who have. If we consider the holistic notion that everything we experience in this body and on this planet serves a purpose, then one who lives only in the middle of the continuum between the holistic and the dualistic might be missing out on something, just as someone with very limited cultural experience (or who has never traveled) might be missing out on something. For a spiritual example of the effect of not understanding the extremes, consider our experience with war and peace. If we lived on a planet where violence was unknown, where there was always peace, we would have no occasion to delve deeply enough into ourselves or our world to understand the value of peace. Having had no experience with violence, we wouldn't know what peace meant. We would have peace, but we wouldn't understand peace—and that could actually be a block to a deeper, heart-centered appreciation of peace.

The preceding example describes a relatively simple variation; however, the complexity and diversity of the system of perspective (and life in general) is such that any combination is possible. For example, one might occupy a relatively central position on the continuum of perspective but nevertheless have access to the extremes. One might also have an extreme left-brain perspective that is more or less balanced by an extreme right-brain perspective—or a combination of lesser extremes of one or both. To the extent that individuals are able to access their non-dominant perspective (or, in the case of a person "in the middle," both perspectives), they are able to achieve a relatively balanced perspective and still understand the essence of the two extremes.

Because each perspective has its advantages and its disadvantages, ultimately the place on the dualistic/holistic continuum where our brain functions is not important. What matters is that we recognize our strengths and weaknesses, use them judiciously, and integrate the two perspectives—something that happens, more or less automatically, once respect for the non-dominant perspective is restored and the two are no longer fighting. The two brain hemispheres are designed to work as an integrated whole, but this natural state can be interrupted by cultural programming. One such example is belief in war as a solution to our problems, a belief that often incites polarization through "patriotic" appeals, organized propaganda, and the stifling of dissent by government, the media, and powerful individuals and organizations generally. We see our individual and collective polarization acted out (and mirrored back to us) by our polarized representatives (elected by us) and the polarized governments that they form.

Wherever we might find ourselves on the continuum (or in the sphere) of perspective, most of us only become conscious of the existence of our nondominant perspective over time, often as a result of living with or otherwise being close to someone whose perspective corresponds with our nondominant perspective—as when left-brain-dominant men and right-brain-dominant women try to coexist. Finally, bear in mind that left-brain and right-brain forms of dominance do not dominate equally. Left-brain-dominant individuals seek to dominate right-brain-dominant individuals, and left-brain-directed cultural expressions tend to dominate right-brain-directed cultural expressions. The left brain is compelled to dominate in order to do what it is designed to do—protect individuals against powerful collectives (cultural and societal influences, government and business, for example). To protect us from the collective, the left brain seeks domination over the perspectives and processes favored by the right brain as a method of establishing control. The right brain, being holistic, is naturally harmonious and cooperative, and therefore is not oriented toward achieving dominance. In addition, left-brained individuals are willing to use force or threat of force to achieve their goals. And since males as a whole are not only left-brain dominant but *physically* dominating, they have been able to dominate and control the mechanisms of wealth and culture for centuries, and have created cultural systems based on their dualistic perspectives. The result is a cultural environment that is largely left-brain directed—a culture that encourages, through formal teaching as well as behavior, the strongly polarizing responses and solutions of the left brain.

The dualistic brain is rational.

The two brain hemispheres differ in the way they acquire the information they process. The rational left evolves ideas *sequentially* through the process of *thought*. This is a deliberative process that helps filter out error.

In *The Tao of Physics: An Exploration of the Parallels between Modern Physics and Eastern Mysticism*, Fritjof Capra writes, "Rational knowledge is derived from the experience we have with objects and events in our everyday environment. It belongs to the realm of the intellect whose function it is to discriminate, divide, compare, measure and categorize. In this way, a world of intellectual distinctions is created; of opposites which can only exist in relation to each other, which is why Buddhists call this type of knowledge 'relative.'"[8] The hemisphere that discriminates, divides, compares, measures, and categorizes is the dualistic left.

In contrast, the intuitive right brain's ideas are born fully developed. The right brain doesn't have to look around and analyze what is happening. It doesn't need to measure and compare, and then to come a conclusion. The right sees and knows everything within the range of its perception, all at once—although it still must rely on the left brain for details. Of course, in reality the right brain's instantaneous, holographic processes do not operate in a vacuum but in the context of a lifetime of communication between brain hemispheres.

The dualistic brain is competitive.

Another distinguishing quality of the left hemisphere is its competitive nature. To help us recognize and process the different options we encounter, the left evaluates and judges them, creating sequential rankings that facilitate the comparison of things, ideas, and relationships. The left brain is impressed by winners, and places a very high value on winning and on separating winners from losers.

A few years ago, I was waiting in line to buy a movie ticket. As the long line slowly moved forward, two teenage boys ahead of me tried to decide what they wanted to see. Even after they got to the window and the ticket seller was waiting for them to respond, they discussed the subject. Finally, unable to decide, they asked which movie was selling the most tickets. And even though neither one knew anything about it, based on ranking, they bought tickets for it. Even more than dominance, the idea of Number One symbolizes victory and, above all, survival, the ultimate goal of competition.

In contrast, the right brain is cooperative. The right brain is looking for harmony, for truth, and might or might not have an interest in competition or rankings. The right is seeking to unify the left brain's facts. To the right brain, a high competitive ranking just does not have the interest or charge that it has for the left brain.

The dualistic brain is self and survival oriented.

The left brain, being focused on survival issues and other needs of individuals (individual wholes), is naturally selfish in its actions. We often think of selfishness as being bad, but to the degree that it protects us, it is good. And after all, that's its job, to take care of us. Thank your left brain for being selfish.

This is not to say that left-brain-dominant people don't sometimes put the collective first. "Me" often transitions into "my," by which I mean that our selfish tendencies can be expanded to include areas with which we selfishly identify: *my* family, *my* tribe, or *my* country. This is why we are sometimes willing to give our lives for a collective in spite of being strongly left-brain directed. However, even this is an act of selfishness, although it can appear as selflessness to others. To cite another example, the apparently altruistic act of helping our child is still rooted in selfishness to the extent that it is done with the goal of being a good dad, or in order to gain the respect of others. We might appear to sacrifice our own interests for the company or the country but actually do it for a promotion we want, or to prove to ourselves or to others that we are brave—or something else that satisfies the self. Of course, we all have a right brain, and it also influences our decisions, so even though we might be left-brain dominant, our responses can be influenced by our right brain. Nevertheless, to the extent that our actions are directed by our left (dualistic) brain, they are intended to benefit the self.

In contrast, the right brain is focused on the collective, so those who are right-brain dominant (to the extent that they are right-brain directed) are naturally focused on helping others. They see themselves in others. They innately know that we are one and often seek to support their collective self at the expense of their individual self. However, because we all receive input from both sides of the brain, this situation is often modified. Thus, for example, we often find a tribal mentality in right-brain-dominant people (typically women), in which they tend to be more protective of their own families and associations than those of outsiders.

The dualistic brain focuses on smaller wholes.

Speculating about the system that feeds our consciousness, Robert Ornstein concludes in *The Right Mind* that it "divides into the large elements of perception and action and the small [elements of perception and action]."[9] Considering the brain's propensity to process visual information with respect to size, Ornstein's studies suggest that "the right is much quicker and much more accurate at detecting very large waves of visual information, whereas the left is much better at detecting the very short waves."[10] This of course reflects the pattern we have been discussing, one in which the right brain is designed to look outward at the universe (which reveals a greater whole in size and complexity), whereas the left brain is designed to look at reality with an inward perspective (which leads us to find smaller, simpler elements). It should therefore come as no surprise that in studying auditory processing,

Ornstein found that the left is "specialized for hearing the high auditory frequencies," the details, whereas the right hemisphere seems to be specialized for hearing low-frequency sounds.[11] (Low-frequency sounds produce larger waves, whereas higher frequencies produce smaller waves.)

We see this response to size reflected in the ways in which the two hemispheres approach ideas. The dualistic brain, being narrowly focused, seeks out (and sees) the details, the facts, the smaller constituent elements of truth. The holistic right, being focused on the big picture, sees an overall pattern that reflects truth (but must rely on the left brain's facts to give its big-picture understanding the clarity of detail). The narrowly focused left naturally seeks out *specifics* and speaks in specifics. The right brain is specialized to observe the broad scope of *generalities* and to express itself in generalities—something that is problematic from a left-brain perspective, as the right brain's broad perspective is often open to interpretation (and viewed from a left-brain perspective is sometimes seen as too vague to be useful).

Notice the unity of the left brain's approach. When *perceiving* reality, the left focuses on smaller wholes rather than the larger, more complex multi-whole collectives. Likewise, when *processing* (acting on its observations), the left focuses on individual wholes and smaller elements (culturally this might mean the family, or the tribe). The left sees and processes the shorter (smaller) frequencies (waves) of light, and its response to sound is similar. Receiving auditory signals, the left's response is to focus on and process the higher musical tones, the ones with shorter (smaller) cycles. And in terms of the left brain's interaction with ideas (ideological wholes), in harmony with the physical, the left explores the smaller parts of ideas (in other words, the specifics, the details).

Of course, size is relative. This is especially true when one considers the infinite size and complexity and dimensions of creation. The left hemisphere in particular can be easily misled into believing that it has the whole picture in front of it, and yet be missing something critical. In fact, every whole we can perceive or imagine is a part of something even larger that lies beyond our view.

The dualistic brain is analytical.

The two hemispheres offer us fundamentally different processes with which to respond to life's creative challenges. Left-hemisphere processes, for most individuals, are analytical.

The left brain's analytical approach to understanding reality is perhaps its most well-known trait. (Indeed, the terms *analytical* and *left brain* are often used synonymously.) The left brain takes wholes apart and studies (or analyzes) their parts in an attempt to understand how they work, to see what "makes them tick"—to see if they are what they appear to be. Analysis, whether focused on physical, mental, or spiritual holons, or some combination, always attempts to disassemble or deconstruct the holon in some manner as a way of trying to understand it. As such, analysis focuses us on the parts—and on the parts of the parts of the parts, and so on. Thus, analysis zooms in on the insides (or interiors) of wholes.

The right hemisphere's approach to exploring reality and processing wholes is, as always, the exact opposite of the left's (when seen from a dualistic perspective). The right is expansive and outwardly vigilant. The right seeks the unification of holons, a process known as *synthesis*. To achieve synthesis, the right *assembles* holons—physical, mental, and spiritual; things, ideas, and people. Seeing the big picture, the right hemisphere (as we have observed) is designed to perceive the exteriors of wholes, but being all-encompassing, it also incorporates the left hemisphere's internal-oriented perspective into its own. Because the right hemisphere assembles wholes, the more we look at reality with our right hemisphere, the larger each whole is seen to be. Ultimately, we see that everything is part of one vast whole—even if we see it only through our imagination, or through mystical contemplation.

The dualistic brain disassembles wholes.

Disassembly, the act that reflects the left's analytical process, is an act of simplification. When you tear down an engine, dissect a frog, or look at elements of a relationship, you end up with smaller, simpler parts on which to focus. By reducing the complexity of wholes, you make them easier to understand.[12]

Disassembly, obviously, is an act of separation, and this is what we refer to when we speak of the left brain as being separative in nature, or when we speak of it as using a separative process in its interaction with wholes. I have long been greatly impressed by the quality of early American mechanical devices, and as a former antiques collector I am still haunted by the memory of two beautiful old oak-cased telephones that I disassembled as a young child and never reassembled (which meant they were discarded). I find that, being left-brain dominant, I have too often disassembled things, changed my focus, and then failed to reassemble them (and often have trouble reassembling things). In the process of disassembling a whole, we separate the whole's parts, and this tends to interrupt a whole's fundamental functions. When separation occurs, individual wholes lose a part of their role in the collective wholeness. Separation can be destructive. Separation can kill—as in the case of a dissected frog.

Although the left brain is separation oriented in its processes and in its perspective, keep in mind that the left brain itself is internally holistic. When we refer to the left brain as dualistic and separative, we are referring to its perspective and to the nature of its actions. The right brain is clearly the more holistic of the two brain hemispheres in terms of perspective and process—and by a wide margin. Nevertheless, the left is holistic in that its various processes—analysis, disassembly, force, separation, destruction—all work in harmony with one another to achieve common goals. We can relate these functions by saying the following: To *analyze*, we *disassemble* the whole, forcing the parts to *separate*, and at least temporarily, we *destroy* the whole; we destroy its ability to function.

The dualistic brain processes information sequentially.

The separative left brain is designed to focus on *individual* wholes and to process reality *sequentially*, meaning one whole (or part) at a time. Since the holistic right brain sees *collective* wholeness and sees everything at once, it naturally processes reality *simultaneously*. It's an efficient and complementary process: the right brain sees the universe around us as a whole, and the left brain (based on our intention and where we direct our attention) probes its individual parts. At our command, the left brain looks into whatever interests us and analyzes it. We might characterize the behavior of our linear left hemisphere as peeking through a series of keyholes at the universe, examining the details seen through each keyhole (perhaps with the aid of magnification), intently focused on fact gathering, never seeing more than a small part at one time, but seeing those parts relatively well.

The left brain, because it separates everything and processes it sequentially, naturally perceives a world of time. Time is a measure of separation. The simultaneous right naturally sees a timeless world—an eternal present. Time is of no concern to a brain that sees only oneness and lives only in the Now.

Relative to the instantaneous right brain, the left brain's sequential processing tends to be slow. Perhaps that is why most men tend to speak more slowly than women. In any case, that's not to say there are not some very quick left-brain-dominant individuals, or slow right brainers—after all, we use a combination of the two hemispheres, and there always seem to be exceptions. However, individually, the difference in speed between the two processors is significant. Ironically, women, as a whole, tend to take longer to make important decisions than do men, and that is probably because they see more options from which to choose and are not as practiced in getting to the details as left-brained men (who, in most cases, are specialists in finding details by nature of being left-brain dominant). There must be other reasons as well, such as women being more holistic and therefore more willing to take the time to try to understand how their decisions might affect other people.

The dualistic brain is change oriented

Given the left brain's sequential processing and the limitations of focus (which can see only one whole or one part of any whole at any one time), we should not be surprised to find that the left *jumps from focus to focus.* Like a bee that must constantly move from flower to flower in order to satisfy its needs, the left brain is never able to find satisfaction in its partial view. As a result, it changes its focus relentlessly. We see this "jumping" behavior in the stereotypical TV channel surfing of left-brain-dominant males. We also see this in male sexual behavior.[13] The right brain, which sees everything (meaning everything in sight, everything within its range of experience) and knows that it is one with everything, doesn't have that need to jump around.

The dualistic brain is limiting and exclusionary.

The left brain, being narrowly focused, is naturally *exclusive.* That is, it excludes greater wholes; it excludes larger contexts; it excludes considerations that are not within its narrow focus. When we focus on certain parts, we can't help but exclude others; thus the left brain's narrow focus is naturally limiting. (The right brain's perspective is the opposite in every respect. Being outward looking, it is inclusive and unlimited.) The left brain's exclusive/limiting response can be very helpful when properly applied. For example, by being more exclusive with respect to what we eat, we might eat less and/or eat more healthful foods with the result that we feel better. Similarly, by cutting out extraneous things in our lives and forcing a discipline of limitation, we create the conditions to have more free time and save money. Limitation, including self-limitation, is to people what brakes are to a car. Limitations slow us down. A limiting and exclusionary perspective can be a valuable tool when used in concert with the holistic, big picture of which it is a part. The left brain's perspective is a problem only when we become identified exclusively with its processes and mesmerized by its narrow focus.

The dualistic brain perceives reality as linear.

Reality has a fundamental linear component, and it is the left brain's job to perceive and report linear information to the holistic right brain.

Being linear, in its primary sense, simply means being line-like in shape. Although we don't always notice their contribution, linear structures provide the basis for three-dimensional structures. Linear proteins, for example, make up the bulk of our body.[14] Our skeleton, the foundation of our body, has a central linear axis, the spine. A geodesic dome, though its overall shape is spherical, nevertheless reveals a linear foundation at the root of the triangle-based icosahedrons out of which one is typically constructed. Perspective, too, can be partially described in terms of its linear component. By combining movement along three linear axes—up–down, right–left, and forward–back— we can position ourselves anywhere and obtain any perspective. Of course, it's much easier said than done, but those are the basics. What we see of anything depends on where we are positioned in relationship to it.

The left brain, designed to detect the linear component of nature, naturally views holons in terms of a continuum. A continuum is "a continuous whole, no part of which can be distinguished from neighboring parts except by arbitrary division."[15] Graphically, a continuum can be expressed as a straight line that runs between two separate positions that are sometimes viewed as poles of energy, one having a negative charge and one a positive charge, and are typically perceived by the dualistic left brain as discrete opposites. Although a continuum does not have parts, we can create parts through arbitrary divisions—as we do when we create continuum-based numerical scales with which to measure and evaluate (such as 1 to 5, 1 to 10, etc.).

As a consequence of the separation initiated by dualism, the left brain perceives a world of black and white, good and bad, winners and losers, passing and failing, and war and peace. The two (dualistic) poles of such pairs effectively serve as guiding beacons that can tell us where we are within the spectrum of fullness and lack of fullness. This structure resembles that of the polarized molecules that populate the brain.

The holistic perspective can appreciate the information that such polarized continuums provide, but sees such linear structural components as small parts of a much greater whole.

The dualistic brain ranks, measures, and divides.

The gap between the two poles of a continuum creates, in effect, a field of variation. As we look across a broad continuum, we see that the change in a whole is *variable* in intensity and *constant* in character—think of light or heat or love, for example. The continuum-focused left brain sees a world characterized by degrees of goodness, degrees of truth, degrees of beauty—*degree* being the left brain's system of comprehension where the continuum has been divided up for the purposes of measurement and comparison. It does this to help us determine where we—

or the thing, idea, or person in which we are interested—are positioned in comparison with some standard such as truth, beauty, or goodness. In contrast, the right brain neither compares nor ranks, nor measures, nor divides wholes. The right brain views variation in a much different way. The right sees variation as novelty, as diversity; accepts it for what it is; and is uninterested in comparing, counting, or measuring it (though respectful of the information and guidance this information supplies).

When change in variation is small enough, the left brain can fail to notice it. Add a couple of drops of black paint to a gallon of white, stir it up, and we are unlikely to notice any difference. However, if we continue to add black, the white will darken into gray and will be noticed. If we chart these changes across a continuum, we create a line that gradually changes from white to black, and is symbolic of the continuum of light and its absence. The left brain can also symbolize truth this way; it can symbolize trust; it can symbolize any whole in terms of a continuum.

Within the continuum, we find a middle point at which two extremes might be said to effectively cancel each other out such that we have neither black nor white, hot nor cold. Imagine being at a point on a continuum where no change can be detected—either over time or within your field of perception. If your view does not contain features or contrasts—if, for example, you are in the middle of a desert or ocean that is totally flat to the horizon and devoid of features—then you would be unable to see any difference in direction, and you would easily become lost and disoriented. The same is true when we lose contact with the boundaries that guide us within the world of ideas and spirit—we can become lost, and ideological mirages can become confused with truth and mislead us.

The linear perspective plays an essential role in the creative process. In spite of the negative image it receives in some progressive circles due to its simplistic, exclusive nature, this perspective is extraordinarily valuable in providing accurate and complete details that we would otherwise not have. The failure to integrate these details can prove to be a major weakness in the right-brain-dominant individual.

Brain Perspective and Directionality

Although the right brain provides the big-picture view, there is one aspect of the whole that it fails to see, at least directly: it doesn't see *into* wholes. For that we have the left brain, which then passes its information on to the right brain so that it can see holistically. The left brain with its zoom-in capabilities probes and dissects, one part after another, to find out what might be hidden beneath the surface—to see the details, to check the authenticity, to check for Trojan horses. And all this happens, on demand, automatically, based on our intent plus attention or focus.

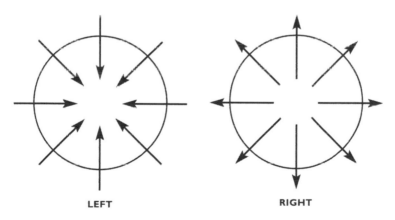

LEFT   RIGHT

Figure 3.   *Figure 4.*
Left-brain perspective.   **Right-brain perspective.**

The left half of the brain, science tells us, uses analysis, meaning that it probes the interiors of objects, ideas, motivations, causal chains, whatever, with a view to achieving simplicity (and through simplicity, an enhanced understanding). The deeper the left brain probes, the simpler things get. Clearly, it is a process that looks *inward into* wholes and wholeness. We see collective wholeness illustrated two-dimensionally in figure 2, which depicts collective wholeness, and figure 3, which depicts an individual whole. Always the complement, the right brain looks *outward*—into an ever expanding unity with (and within) the collective, and ultimately, All That Is (see figures 2 and 4).

When exploring mental energies such as ideas, the cautious (self-protective) dualistic left brain reacts in the same way as it reacts to physical energies: it zooms in and unearths the insides to find details—wrong data or a revelatory piece of data, flaws or clinchers in an argument, subtexts, proofs or contradictions, bad motivations, the list is endless. Ideas can be born of deception and need to be taken apart or analyzed. In contrast, the holistic right brain, which is fearless and inclusive (open to all ideas), focuses on our ideas as a whole (our ideological context, the big picture). Just remember that since the right brain is dependent on the left's skeptical abilities to identify and screen out flawed ideas, a poor performance by the left can severely limit the right brain's ability to do a good job.

When the two brains explore spiritual realities, we find similar patterns. The image that people present to us (the appearance of peacefulness and honesty, for example) is not always a true representation, and so we sometimes need to look behind the spiritual facade. Although the limitations of being linear based largely disqualify the left brain in terms of *understanding* the multidimensional reality of spirit, the left brain can discover details that can sharpen our understanding of spirit. As we move outward in consciousness and encounter expanded spheres of experience, we perceive ever greater feelings of joy. Through felt responses such as joy, we are aided in determining the direction in which our perspective is taking us. For example, when our spiritual movement is metaphorically inward or backward—as when we withdraw spiritually from our collective self (our environment) or are spiritually lost—we feel depressed. Rather than taking a pill to mask our depression, we might use this clue to help us reverse our direction.

Because the left brain is linear and oriented principally toward the physical dimension, we might ask how the left brain's focusing activities apply to mental and spiritual dimensions. A clue might come from those interior explorers from the past and present who have often provided descriptions of these nonphysical realities that are as detailed as any that a geographical explorer or laboratory researcher might give—and often with the same apparent scientific precision. Such descriptions are also common in the various scriptural revelations past and present, and cross-studies have shown amazing similarities of detail in the various accounts. The simple answer to the question is that the left brain's contribution to the exploration of mental and spiritual realms is the same as with the physical. That is, it searches for information to help the right brain fill in the details of its big picture.

Helpful to the discussion of perspective and movement is an understanding of sacred geometry. Euclidian geometry and systems of mathematics are a part of our public knowledge, and we all are exposed to these in our educational system. Sacred geometry is much less well known, even among mathematicians, scientists, and academics. And yet these principles have been consciously utilized by nearly every culture through most of recorded history.

Sacred geometry (which we will discuss in more detail in chapter 5) refers to the ways that shapes and patterns are repeated throughout nature and even in the mental and spiritual worlds. Although we can scarcely scratch the surface of this subject in the present book, full study of these patterns reveals the myriad ways that we are connected at (and to) all levels of life.[16] Every discipline, every way of knowing (such as chemistry, physics, architecture, music, even one's emotional states), can be shown to have a correlation in sacred geometry. Even mathematics would not be possible without sacred geometry, for numbers and their laws arise out of (and could not exist without) shape, form, and proportion, and the relationships these reveal.

The most basic and fundamental of all geometric shapes at the two-dimensional level is the *circle*; within three-dimensional space it is the *sphere*. Just as the circle is a curved, closed line in which all points on the line (or circumference) are the same distance from its center point, a sphere (in its ideal, perfect shape) is a single, completely symmetrical surface—and as such, it expresses oneness and unity in a way that is unique among three-dimensional shapes. (It also has the greatest ratio of volume to surface of any imaginable body.) Given sufficiently fluid boundaries, everything tends toward symmetry around a center. The entire universe—every single thing in existence—can be seen as being the inside of a sphere. Combine this with the demonstrable, scientifically grounded knowledge that structures nest within one another, and we can imagine the universe as a series of nested spheres (depicted two-dimensionally in figures 1 and 2)—starting with minute particles that collect to form atoms, which then form into molecules, which then form into ever more complex wholes. These include our own perspective from Mother Earth and the body of our ideas and experience.

In similar fashion, increasing complexity can be seen as one's perspective moves out to ever greater, more inclusive wholes (or holons). The complementary nature of the highly focused, detail-revealing left-brain perspective and the context-

and relationship-revealing right-brain perspective gives us the fullest understanding of the patterns and revelations of sacred geometry, and what they tell us about everything—money, knowledge, personal relationships, the connectedness of life, or anything else.

Looking at an issue raised by directionality and perspective in the previous chapter, we mentioned that religion is divided over whether to look inward or outward to find God. As we suggested there, the confusion seems in large part caused by a misunderstanding of what it means to go inside. Primarily, it means that we get in touch with spirit. We apparently call it "going inside" because to get there we must escape the "outside" world. But do we truly move in an inward direction to get there? Might not this simply be a couple of words that are used to describe a process of directing our attention away from physical energies and *onto*, rather than *into*, spiritual energies?

Yes, there is a spiritual dimension inside our bodies; but that same spirit also exists outside our bodies. Perhaps the language we use arises from a failure to recognize that *no one is outside the spiritual world*. It is impossible to be outside; spirit is unified. Therefore, *it is impossible to "go inside," impossible to move into the spiritual dimension*. We are already there! When spiritual leaders suggest we go inside, they are suggesting that we move out of a state of consciousness that is distracted by our interaction with the physical dimension. This leaves us perceiving only the spiritual dimension and the dimension of mind (thought). Of course, when we are able to stop thinking, at that point only spirit is left to interact with. And that's where we want to be when we want to experience the peace and happiness that come with being a god.

Since spirit is everywhere, it doesn't matter whether we think we need to go inward or outward to find God, nor does it matter which words we use to describe where we seek to go—

spirit is everywhere we look—but it does matter which brain hemisphere we use. One brain is the ego brain; the other is the God brain. One faces us toward oneness and inevitably takes us closer; the other takes us on side trips to check out details that might or might not help us toward our goal.

God is everywhere. The illusion of going inward to find God appears to be what is sometimes referred to as an ego trap. An inward journey (which takes us into the ego's perceptual territory and largely turns our back to oneness—and suggests that the ego is involved) can take us only part of the way. Only by moving outward in complexity (such as through communion with God, with gods—other people, and with revelation) can we grow our experience of God. On the other hand, the inward-focused left brain assists this process by helping us to expand our knowledge, detail by detail, so it too plays a valuable role in our quest to understand wholeness. Nevertheless, if the devil is to be found in the details, then God must be found in the context, and of course, we find context as we move outward onto the next level of complexity or unity—as when we expand our understanding. Mentally, we achieve outward movement within the whole of knowledge by assembling information. Spiritually, we expand the size of our wholeness—become more holy—by assembling experience.

Keep in mind that our inward and outward perspectives can take two fundamental forms because we possess two bodies, an individual one and a collective one (which, of course, can take many forms, since we are a part of many different collectives). Both our individual body and its encompassing collective body possess inward- and outward-looking perspectives. Our collective self, for example, can be focused inward on its individual selves—as we see exemplified by most political cultures in which the reelection of individual politicians, rather than the welfare of the country, is the primary goal. Our collective self can also be focused outward on our collective body. We see this in our efforts to build cultures that are supportive, as well as competitive, and fair to all.

In *Why We Believe What We Believe*, Dr. Andrew Newberg, director of the Center for Spirituality and the Mind, and Mark Robert Waldman, associate fellow at the Center, explain the relationship between the two brain hemispheres this way: "We are born with two hemispheres that will, over time, develop two distinctly different worldviews, and our consciousness does not seem to like this very much. The right side of the brain wants to exclaim, 'This is it—this is the whole picture.' But the left side intrudes, saying, 'No, you're wrong—look at all the inconsistencies and differences and pieces of the puzzle that have been ignored.' Neurological studies seem to confirm this inner conflict by showing that each person is capable of thinking both ways, though not necessarily at the same time."[17]

Newberg and Waldman explain that the brain's left hemisphere "turns reality into sets of ideas that can be communicated through language to others," whereas "the right side spatially grasps the wholeness of the world through feelings." They found that "both halves of the brain, when working together, give us a sense of reality that is clearly different from the sense formed when either side acts alone. Experiments have even found that each hemisphere creates a separate consciousness, functioning independently of the other."[18]

"Most of the time the marriage of our two brain hemispheres is completely harmonious," Rita Carter observes in *Mapping the Mind*. "Conscious decisions, although they may seem to be made by the dominant partner [brain hemisphere] alone, are in fact fully informed by the findings of both hemispheres. Sometimes, though, the conversation between them falters. The dominant hemisphere may ignore the information supplied by its partner and make a decision based purely on what it thinks. The result may be an emotional disquiet that is difficult to explain. Conversely, the non-dominant partner sometimes bypasses the executive control of the other side and triggers an action based purely on instinct."[19]

Our choice of perspective determines what we *see*. And what we see affects what we *believe*, which influences what we *do*. What we believe and do then reverberate in what we *feel* and *create*. Brain perspective—whether of the left or of the right—resonates in everything we encounter.

Our two perspectives serve as our windows on the world. Energized by life, we create through the energy of mind, guided by feeling and judgment. As with our physical perspective, our mental perspective determines what part of the whole we see. In one case, we are working with physical objects in a physical environment; in the other, we are working with ideas in a mental environment. We see the same patterns being expressed, but through two different yet harmonious energies. Much can be learned about mental perspectives simply by recalling what we know about physical perspective and transferring the pattern.

The brain is our communications tool. It processes the information that creates our belief systems. It runs our body, and it can heal our body. When we are able to understand the relationship of the two perspectives, we create a mental environment in which we can more easily find our bearings, and thus more easily find truth and healing and achieve success in our efforts to create. And the brain is easy to operate. Ask right-brain questions—questions the right brain is equipped to answer, holistic questions that seek generalities—and the right brain will answer (but not necessarily via thought). Ask left-brain questions, questions that seek details, and the left will answer.

We believe and act based on what we see and hear. And mostly, what we see and hear is a worldview that sees and discusses reality from a left-brain-dominant perspective, a competitive view that often ignores the holistic perspective. When we act based on this worldview, the loss can be substantial, because the combination of any two parts is greater than the sum of the individual parts.

Deep within our consciousness, we routinely and instinctively ask, What is real? What is true? The answers that come back to us are almost always two—from two very different voices, typically one loud and one soft, one perhaps in the form of a thought, the other in the form of a feeling. We are then left to find a way to harmonize them, to find where we want to be physically, mentally, and spiritually in relation to them.

When forced to make a decision, we usually find a position somewhere between the extremes: where we *feel* the best, where we *think* we belong, perhaps a combination of the two, perhaps where the pressure is least. For some of us, the extremes themselves are the places where we feel best; we may be addicted to intense experiences, or even to pain or high-risk activities. On the other hand, we often do not make big decisions unless we have to. When we are not challenged, many of us stay mired in current patterns and end up living a placid, passive, and rather stuck existence.

Chapter Four

Separation and the Left Brain

> Until the left brain is able to see the unity running through
> everything, to know that there is truly one spirit, one force, one
> consciousness moving through absolutely everything in existence—
> until it knows that unity beyond any doubt—then the mind is
> going to stay separated from itself, from its wholeness and from
> the fullness of its potential.
>
> — DRUNVALO MELCHIZEDEK, *THE ANCIENT SECRET OF THE FLOWER OF LIFE,*
> *VOLUME 1*

After reading the previous chapter, some readers might be thinking, "I'm analytical. I must be left-brain dominant. If the left brain is limited, selfish, and destructive, aren't left-brain perspectives and processes inferior? What does that say about me?" In the present chapter, we will examine both the perils and the usefulness of left-brain dominance, and its relationship to separation. We will look at how to avoid its pitfalls and how to integrate the left brain's unique skills with a whole-brain perspective. When we take in the big picture and don't get trapped by a narrow-focus perspective—something we can all do, since we all have two brain hemispheres—any perceived disadvantage in left-brain dominance will disappear.

We are much more than our perspectives and the processes with which we respond. Brain dominance plays a major role in what we perceive, what we create, and how we feel, but this is not who we *are*. It's just another dualistic option that comes with life in a dualistic system. The two hemispheres are processing centers whose function is to absorb streams of energy-charged information and then respond to that information. Energy comes to us and registers as perspective. We process that information into perception, and creative energy goes out: *information in* (from perspective), *response out* (through process). Energy is always moving. Our hemispheric dominance is reflected in our choices to a degree, and often it temporarily channels us into certain roles, but it does not ultimately define or circumscribe our deeper purposes, value, and character.

There is no such thing as superior or inferior perspectives and processes; therefore, there is no point in judging them. Judgment is an essential tool of discernment, but it needs to be applied correctly. When we judge the left brain's linear perspective and compare it with the right brain's holistic perspective, it's like judging a room and a building and pronouncing one to be superior to the other, or like comparing a single personal attribute (size, skin color, age) with the complete person. It makes no sense. Judging is useful when it helps us to sort out our options, but brain dominance is not an option we can choose. Furthermore, both brain hemispheres are needed because they are complementary; taken alone, both are limited. As we have seen, the right brain sees on a macro scale but is lacking critical details. It sees the map of reality and knows where to end up but does not possess the details for discerning how to get there. The linear left brain has the ability to figure out how to get there but is often lost in terms of where it needs to end up (or thinks it knows how to get there but doesn't). The complexity of choices and details is overwhelming, and the left brain can "crunch the numbers" (or the details) without remembering why (or even if) the details are necessary in the first place. It can miss the big picture altogether and needs the right brain's holistic context for guidance.

From a holistic perspective, there is no disadvantage to having left-brain dominance. The holistic perspective itself encompasses detail, and therefore it encompasses the left-brain perspective; it takes in duality just as it takes in all points of view. From the holistic perspective, therefore, no supporting perspective is rejected; the whole cannot reject parts of itself. We all have and need the left brain and its ability to separate out and analyze the parts. Ultimately, it is most advantageous to use *both* sides of the brain when viewing a problem or situation. It so happens that women are more likely to integrate the two brain hemispheres than men. As Rita Carter states in *Mapping the Mind*: "There is a tendency for women to bring both sides of their brain to bear on [a] problem, while men often use only the side most obviously suited to it. This pattern of activity suggests that in some ways women take a broader view of life, bringing more aspects of the situation into play when making decisions, for example. Men, on the other hand, are more focused."[1]

Keep in mind that left-brain dominance itself does not prevent us from fully accessing and utilizing the right side of the brain. Being left-brain dominant does not mean you are one- or two-dimensional. In a generalized sense, that is true of your dominant brain hemisphere—but not of you. If, like me, you are left-brain dominant, rather than focusing on the left's limitations, you might think of yourself as a specialist—specialized for focusing, for seeing linear perspectives, for getting to the root of things and seeing the critical details. It is an important and necessary perspective.

On the other hand (as we have seen and will continue to see), left-brain dominance does come with some baggage, particularly in men, selfish and destructive tendencies being examples. Although these tendencies are often negative in their expression, they are not necessarily so, and they can in fact be quite beneficial.

Given that the two hemispheres are so different in their visions and in their approach to problem solving, in order to avoid a deadlock between the two, one hemisphere or the other must act as director of operations. Each hemisphere has its advantages and disadvantages, and an advantage in one circumstance may be a disadvantage in another. As we have seen, one constructs, the other deconstructs (and deconstruction can be destructive, but not necessarily); one is designed to protect us as individuals, the other is designed to protect us as a collective. Because the hemispheres work as a team, the choice of action is ours, and circumstances dictate which perspective and process will best serve us. The left brain's perspective is at a disadvantage only when trying to understand something it is not equipped to understand; the same applies to the right brain's perspective. The dualistic (left) hemisphere is the fact gatherer, the explorer—independent, free, roaming, and aggressive. It analyzes facts to try to determine if they are accurate before sending them to the holistic (right) hemisphere to be integrated into the whole, the big-picture perspective. They are both extremely valuable perspectives.

Aggression and the Left Brain

With this in mind, let's explore the pitfalls that often accompany left-brain dominance, and also look at how we can help our two brain hemispheres to cooperate for achieving optimum clarity, harmony, and (ultimately) both internal and external peace.

Left-brain-dominant individuals tend to be more aggressive than right-brain-dominant individuals. This corresponds (harmonizes) with the energetic charge of most males, which is electric—think of the charge that invades you aggressively if you touch an electric line. Most females, on the other hand, are magnetic—magnetic energy draws us in. (This structure reflects the polarization of electromagnetic energy into either a propelling/repelling force—electricity—or an attracting, unifying force—magnetism.) The left brain tends to be aggressive. It needs to be. Its job is to isolate wholes, focus in on them, and take them apart (analyze them) to see what's inside—perhaps to see if they are what they appear to be.

The Destructive Nature of the Deconstructive Left Brain

The aggressive, analytical nature of the left brain leads us to disassemble wholes. In keeping with their opposing natures, the right brain constructs; the left brain deconstructs. Although destruction does not necessarily result from aggressiveness, it is a common response when we are overly aggressive. Whether it's a bullet shot into someone, a car that moves too aggressively to change lanes on a crowded highway, or the use of dismissive or obstructive conversational strategies, when one individual or object moves into the space of another, destruction is a common occurrence.

Thus, the left brain's approach to understanding, being inherently aggressive, often tends to be destructive. Whether its deconstructive process becomes destructive depends on the nature of the object or process to which deconstruction is applied, as well as the *manner* in which it is applied. Take an engine apart, and no harm is done unless we break or lose a part; we can always reassemble it. But take apart a cat or a tree, and the result is destruction. And while destruction might seem a purely negative process—and it certainly can be—it is sometimes necessary and good, as when the lumber of a tree provides someone with shelter. Or consider ideas. The left brain approaches ideas with the same aggressive, deconstructive attitude with which it approaches physical reality. New and unknown ideas are met with a skeptical, combative attitude in an attempt to detect deceit, to prevent us from being misled. As a protective security measure, the process of analysis works to break down ideas and reveal their fundamental weaknesses.

We see the destructive character of the left brain expressed graphically in the frequency with which young men (with their left-brain dominance) destroy lives and property, relative to young women. This destructive tendency continues through male adulthood in many ways—such as in men's use (and belief in the effectiveness) of war and weaponry as means of effecting change, and in their almost psychotically obsessive focus on short-term profits at any cost, especially in the corporate world. In these examples, the outcomes on the future and on the broader collective are almost invariably disastrous and unsustainable—but the left brain doesn't notice this, because its concentration is on immediate, narrow gains. The left brain also has a fascination with technological fixes as shortcuts for real understanding—for example, "smart bombs" whose accuracy in destroying a given target is erroneously confused with effectiveness in accomplishing ultimate goals. In such cases, the left brain is so mesmerized by its own ability to view things in isolation that it forgets the big picture altogether. A further indication of the destructive tendencies of left-brained males is the fact that nearly 93 percent of the U.S. prisoner population is male.[2] Imagine how many people have been killed and tortured throughout the history of the planet, and try to guess what percentage of these deeds have been done at the hands of males.[3]

For all of its activities of splitting off and examining and manipulating pieces of the whole, the left brain understands the value of harmony and seeks to achieve it through dominance

("Come into harmony with me"—in other words, "Do what I want"). Force, when determined enough, almost always pre-vails—look at how water is able over time to erode rock. The left brain is internally harmonious—it is not self-divided—but its vision is one of separation, resulting in a competitive world in conflict. The left brain, focused on security, sees domination over people and things as a way to ensure it—but, having a par-tial perspective, can easily overlook factors such as future consequences.

The fact that many of our global friends opposed the United States' war efforts in Iraq and refused to help us invade should have caused us to take pause, but we did not, because the collec-tive left brain was so concentrated on its narrowly focused tactics that it chose to ignore this external feedback. As a result of our "selective perception," we created a breeding ground for terrorists (one of many unintended consequences). We created in Iraq what we went to war in Afghanistan to destroy—a school for war. Rad-icals went to Iraq, fought, learned their craft, and went home to spread their knowledge. Opponents of the war pointed out this obvious response for years, but their unpopular views were dis-missed as partisan or unpatriotic until they were finally vindicated by a leaked secret National Intelligence Estimate.[4]

Our collective (cultural) left brain, having a narrowly focused, force-oriented, go-it-alone perspective, naturally led us to ignore our old international allies and rush ahead with our plans for war. This is how the left brain is designed to respond, but it does not mean we need to make that choice. The two hemispheres simply convey to us what they see of reality, but ulti-mately, responsibility for the direction we take lies not in our brain, but in our personality, in our temperament and character.

People heavily under the influence of a left-brain-directed perspective are almost always willing to use force—or at least to sanction its use by others—when something stands in the way of their goals. The weapon of choice might be a gun, a threat, innuendo, or a vote, but whatever the tool, the intent is always to remove, damage, or destroy obstacles to their left-brain-driven goals. And we don't have to be left-brain directed to respond with force. Just as left-brain-dominant people are able to utilize the holistic right brain, all of us can utilize the dualistic left-brain perspective, for good or for ill. Therefore, when any of us encounters a problem, our left brain is likely going to advise us to engage in a separative activity to solve it—to break up the problem into chunks that we can dominate and thus control. This involves separating the whole (the problem) from its influence, from its power, even from its life if necessary (if our goal is seen to be important enough). In this mindset, whatever is necessary in order to win, or to achieve one's narrowly focused goal, is justified. Because the left brain's attitude is fundamentally self and survival oriented, its narrow focus tends to preclude long-term outlooks, just as it precludes broad collective interests.

The destructive methods of the left brain can be put to a lot of good uses as well—for example, when we need to break a habit; or when we need to destroy obstacles in order to make a fresh start; or when we need to expose deception. The destructive nature of the left brain is part of the yin and yang of reality. The destructive option is a choice. It's a force that we have available to us. We truly are gods, in that we have access to all creative and destructive forces present on this planet. We are not compelled to use destructive means to solve our problems. It's a conscious choice that we make.

A Course in Miracles describes the destructive action of the left brain in terms of fragmentation: The ego (a fear- and separation-based thought system[5]) "believes in 'solving' conflict through fragmentation, and does not perceive the situation as a whole. Therefore, it seeks to split off segments of the situation and deal with them separately, for it has faith in separation and not in wholeness."[6] Elsewhere, the Course states, "Obsessed with the conviction that separation is salvation, the ego attacks everything it perceives by breaking it into small, disconnected parts, without meaningful relationships and therefore without meaning."[7]

You will notice that what the Course describes as a thought system of fear and separation perfectly coincides with our description of a left-brain-directed thought system. In my research to understand how the left brain perceives reality, it became progressively clear that the ego is nothing more or less than the perception that results when we look at reality through the lens of the left brain. The ego is that part of us that reacts from a purely left-brain perspective. It is what it is because it is, by itself, narrowly self focused and lacks holistic perception.

Controlling Our Perspective

Since our perspective is so heavily tied to perception, and perception is tied to action (we act based on what we see/perceive), our choice is either to take control of our perspective to the degree that we are able, or to allow it, in effect, to largely control us through our beliefs and actions. Though we assume that others are separate from us, when we look closely, we find that we live in a complex matrix of energetic connections and relationships. Our perception of people and things largely determines our *understanding* of people and things, and our understanding of people and things affects the way we *treat* people and things. Of course, how we treat others affects the way others *feel*, and their feelings produce energies that are often redirected back at us. When we stir people's feelings, we stir energies that often affect the way we are treated and the way we subsequently feel. By recognizing how our energies affect the feelings of others, we can learn how to protect ourselves from debilitating energies, and we can feel good in spite of those around us.

Viewing reality from a right-brain perspective, we perceive others as one with us, cooperative, and supportive in many ways. Viewing the same reality through our left brain, we see those same individuals and groups as separate and in competition, and this often leads us to view them as being in opposition to us—in opposition to our goals, to our ideals, to our values. It's a view that intensifies polarization and effectively provides the fuel for war and other activities with destructive and tragic consequences.

Eastern cultures refer to our two fundamental perspectives in terms of the knowledge they produce. In *The Tao of Physics*, Fritjof Capra explains,

> The *Upanishads*, for example, speak about a higher and a lower knowledge and associate the lower knowledge with various sciences, the higher with religious awareness. Buddhists talk about "relative" and "absolute" knowledge, or about "conditional truth" and "transcendental truth." Chinese philosophy, on the other hand, has always emphasized the complementary nature of the intuitive and the rational and has represented them by the archetypal pair *yin* and *yang* which form the basis of Chinese thought. Accordingly, two complementary philosophical traditions—Taoism and Confucianism—have developed in ancient China to deal with the two kinds of knowledge.[8]

Have you ever asked a question of God and received two very different answers? Have you ever thought, "There's a part of me that believes in this idea (or plan or solution) but another part that doesn't"? Or perhaps you've sensed that a part of you wanted to change something and another part didn't. That's likely your two hemispheres responding to you. Each processes its perspective of reality in its unique holistic manner so that you get a minimum of two different answers, directions, perceptions, or possible responses. And remember that answers are not always verbal. Answers can also come through feelings, symbols, connections, and other means.

The Challenge of Left-Brain Dominance

Those of us who inhabit a body that is effectively directed by a polar-based, dualistic brain—most men and more than a few women—face a unique challenge. We have come into this body with a controlling brain hemisphere that sees and seeks separation and polarization, and has a narrow focus that ignores or even sabotages broader collective as well as long-term interests. The result is a tendency to perceive God and everything else as being separate from us. That's what it means to be separative: to see the separation between wholes (to the exclusion of their oneness) and to act to separate wholes. The left (or dualistic) hemisphere separates, while the right (or holistic) unites; together the two perspectives encompass the entire range of connectivity.

The planet and universe we inhabit are fraught with dangers. Relying on the left brain for guidance rather than the right (or, better, a fully integrated) brain in this treacherous environment is something like choosing a sporting event like diving where the more difficult the dive, the more points you can earn. Although the payout from finding our way back to unity after being separated from it is likely to be exceptional, this option involves substantially greater risk and hardship. When we are directed by a dualistic brain, we experience a greater separation from love, and from its connections, insights, and nourishing qualities. The dualistic brain is essentially blind to oneness, blind to timelessness, blind to feeling, perhaps even blind to God. Only because we have holistic brain input can we sometimes escape the limiting extremes of the dualistic perception as described. On a planet where many people feel abandoned by God, the ones most likely to feel this way are surely those who perceive the world from a perspective of separation.

Nevertheless, the limitations of being directed by a left-brain perspective are mostly those we place on ourselves by refusing to respect and accept (and often, through reflex habits, not even noticing) the vision offered to all of us by the harmonious unity of the brain's right hemisphere. If left-brain dominance has been limiting up to now, it is no longer. Once we know that we have two distinct perspectives, our only limits are those we impose on ourselves through inaction. And there is only now. The past and the future are but ideas we believe in, ideas that tie us to an inaccessible past and an imaginary future. It doesn't matter what we were 10 minutes ago. We don't have to be that any more.

In *Conversations with God: An Uncommon Dialogue, Book 2*, Neale Donald Walsch asks God about separation and receives this answer: "Consciousness of separation, segregation, superiority—of 'we' versus 'they,' of 'us' and 'them'—is what creates the Hitler Experience. The consciousness of Divine Brotherhood, of unity, of Oneness, of 'ours,' rather than 'yours'/'mine,' is what creates the Christ Experience."[9]

The peace and bliss of Oneness is a great place to be in— so what might account for our *not* being in that place? Why might Higher Powers have created such a state of apparent separation? As a possible answer, we might consider the following: If we crave a *supreme* challenge and *supreme* excitement, what could possibly be more challenging than to separate from the Oneness, separate from our knowledge of unity, and start over in an environment where we see ourselves as separate from God? Perhaps being separated from unity and finding our way back again gives us an added dimension of understanding and even deepens our compassion. Perhaps experience of such extremes of apparent loss (or estrangement from the whole) add to our sense of the whole, just as our experience of extremes of pain adds to our appreciation of ordinary pleasures.

The Fundamental Separation: Unity into Duality

To understand separation at its most fundamental level, the best place to start is probably at the point of Oneness just prior to the birth of separation.

The left brain, in response to encountering the oneness of a whole, seeks to process it analytically. This involves separating wholes into as many parts (details) as possible, beginning with a simple division into two parts. A two-part separation is the one we usually discover first because it's the most obvious division. Nevertheless, in trying to separate a whole, the left brain is trying to do the impossible. We cannot truly separate individual realities from collective realities. Nor can we separate parts from the wholes in which they nest, or get a true picture of anything (fact, object, process) apart from all the ways in which it is related to other things. As we have seen, every part is a whole comprising other parts, and every whole is a part of another whole. Viewing a whole and taking it apart in isolation only destroys the whole.

Let's look at some examples. You can remove the interior parts from a car's engine, but then you no longer have an engine—it no longer converts energy into mechanical force and motion, which is what an engine does. Remove all the people from a community, or from a school, and that collective (community or school) ceases to exist (except perhaps as an inherently fictitious legal entity or a set of buildings and infrastructure). Remove one or more of the individuals from such a collective and we change the nature of the collective—it becomes a different collective (even if it has the same name and some continuity of purpose). Wholeness is a relationship, and relationship is born of spirit energy. Wholeness, being spiritual in nature, being Oneness to its very core, cannot be divided. When we try to divide it, it loses its wholeness.

Wholes can, however, be arbitrarily separated, as when we cut a cake. There is no fixed way of separating a cake. We simply choose how many slices we need. We can divide goodness into *good, better*, and *best*, but we can also divide it into *good* and *bad*, or make four or five divisions. To the limited perspective of the left brain, it appears that we can separate parts from wholes to get to the truth of them. Separation is indeed the left brain's function, and it can be very useful—but by itself it leads to wrong conclusions and destructive outcomes. We see the destructive results of separation when someone's words are taken out of context in order to create an advantage for someone else, such as we so often find in political wrangling and personal disputes. When we take someone's words out of context, we are arbitrarily separating the whole in a way that destroys its integrity for the sake of some perceived personal advantage.

The dualistic left brain tries to separate based on facts, but when it doesn't have the facts, it will separate based on assumptions, or its goals, or some other criteria. Its underlying assumptions or goals can then seriously get in the way of its ability to discover what is true. When we act out of our left brain, we are naturally focused on separation, and our creations are likely to reflect the separation we perceive. This separation usually begins as a two-part division into good or bad, right or wrong, black or white, yes or no. From an evolutionary standpoint, this is a necessary and perfect first step, because the first thing we need to know as we set out on a quest into the unknown is the nature of any extremes that we might encounter. As holistic teacher and author Gregg Braden asks in his video *Beyond Zero Point: The Journey to Compassion*, "How can you ever find your balance in life until you know what the boundaries of that balance are all about? How can we know our balance until we find our extremes?"[10] Sometimes one question is worth many answers.

To understand full well the effects of the extremes we encounter, we need to understand the effects of too much of anything, as well as the effects of too little. This applies whether we consider light, love, money, or work—in fact, almost anything. Once we understand the two extremes, we are more capable of understanding what we will find in the territory between them. The two extremes of a dualistic system frame the stage for the unfolding of knowledge that occurs as we explore different positions between those extremes.

The separative effect of the left brain can often mislead, however. One such example is when we look at one thing that has variable expressions along a continuum and see it as two irreconcilable, opposing things. This kind of mistake has been known and described since antiquity. Ancient Hermetic teachings, for example, state that

> love and hate are generally regarded as being things diametrically opposed to each other; entirely different; unreconcilable. . . . [But when] we apply the Principle of Polarity [the Fourth Hermetic Principle] we find that there is no such thing as Absolute Love or Absolute Hate, as distinguished from each other. The two are merely terms applied to the two poles of the same thing. Beginning at any point of the scale we find "more love," or "less hate," as we ascend the scale; and "more hate" or "less love" as we descend, this being true no matter from what point, high or low, we may start. There are degrees of Love and Hate, and there is a middle point where "Like and Dislike" become so faint that it is difficult to distinguish between them. . . . Where you find one thing you find its opposite.[11]

Needless to say, we sometimes make mistakes when we try to separate wholes. For example, we've traditionally separated love into two parts: love and hate (with gradations in between). But the absence (or opposite) of love is actually fear, and this suggests that, as a culture, we understand love so poorly that we have yet to widely recognize its true opposite. Hate is a response of fear, a component of fear.

A certain amount or kind of information is necessary in order for the left brain to divide a whole into two fundamental parts (or, put another way, to dissect a unified whole into a set of polar opposites). Another amount or kind of information is necessary if the brain is to divide a whole into three or more parts. An example of a primal three-part separation is the famous truth/beauty/goodness triumvirate. These are the three objects of love—or, as love is described in *The Urantia Book*, their ancestor.[12] In spite of our best efforts to separate these qualities, at this fundamental level of reality, evidence of the Oneness of the three comes through. Truth is both beautiful and good. Beauty is both true and good. Goodness is equally true and beautiful.[13]

Sometimes the number of parts in the division is itself important. Two, for example, is the primal number for polarity (love/hate, heat/cold, etc.). Three can indicate a balanced set of attributes, as in the truth/beauty/goodness example above. Four is often the result of further division of each of two parts (although four can also come directly out of one). Of course, we can separate wholes into any number of parts—2 or 12 or 1,000. Sometimes certain rules govern the number of parts; at other times the division is arbitrary, as we saw in the cake example. When divisions are made in an attempt to provide or receive clarification (in contrast to something like cake cutting), then the more we know or want to know, the more details we have and the greater our ability to differentiate the parts of a whole. In other words, *the more we know, the more parts we find*. And of course, the more parts we find, the more we know—at least in the left brain's sense of knowing. As science clearly demonstrates, you can learn a lot about a whole by looking at its parts. Fact by fact, whole by whole, slowly we expand the unity of our understanding.

Rather than continuing to expand their understanding, many people are content with their current understanding (or lack of it) and as a result are stuck in a position where their current level of ignorance remains or even gets reinforced by the preselected nature of their inputs. Because separation as a state and process is so widely accepted in our culture, people are able to create ideological moats around themselves, their ideas, and their actions. They are able to build philosophical defenses to wall off (separate) and hide the philosophical conflicts that reveal the errors in their beliefs and actions. Because so few people look to achieve deeper unity in their ideas and understanding, people (including many governmental and business leaders) are able to separate and hide parts of the truth from one another in such a way that ideological conflicts go unnoticed and, as a result, often go unchallenged. It is through separation, coupled with the failure of people to notice the inherent conflicts that separation obscures, that some people (and their mosques, churches, and synagogues) are able to justify their support for war, and get away with it.

In Neale Donald Walsch's *Tomorrow's God*, God tells Walsch, "The only way you can justify treating other countries, other cultures, other people, the way that you do is to imagine—no, to *insist*—that they are separate from you. To make this separation more vivid, and to give yourselves justification for acting the way you do, you also insist that these others are separate from God. Only YOU are united with God, only YOU are God's people, only YOU are following God's plan for salvation."[14]

We must always remain vigilant against the dangers presented by those who become too focused on left-brain-generated perspectives and perceptions, and fail to be moderated by those of the holistic right brain. The perceptions we create, based on the left hemisphere's selfish, separation-based perspective, are always going to suggest that separative activities and processes can solve life's problems. Money, for example, can separate us from having to work, from having to support society. Need more than you earn? To some (including many white-collar criminals), the solution is theft—separating money or possessions from the rightful owner. Is someone a major problem? Murder separates, as do capital punishment and prison. The purpose of jail is, more than anything else, to separate us from problem people. Another tool of separation is bribery. Bribery works in that it separates us from the system of law and justice designed to protect us. Corruption, lack of transparency, and favoritism all separate honest government from the people and from accountability, and are so endemic in Washington that we can hardly imagine government operating in any other way.

The effect of separation drives us to live in the suburbs or the country or a monastery. We retreat as a way of separating from the collective and from the conflicts that our neighbors present us with. That way, we don't have to make some of the difficult internal spiritual adjustments that are necessary if we are to live in peace among the other members of our culture. *And these spiritual adjustments may be exactly what we need as individuals and as a society—and might even (according to many sources of spiritual wisdom) make up our deeper purpose for being here.*

Separation and Feeling

We've touched on the importance of feeling—the right brain's signature response to reality—as a way of understanding our experiences. You might be wondering, does separation have a feeling?

Separation has many feelings. If you want to know how separation feels, remember how it feels to be jealous. Remember how it feels to be lonely. Remember how it feels to be separate from something you want really badly. Remember, if you dare, how it feels to hate.

To describe the attitude of a left-brain-dominant individual or collective that lacks a right-brain-augmented perspective, we need look no further than the synonyms of separation: *withdrawal, alienation, segregation, disconnection, isolation.* True to form, this was left-brained America's response to the rest of the world when given the opportunity to go to war in Iraq. We *withdrew* our respect for the opinion of our allies and acted against their strong protests. We *segregated* ourselves from their criticism and choice of action, and ignored the feelings that these actions provoked. In taking these actions, we *alienated* much of the world, *disconnecting* from the strong bond of unity created by the events of 9/11, thus *isolating* ourselves from our traditional friends.

"Is there any way out of this mess?" Walsh asks God in *Conversations with God: An Uncommon Dialogue, Book 2.*

"Yes," God answers. "Shall I say it again? A *shift of consciousness.* You cannot solve the problems which plague humankind through governmental action or by political means. You have been trying that for thousands of years. The change that must be made can be made only in the hearts of men. . . . *You must stop seeing God as separate from you, and you as separate from each other.*"[15]

Selected Left- and Right-Brain Characteristics

This table summarizes how the two brain hemispheres view and process holistic elements. Perspective, process, and structure are interrelated, so there is necessarily considerable overlap in the descriptions.

Dualistic (Left) Brain Hemisphere	Holistic (Right) Brain Hemisphere
PERSPECTIVE	
Polar	Nonpolar
Individual oriented	Collective oriented
Inwardly focused (self focused)	Outward looking (collective-self seeing)
Views interiors (individually)	Views exteriors (as one)
Limited	Unlimited
Relative	Absolute
Smaller elements	Larger elements
Specifics	Generalities
Part seeing	Whole seeing

Dualistic (Left) Brain Hemisphere	Holistic (Right) Brain Hemisphere
STRUCTURE AND PROCESS	
Polar	Nonpolar
Individual oriented	Collective oriented
Focuses sequentially	Perceives wholes simultaneously
Analytic, deconstructive (often destructive)	Synthetic, which is constructive
Separative or disintegrative	Connective or integrative
Exclusive	Inclusive
Electric	Magnetic (which is inclusive)
Reason-based sequential processing, rational	Processes intuitively
Serial processing	Parallel processing
Competitive	Cooperative
Judgmental	Nonjudgmental
Skeptical	Trusting
Rejective, intolerant	Receptive, tolerant
Selfish	Serving
Force oriented	Attraction oriented
Conserving	Liberal, nonconserving[16]
Energized by fear	Energized by love
Simple, dualistic relationships	Complex, holistic relationships
Linear based	Nonlinear, but incorporating the linear
One- and two-dimensional	Multidimensional
Time oriented	Now oriented
Actuality	Potentiality
Tactical	Strategic
Ego perception	God perception

Chapter Five

The Right Brain's Vision

If your head tells you one thing, and your heart tells you another, before you do anything, you should first decide whether you have a better head or a better heart.

— MARILYN VOS SAVANT

The whole-istic right brain is sometimes referred to as the feminine brain, as it is the predominant brain hemisphere for most women. To ground our exploration of right-brain perspectives, processes, and perceptions, we turn to brain researcher Jill Bolte Taylor. Taylor, a neuroanatomist, gained international fame after posting a video on the Internet in which she discusses her experience with a massive left-hemisphere cerebral hemorrhage (a type of stroke), also chronicled in her book, *My Stroke of Insight*. Her insights are based not only on her impressive professional qualifications, but also on her personal experience and observations of an event in her brain that temporarily gave her only one normally functioning brain hemisphere (the right) and resulted in a spiritual epiphany. "For those of you that understand computers," Taylor says, our right hemisphere functions like a parallel processor, while our left hemisphere functions like a serial processor. . . . The two hemispheres . . . process information differently. Each of our hemispheres thinks about different things, they care about different things, and dare I say, they have very different personalities. . . . Our right hemisphere is all about this present moment. It's all about right here, right now. Our right hemisphere . . . thinks in pictures and . . . learns kinesthetically through the movement of our bodies. Information in the form of energy streams in simultaneously through all of our sensory systems, and then . . . explodes into this enormous collage of what this present moment looks like, what this present moment smells like and tastes like, what it feels like and what it sounds like. I am an energy being, connected to the energy all around me through the consciousness of my right hemisphere. We are energy beings connected to one another through the consciousness of our right hemispheres as one human family.[1]

In chapters 3 and 4, we outlined the fundamental nature of the holistic right brain's perception in our exploration of the dualistic left brain. Here we continue to explore these fundamentals, but with a greater focus on the right brain's perceptual attributes as a whole. This exploration should enable us to better perceive the connections (relationships) between these perceptual attributes and thus help to confirm their place in the unified system that is right-brain perception. Whether it's a watch, a couture ensemble, or an ideology, the precision with which the parts of a whole connect, or relate harmoniously, suggests with a high degree of confidence whether they are authentic parts of the whole. Connections both create and reflect unity, unity being a fundamental characteristic of truth. But connections can also be found in distortions and lies, so connections can be misleading. The key to confidence is having sufficient harmonious context with which to connect. It is analogous to having the surrounding pieces of a jigsaw puzzle confirm that the piece we have just inserted is correct.

We will explore four main areas in this chapter: perspective, process, sacred geometry, and relationship. Two of these areas, perspective and process, we have already explored at some length. The third, sacred geometry (already introduced briefly in chapter 3), fleshes out perspective in an often-dramatic fashion. And the fourth area, relationship, takes us into the spiritual realm, wherein we perceive that unity reigns and separation is illusory; every whole has some impact on every other whole. Rather than expand on Taylor's ideas, we will use them as our context, always choosing definitions and interpreting ideas in light of her insights.

Before we continue, I would like to point out that I use the word *perspective* in conjunction with the right brain hesitantly. Because the right brain sees everything around and within it, this is technically not a perspective. By definition, a perspective tends to suggest a limited view. However, considering the limitations faced by our right brain—the distortions, the barriers, and the vast holes in our knowledge, for example—in effect, the right brain's view is partial; therefore, the use of *perspective* here seems reasonably accurate.

Perspective, Perception, and Control of the Creative Process

Before we focus our attention on right-brain perception and its perspectives and processes, let's review some of the fundamentals of perception. Perception has two fundamental meanings. Scientifically, the process of thought is known as *cognition*. Cognition is a whole, of which perception and judgment are the main parts. It is a sequential process in which we do two things: we *grasp* the vision that unfolds in front of us (based on our perspective), a process known as *perception*; we then *judge* that perception. And the process is cyclic. Perception is continual, as is judgment; they alternate back and forth, checking and rechecking, processing and reprocessing the thing, information, or experience until we are satisfied. From a *left-brain* perspective, it's a sequential process with a zigzagging linear flow that takes the form of a wave. From a *holistic* perspective, this linear zigzag flow appears to spiral. When we stretch out the spiral shown in figure 5, its waveform structure is most readily apparent, as seen in figure 6. Thus we have a pure perception—which flows to us as a stream of information-based energy (the scientific perspective)—and we have perception after it has been processed through judgment (reflecting the most common usage of the term). Since most people think of perception as inclusive of judgment, and since it is the more holistic of our two options, we will continue with that definition.

Although brain dominance plays a rather substantial role in determining our perspective, perspective is also very much a creative choice. We can adopt the perspectives that members of our culture want us to have, or we can develop perspectives that reflect who we are and what we have to contribute to the collective self by being our authentic selves.

Physical perspective, as we know, reflects our position (physical attitude) within our environment. Our physical perspective is limited by where we choose to go and how attentive we are. It depends on what our eyes (and other sense organs) reveal to us. Our mental perspective likewise depends on where we position ourselves and how attentive we are.

Since spirit controls mental energy, and mental energy controls physical energy, our three perspectives—physical, mental, and spiritual—tend to be in close alignment, sharing significant

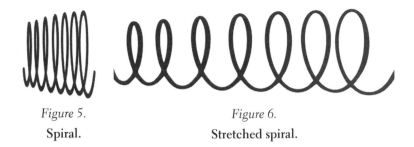

Figure 5.

Spiral.

Figure 6.

Stretched spiral.

patterns with each other. Each of the three energetic perspectives reflects the others in fundamental ways (reminding us of the aphorism "As above, so below; as below, so above"). By applying our understanding of a physical perspective to mental and spiritual perspectives, we are able to gain valuable insight into the latter two.

As we move through a physical environment, our position changes, and with that change we experience a change in our perspective, which then affects our perception. Perspective is instantaneous; perception develops over time (but that can be very short). Of course, when we turn our body and face in a new direction, the change in perspective is more pronounced than if we only move straight ahead. Another way to increase the scope of our perspective is by simply turning our head and turning our eyes. Although movements such as these broaden our perspective, it's still a limited perspective. And if our neck or eye movement is limited, our perspective is narrowed further. At the extreme (for example, if we are sitting paralyzed in a chair with no neck movement and loss of eye muscles), we can lose all but one perspective.

Much the same can be said of our position within an environment of mind and ideas. Our mind can become fixated in one direction with the result that we are unable to see essential information and suffer because of it. When we lose much of our ability to exercise our beliefs, we call it tunnel vision or narrow-mindedness. But we can lose mental movement even though we remain mentally flexible. This happens when we become fixated on a person, thing, or idea for some reason (because we like it, or fear it, or feel traumatized by it, for example). Eventually, stealthily, a fixed position can become habitual and comfortable, with the consequence that we lose part of our mental perspective: we become unable to think or feel or explore in other directions. Our mental body is like our physical body in that when we keep our mental body healthy and flexible, we naturally see more of the mental world, the world of ideas, and we understand it better.

In the physical world, once we find a place where we would rather be or need to be, we move to that place. Movement is initiated by intent. Movement to or away from a *mental* position is initiated in a similar manner—by our intention to seek new perspectives and by the changing perceptions and judgments that we develop in the process of seeking new mental vistas. In effect, perception and judgment (or simply perception as it is commonly thought of) guide our mental movement.

$$\circledcirc$$

The right brain's perspective vertically nests the left brain's perspective within itself. We know this because the right brain's holistic perspective is achieved, in part, by integrating the left's dualistic perspective into its big picture. This structure, this relationship, is one of text and context. Whereas the left brain focuses on exploring and understanding the *text* of our lives, the right brain specializes in showing us the *context*. Although the two brain hemispheres are physically and (to a large extent) functionally connected via the corpus callosum, we discuss them as if they were separate. We do this not only to highlight the differences in their perspectives, but also because the dualistic left and the holistic right can become functionally separated, not only in individuals but (perhaps to an ever greater degree) collectively. Witness the cultural polarization we see in the United States between "red" and "blue" states, for example. Even right-brain-dominant individuals contribute to this polarized mentality, as when they reject rational thought and blame it for the dysfunctionality of our culture, ignoring the fact that people guided by the "rational" left brain are not always rational, just as those guided by a holistic brain are not always holistic. Another reason we find a functional disconnect between the two brains, especially with regard to culture, is that the left brain, because it looks after its self-interest, naturally resists being integrated with the holistic right-brain perspective. It sees survival value in maintaining its distinct identity. We see this clearly in the area of sex-role identification. For example, most males in our culture (governed by a left-brain defense of male sexual roles) would not be caught dead in women's clothing (even women's shirts and jeans, for example), whereas women tend to wear anything they like, from formal dresses and high heels to clothing from the men's department.

Keep in mind that the word *holistic* is a relative term. Obviously, not all wholes are complete. Wholes that are incomplete and only *tending toward* wholeness (something that is common when we deal with highly complex wholes such as governments, ideas, and human emotions) are perhaps best described as whole-istic, rather than whole. That is perhaps especially true in the case of holistic perspectives. Because we don't always know how much of a given perspective is missing, the word *holistic* suggests a degree of wholeness that is variable and often unknown.

Not knowing how complete or incomplete something is tends to trouble the cautious left brain and those who rely heavily on it for guidance. Since the left brain is responsible for our safety, not only is it wary, but also it probes for weaknesses. It seeks to find out if there is any incompletion, any parts missing. The trusting, fearless, collective-oriented right brain, on the other hand, simply accepts things as they are without judgment. From a right-brain-directed perspective, a glass filled halfway to the top is half full. From a left-brain-directed perspective, the same glass appears to be half empty.

To begin to approximate what it means to have a holistic perspective, imagine having a clear view of an environment containing an immense and rich landscape, such as a great city. To be in position to see all of it, the whole of it, we must have a distant perspective. However, being that far away, we can clearly perceive only the larger elements; the details cannot be accurately perceived. We can use binoculars and focus in on the details, and obtain the information that way, *but then we lose the big picture*. In any moment, we have to choose one perspective or the other. Mentally, our situation is similar. Although we have access to both perspectives to some degree, one or the other usually dominates the feed of information flowing to consciousness, and thus feeds our perception. We are (to a degree) what we physically, mentally, and spiritually consume.

We can, of course, choose to not look, or not respond to what we see from our perspective; which is to say, we can suppress a perspective and the perceptions we draw from it, as we sometimes do when we encounter disturbing ideas. Attitude and the perspective we obtain from our attitude are mind-based energies, energies over which we have considerable control. We must, however, have sufficient willpower to actually exercise control. Willpower, like muscle power, needs to be correctly exercised if we are to maintain strength.

Given that the right brain's process for dealing with reality is synthetic, or unifying, the right hemisphere naturally is all-inclusionary, taking in all that appears around it (in contrast to the left brain, which focuses in on some aspects of the big picture in great detail to the exclusion of others). Looking at the world through the lens of the right brain, reality is seen holistically, in its full multidimensional state. The right hemisphere, in contrast to the intentionally limited, one- and two-dimensional-based left, enjoys an unlimited perspective. The right brain is positioned to perceive unity and its identical twin, harmony.

From our habitual perspective as left-brain dominants (or as right-brain dominants under the spell of a left-brain-dominant culture), the foregoing description of the right hemisphere's unlimited, multidimensional, harmonizing perspective might seem rather fantastical, unbelievable, in direct conflict with what we see around us—a multitude of right-brain dominants who seem no more capable of understanding reality than left-brain dominants. But there are reasons why we are culturally unable to perceive the right brain's multidimensional scope. The broad, flawed perceptions that we create from our narrow perspectives naturally limit us—limit what we perceive as well as lead us to believe in limitations. But these are limits we impose on ourselves. They are the creation of an attitude that fails to recognize our potential. This response ignores the fact that we are almost unlimited in where we can go and what we can do in our dreams, which, of course, the left brain distrusts as unreal. As children, when we express our absoluteness, we quickly learn that it often interferes with other people's goals and can bring painful responses. And so we withdraw our belief in the value of extraordinary, transcendental events and thereby suppress portions of our natural potential. By simply accepting that the potential is there, rather than resisting, we free our mind to let it show us greater visions.

We are all, to one degree or another, programmed by cultural influences to act against our best interests—programmed to see a perspective that others want us to see. And often we choose to take in these influences even without understanding *what* we are taking in, just as we have chosen to eat junk food without understanding what it might do to our body. But cultural influences, however strong, can always be reversed, and the more we understand how and in what ways we became influenced, the easier they are to reverse.

To regain control of the fullness of our perspective, we must establish an internal environment of stability and honesty. Stability means we have a clear, focused internal center, and it is achieved by harmonizing our holistic and dualistic perspectives to the degree that the two are no longer at war with one another. Honesty entails openness to our higher self, allowing the higher self to be expressed in our creative processes. The process by which we gain greater control of our perspective unfolds in a holistic spiral whereby both of these qualities develop and integrate.

Although perspective might be thought of as the foundation of perception, perception is the product of a number of factors, including personality, brain functions, intent, and self-honesty. And affecting these and other factors is our context, or environment—culture's impact on our perception. Because of these, perception is sometimes freely chosen, sometimes imposed (willingly and unwillingly). Although two individuals might at times view reality from nearly identical perspectives (as a result of having nearly identical brain dominance and educational experiences, for example), because of the unique way they process their perspectives, they will tend to develop different perceptions, and from those perceptions, a variety of different creations. Perception is a process that can take a nanosecond or take years, but more often it takes place in a matter of seconds or days. It might take only a second to perceive that the man with a gun in the bank is a thief, whereas it might take years to perceive that the manager of the bank is a thief.

Right-Brain Processing

The complexity of the Whole (speaking here of the Whole in the sense of All That Is) is such that it is impossible to comprehend in any detail except over time. One either already lives it and understands it as God does, or evolves it into such an understanding over eons. For such an understanding or comprehension to manifest, layers or waves of experience must be added and integrated, a process of assembly sometimes referred to as *synthesis*.

Synthesis is a *connective* process that works toward oneness. *Constructive* is another term we can use to describe this process, a process of evolving toward unity through growth or addition. Being oneness oriented and synthetic in process and action, the holistic right brain is naturally *acquisition* oriented. It is driven to *assemble*—which is what it takes to arrive at greater oneness. One imagines that this drive is intended to acquire information and experience (mental and spiritual things) as part of the process of attaining oneness in its various forms. In a consumer-oriented society focused on the physical, this drive naturally unleashes an urge in many right-brain-directed individuals (women and men) to shop and to acquire physical things.

As our connection with the source of love, the inclusive and constructive holistic brain is inherently nurturing and receptive to the needs of others. The holistic right sees and knows that everything is part of a wholeness that is, by definition, *holy*, as is implicitly recognized in the common root of these two words.

The right brain, being harmony seeking, is *cooperative* and gentle in disposition. Drunvalo Melchizedek, a healer and spiritual teacher focused on sacred geometry, human energy fields, and living in the heart, provides the following illustration:

> In the Shiva religion there are 113 ways to meditate. They believe that there are exactly 113 ways and no more. They

feel that no matter what way you meditate or what you call it, even if you invent a new form, your way will fit into one of these 113 ways. The first 112 ways are male, and the last (or first) way is female. The male ways are pathways that can be written down or verbally described to another person. Exact descriptions are possible and logic is the rule. . . . The single female way has no rules. It is never done the same way twice (it could be, but that would not be known beforehand). The female pathway has no logic in the normal male way of thinking about things. The pathway moves according to feelings and intuition. It is like water in its movements, following the path of least resistance.[2]

Right-brain processes, like right-brain perspectives, are holistic, unlimited, and infinite (in potential), and therefore are unlimited with respect to time. Because time is meaningless in the absence of separation, the brain's right hemisphere lives in the Now and has no need to be in a hurry. The left hemisphere, on the other hand, being selectively focused in perspective and linear (and thus looking at the past and the future), sees time as a fast-moving, limited resource (one that we can "run out of") and thus feels pressured by it.

The holistic right hemisphere, being unlimited by time and seeing all that surrounds it, processes the information that lies before and around it simultaneously (or, put another way, nearly instantly). Everything is connected, and everything we need is just a thought away. Its perspective is all-encompassing, and from this perspective comprehension is immediate. This is not to say that our right brain literally knows everything. Nor is it to say that this description represents the typical experience of right-brain dominants, let alone the rest of us (who, after all, also have a functioning right brain). Most of us tend to ignore the right brain's revelations once we become acculturated into left-brain ways as children. But our acculturation does not change the inherently unlimited perspective that the right brain hemisphere is capable of providing. Even though we do not generally recognize it, the right brain has a direct connection to everything, and given our cooperation and the need and desire to know, it can access almost anything for us.

Being unlimited in perspective and simultaneous in processing, the right brain is, as we have pointed out, instantaneous in its information feed: *intuitive*, we call it. Although culture tends to exalt the rational above the revelatory mystery of the intuitive, in *Stalking the Wild Pendulum: On the Mechanics of Consciousness*, Itzhak Bentov reminds us that "meaningful breakthroughs in science, art, and technology come not by 'figuring out' things to the nth degree, but through intuitive leaps or insight, which are later rationalized." When operating in uncharted territory, "intuition is the only thing we can rely on."[3]

The dualistic left hemisphere, with its perspective restricted to a relatively narrow focus that seeks details, is limited to a *relative* perspective of the whole: there is no way it can see everything, given the directionality and narrow scope of its perspective. The tactically rational left brain must work its way to truth bit by bit, in a *sequential* process. *Relative, limited,* and *sequential* are characteristics we associate with humans. *Absolute, unlimited,* and *simultaneous*—holistic brain characteristics—are characteristics we associate with God or the Absolute. In essence, the holistic brain is our God brain; the dualistic is our Earth brain. This might be a radical idea to most Western cultures, but it is traditional to native people. According to Ohiyesa (1858–1939), a member of the Sioux nation, medical doctor, and author of 11 books on Native American life, "Indian people have traditionally divided mind into two parts—the spiritual mind and the physical mind."[4]

Sacred Geometry

"Geometry deals with pure form," Robert Lawlor reminds us in *Sacred Geometry: Philosophy and Practice.*[5] Geometry can be said to be sacred because it reveals the underlying structure of reality, the framework of God's body, of All That Is—the Whole. Our own bodies—which sacred geometry reveals to be god bodies—are also geometrical in form. We see an illustration of the connection between sacred geometry and the body in Leonardo da Vinci's famous drawing of a man with outstretched arms surrounded by a circle (Vitruvian Man).

Mind, which feeds consciousness through the energy of perspective, naturally has its own energetic geometry. Mind's perspective, too, is built with and within a framework of geometry.

Energy appears to disperse along geometric lines. Geometry starts with straight lines (in sacred geometry, straight lines are thought of as male lines) and transitions into curved lines (female lines), such as we find in circles and spheres. If we imagine a line at one end of a continuum and a circle at the other, halfway between we have a structure that combines elements of both, a structure that is rounded but has a linear characteristic, as we find with a *vesica piscis*. Although it contains no visible straight lines—having been created out of the shared space of two circles of the same diameter—nevertheless, it has a rather obvious linear dimension (depicted in figure 7 by a dotted line).

Whereas the left brain shows us a world based on a foundation of linear structures, the multidimensional right brain perceives reality as spherical and ovoid (reflecting the geometry of a vesica piscis). The brain's integration of these two fundamental structures (lines and circles) can be clearly seen in the progression of platonic solids from the simplest to the most complex—from tetrahedrons to hexahedrons (cubes) to octahedrons to dodecahedrons to icosahedrons.

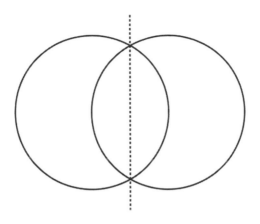

Figure 7. **Vesica piscis.**

Using the left brain's geometric symbology, we could say that the left brain perceives reality as a straight line (the representation of linearity), and the right brain perceives reality as a circle (the two-dimensional embodiment of the holistic), which in three dimensions becomes a sphere. The right brain knows about these one- and two-dimensional aspects—partly from its connection with the left brain, but also to some degree intuitively.

The fundamental quality of a linear structure that allows it to build anything is demonstrated by the fact that it can be used to create perfect spheres, as shown by the following exercise.

Imagine two straight lines, their centers touching and crossing (at any angle), floating in space somewhere in front of you. For the sake of this exercise, let's assume that the lines are of equal length. Now add a third line, then a fourth, and so on. Keep the centers together and keep adding lines. Evenly disperse the lines, and you quickly create what looks like a spherical pincushion with a number of pins in it. Whatever form you initially create, if you keep adding lines in this manner, keeping the centers of the lines together so that they all cross at the exact same location, eventually you end up with a solid, smooth sphere with a very dense core—a sphere created out of linear elements. (To create a sphere of light, use translucent light-emitting lines.) Spheres can also be crafted out of lines laid parallel to the surface, as suggested by the form we see in an icosahedron (a regular polyhedron with 20 identical equilateral triangular faces). Although an icosahedron is not a perfect sphere, if we reduce the size of the triangular faces by increasing the number of them, eventually they become so small that they disappear and we have what appears to be a perfectly smooth sphere. In the first case, you're building the sphere from the inside, and in the second case you're building it from the outside.

Although the dualistic left brain perceives the linear and the holistic as separate and in competition, these fundamental models remind us that they are not. They are complementary and lead to the same place. Even circles possess a linear component. We can see this by evenly bending a line back on itself so that the two ends connect. As the two ends come together and their polar separation is terminated, the line becomes a circle and inclusion is created. These two geometries, like the two brain hemispheres that employ them, are complementary, and we can see this in the precision with which the male and female sexual organs come together.

Linear and Holistic Patterns in Sexuality

The line and the circle can be found in the sexual patterns of linear-oriented (left-brained) and holistic-oriented (right-brained) individuals of both genders. Notice that the masculine sexual organ, being primarily linear in structure (and secondarily holistic), reflects the typical left-brain male perspective (primarily linear, secondarily holistic/round). Likewise, in most women, physical (sexual) geometry and mental (perspective) geometry are in harmony, their sexual organ being vesica piscis in form—holistic, and inclusive behind a linear façade (sup-plemented by one detail shared with males). The mouth, also a vesica piscis, serves as common ground in terms of human geometry and sexuality.

The right-brain-dominant individual (whether male or female) seeks wholeness—completion. Completion is desirable whether the whole on which we are focused is physical, mental, or spiritual—which is to say, whether the brain is focused on sex or ideas or spiritual relationships. Completion, in a dualistic sys-tem, means we require a complement—in the choice of a mate, for example. But the diversity of life ensures that there are excep-tions. *A mate can complement us in one energy form and not in another*—as when our mate complements us physically (sexu-ally), but not mentally—or vice versa. To clearly understand the effects of this somewhat unusual situation, we need to know a bit more about the relationship between brain dominance, its perspective, and human sexual drives.

The typical male perspective—which we have found to be linear based, focused, probing, and designed to penetrate wholes—comes paired with a linear sexual organ that, when focused (erect), is probing like the male mind and seeks to get inside wholes. The typical female mind and perspective, as we have stated, is holistic, inclusive, and focused on the outside dimension. Her version of greater mental completion is achieved by embodying linear elements in an effort to add detail to her innate sense of context. Naturally, we find the same pattern—"As above, so below"—in feminine sexual tendencies, where an *exterior* whole (organ) is sought, and where completion is achieved through the *inclusion* of linear elements—details. Sexually, the detail sought by right-brain-dominant females is, of course, the tail (*tail*, in Latin, is "penis"). But she has her own detail, as men-tioned above. In keeping with the left-brain mental patterns we have been discussing, most males tend to be drawn to smaller wholes, which in the case of sexual organs means the clitoris—and that, remember, is the exact same structure from which the penis develops. It's one of the structural details the two sexes share.

Left-brain-dominant females—guided by the same brain dominance and the same perspective possessed by left-brain-dominant males—tend to have the same physical, mental, and spiritual perceptions and responses as males: they are physically (in our example, sexually), mentally, and spiritually drawn to circular-based structures—holistic structures constructed out of female lines, feminine structures.

Looking closely at this situation, we see that a reversal in brain dominance tends to create a reversal in mating preference. Holistic males—those with the brain dominance of a typical female—tend to be drawn to males. Dualistic women—those with "male" brain dominance—tend to be drawn to females. Ironically, most often a dualistic woman ends up paired with a partner of similar attributes—a dualistic female—rather than with her natural complement, a holistic male or female. Since holistic females are generally drawn to seek a male partner, dualistic women find it difficult to attract holistic women, and end up like holistic men, choosing from a culture that will accept them, that will pair with them—in this case, someone in a similar situation. Although a dualistic female would achieve better *physical* completion with a male, *mental* energies have dominance over physical energies; so the soul's quest for understanding, for mental completion, has dominance over its quest for physical harmony.

As you might infer from this geometry, what we have in homosexuality is simply a situation in which the *mental* energy body (recognizable in the form of consciousness) typical of one gender finds itself in the *physical* body of the opposite gender and trying to integrate the two energy bodies (one polar based, one nonpolar based). For example, we find a polarized male physical body (male physical energy) housing a nonpolarized female mental body (female mental energy — female consciousness), and we find a holistic female physical body (female physical energy) housing a polarized male mental body (left-brain-directed consciousness). Because dualistic women and holistic men fail to conform to our fundamental stereotypes, most cultures are slow to understand them. Failing to understand, people often become fearful. Being fearful, a common response is repression, which, stated another way, is *war* — in this case (as in so many others), war on individuals.

The Power of Geometric Structures

"Fundamentally, sacred geometry is simply the ratio of numbers to each other," explains acclaimed photographer and anthropologist Martin Gray. To late medieval and Renaissance painters, "the positioning of elements within the frame of a painting was considered as important as the subject matter itself." This concern for positioning reflected their belief that a composition needed to be laid out "according to the mathematical principles of the golden ratio, or phi — a geometric ratio occurring throughout the natural world that the ancients believed to be a divine proportion." The golden ratio is reflected in sacred buildings and in the orientation of sacred buildings to one another — and it can be seen in examples that span the globe. In trying to explain the drawing power of sacred spaces, Gray quotes an ancient Hindu architectural sutra: "'The universe is present in the temple in the form of proportion.' Therefore, when you are within a structure fashioned with sacred geometry, you are within a model of the universe. The vibrational quality of sacred space thus brings your body, your mind, and, at a deeper level, your soul into harmony with the universe."[6]

My introduction to the power of sacred geometry came in the time required to take two or three steps. After having visited

Figure 8. **Flower of life.**

numerous temples in Egypt and, with one exception, having felt little different than in my hotel room or on the tour bus, I stepped onto the grounds of the ancient temple complex at Abydos and was suddenly flooded with a powerful and wonderful feeling that I can only describe in terms of waves of love. It was like falling in love, true love, in the space of a couple of seconds. An hour later, on the back side of the complex, I had my first encounter with the ancient flower of life symbol (figure 8).

The flower of life symbol, according to Drunvalo Melchizedek (who probably knows as much about sacred geometry as anyone on the planet), incorporates in one drawing "all knowledge of the universe, both male and female, no exceptions." He acknowledges that this must seem like an outrageous statement, but he believes that the symbol "contains every single mathematical formula, every law of physics, every harmony in music, every biological life form right down to your specific body. It contains every atom, every dimensional level, absolutely everything that's within waveform universes."[7] He then goes on to offer some proofs.

Most of us, of course, think of geometric shapes as interesting but not particularly useful unless one is, say, a mathematician, architect, or engineer. But the evidence is otherwise, and this evidence has been known for thousands of years and in nearly every religious and cultural tradition. It is no exaggeration to say that these geometrical structures are fundamental to our understanding of ourselves and all aspects of manifestation—physical, mental, and spiritual. Their significance lies in their immense creative power. These structures describe—in the abstract symbolism of geometry—the places where the "universes" of the left and right brain hemispheres meet. The process of transforming the linear into the holistic, even on the physical level, is an immensely creative one, producing transformative spiritual consequences.

An example of the spiritual shift that can occur when we transform a linear physical structure into a holistic structure is contained in the story of how the legendary Knights of the Round Table came together. According to the story, an ongoing quarrel among a group of knights over who would sit where at the table was blocking an effort to unify them and bring peace. Tables, reflecting the shape of trees, were linear, and those who sat at the ends had an advantage. Seated at an end, a knight had a more visible presence and could clearly see everyone's face and be seen. In case of a fight, a knight could more easily draw his sword and protect himself. Because the ends clearly had the best seats, they were reserved for those of the highest rank. Given the natural competitive spirit of left-brain-dominant males, some of the knights were unwilling to come to a negotiation if it required them to accept an inferior position.

Eventually a solution was created when someone recognized that by creating a round table, they could eliminate the superior position, and then no one would have a physical or spiritual advantage. The act of getting away from a linear structure and adopting a circular structure—a change of physical dimensional relationships—created sufficient spiritual and ideological harmony to allow the individuals to come to the table and assume the power of their collective self.

The right brain perceives multiple wholes and perceives them simultaneously. We sometimes describe a collective of wholes as a *constellation*. A constellation lacks the precision we normally associate with geometry; a group of knights that have come together to create an alliance for peace is an example of such a constellation. A city is a constellation; likewise, a grove of trees, a flock of birds,[8] and a street gang. Ideas that have yet to be fully integrated and unified can also take the form of a constellation. Notice that when viewed from a sufficiently distant perspective (a right-brain perspective), a constellation (physical or mental) appears to be an individual whole. Sometimes, the difference between a whole and a part comes down to the distance between us and the object of our perspective.

Relationship and Perception

The functional relationship between the two hemispheres is a complex one. Since we all normally have both a left and a right hemisphere that are intercommunicative and are also complementary (and to some extent duplicative of functions as well), the way that interaction plays out can be surprising. Brain scientist Robert Ornstein comments on the relationship between the two hemispheres as well as their relationship with wholes:

> From rats to human beings, the mammalian nervous system views the disconnected pieces of life's puzzle in different size pieces. This distinction is not simple; it's not one side of the

brain analyzing the parts and the other somehow grasping the whole. Rather, there's a precise and isolated meaning, what I am calling a basic text, to any message. There is also a larger view to interpret the text in. We don't somehow assemble three individual lines into a triangle, *but we change viewpoint and see the triangle as a whole.*[9]

Though some of this might seem to conflict with what we have been saying about an assembly-oriented brain, keep in mind that the holistic right brain can and does unleash an assembly process when required, but from its perspective it sees wholeness and completion—no assembly required.

Assembly means two different things, depending on which brain is dominant. From a left-brain perspective, the process of assembly appears linear and takes time. From a right-brain perspective, assembly either comes together instantly or is seen to be already complete. Think of the process of discovery like this: Imagine a plastic triangle lying flat on a table positioned at eye height so that your gaze is horizontal toward the table. From this perspective, looking across the table top at the triangle, all that can be seen is the straight line of its edge. Now, reach over and pick up one corner of the triangle and slowly raise it. Eventually, you will come to see a triangle (from most viewing angles). The triangle was always there—we did not assemble it. All we did was change the relationship between perspective and the whole: we moved the triangle. We also could have left the triangle flat and elevated our perspective. Or we could have changed both of these aspects to a lesser degree. In changing our perspective relative to the whole, we assemble factual information and reach a point where we suddenly are able to recognize the triangle.

Let us be careful here not to confuse perspective with perception. Holistic perception, like dualistic perception, can require a great deal of assembly! Good perception depends on a number of things, among them that a relatively complete and accurate body of left-brain facts be brought into harmony under the onslaught of analysis and the ethics of reason. Good perception requires intelligent, thoughtful processing. We must *judge* the information provided by our perspective (or accept someone else's judgment) in order to arrive at perception. Because of errors in judgment, we can have the perfect perspective from which to view a whole and still have poor perception. Take elected officials as an example. Although electing right-brain-dominant officials would help bring greater balance to the political landscape in terms of *perspective*, we should not expect that it would automatically give our political body greater *perception*. And ultimately, it is perception that guides our decisions. Anyway, more important than whom we elect—*far* more important—is the system. The system is dominant. The system is the controlling factor—the nest. And like most nests, it is fundamentally limiting. Put good people into a bad system, and you are going to get bad results.

When we choose to understand something—whether it is a thing (physical energy); a perspective or idea (mental energy); or a process (spiritual energy, recognized as a feeling)—only by viewing it in *relationship* can we hope to fully understand it. We can return to our Russian nesting dolls to show the impact of relationship on perception. They can be nested inside one another (concentrically, vertically nested) so that only one is seen, and they can be placed side by side in a line or in a circle (nested horizontally) and be seen as a set. Of course, they can also be positioned in an unorganized manner—as when they are scattered so far apart that only one of them can be seen at a time. And individual dolls can also be separated into two parts. Tremendous changes can be made in a whole through changes in relationship. Notice that when relationships change, values tend to change. Together, as a complete set, they achieve maximum value.

Relationships are *felt*. Relationship is spiritual in nature, and as a consequence, changes in relationship create changes in feeling. If a doll goes missing from a set, the change in relationship is felt as loss. This is of course all the more true with people — whether family members, loved ones, or members of a tight-knit group. When a long, close marriage ends in the death of one partner, it is common for the surviving partner to feel as if a part of himself or herself has been ripped away.

The whole that is relationship, like other wholes, has four fundamental parts, each of which has something to reveal to us. We learn from *individual* relationships, we learn from *collective* relationships, we learn from *internal* relationships, and we learn from *external* relationships. For example, looking at *internal* relationships, we might explore our feelings and our thoughts, and ask, do they agree (harmonize)? Looking at wholes in terms of their *external* relationships, we might compare our feelings and thoughts with other people's feelings and thoughts to get a sense of where we stand relative to our culture or our friends. For another example of the insight that comes from looking at what relationship can tell us, consider the relationship between morals and ethics. A *moral* response is an *individual* response. *Morals* reflect a harmonious internal relationship based on our values as an individual. *Ethics* reflect the same fundamental relationship with values, but as applied to *external* relationships — a collective expression of morals.

We can also gain insight into the importance of relationship from physical examples such as building blocks. Building blocks obtain their individual shape — that of a square or rectangle, for example — from the relationships of the various cuts to one another. Individual blocks connect with one another to form a collective block through connective relationships; the more harmonious the connections, the stronger they are. Depending on how we relate the blocks to one another, we can create a plain or purely utilitarian box, an architectural masterpiece, or something in between.

When attempting to assemble mental elements such as words and facts into ideas, we encounter developmental patterns similar to those we associate with building blocks. Close-fitting relationships tend to be strong and durable. Here too, beauty is a function of the relationships we create.

And just as strength and beauty are affected by relationships, so too are understanding and believability. The letters of a word must be arranged in a certain order for us to understand the word. Even the letters themselves often depend on relationships—as we see in the relationships formed by small round dots such as pixels. To convey an idea through print, we depend on a whole series of nested relationships: a relationship of small dots nesting together creates letters, a relationship of letters creates words, a relationship of words creates sentences, and so on. Relationships, like the energetic wholes that they create, nest both horizontally and vertically.

Many in our material- and science-based culture would have us believe that relationships are secondary in importance to elements. However, looking at our examples, we see that it's not the elements, the pixels, that are indispensable to understanding—it's pixel *relationships*. Given a sufficiently distant viewing perspective, we could create and recognize the same relationships using large objects such as pumpkins or trees or airplanes. Reality is found in relationships. Relationship is everywhere. It's in everything we see and say and do.

In exploring the two hemispheres and their perspectives and processes, we have been separating them and focusing on their differences. However, in real-life situations, there is (as we have alluded to) a good deal of interaction between the two hemispheres in virtually all complex activities. In fact, Ornstein found that "if [brain] damage happens in youth, one hemisphere *can* take over almost all of the functions of the other."[10] He also stresses that *there is almost nothing that is regulated solely by the left or right hemisphere.* Very simple chores may be the responsibility of one or the other, but both get involved as soon as any situation becomes slightly more complex." Interactivity and relationship are the rule for the brain itself. "Neither hemisphere operates anything on its own, any more than we walk on one foot or the other."[11]

This is good news, because it suggests that our brain is highly flexible and our limitations often self-imposed. It suggests that we are not captive of the perspective of our dominant hemisphere, but rather are able to access an integrated and all-inclusive perspective that sees the world as it is—sees its wholeness.

Perceptual Problems of the Right Brain

Although the right hemisphere is the relationship brain as well as the brain that sees both perspectives, there are a number of reasons why the right brain can fail to produce a clear and accurate perception.[12] First, as we've repeatedly discussed, if the right brain's perspective is insufficiently or inaccurately informed by the left, it cannot guide us to make accurate decisions. As a result, perceptual problems can develop, leading to flawed conclusions.

Holistic perceptual abilities can also be distorted by *external* influences such as cultural conditioning. One type of external influence is conventions of speech that tend to distort reality. An example is the widespread use of the term "drugs and alcohol" when referring to alcohol and other drugs. Although it is possible to pair the two words in this way and do so correctly, the two words are more often incorrectly related. It's a response that is sometimes referred to as "level confusion."

Alcohol is a drug. Alcohol is vertically nested within the whole that we categorize as drugs. Saying "Drugs and alcohol are a problem in my neighborhood" is the equivalent of saying "Dogs and pit bulls are a problem in my neighborhood," as if the two wholes belonged in separate categories. Because we understand that pit bulls are part of the whole that is the dog family, we would never say this. Nor would we say, or think, "My neighborhood needs more trees and elms." Elms *are* trees. It's redundant to mention elms. Yet we readily accept terms such as "drug and alcohol abuse" and think nothing of it.

If we wish to include alcohol when addressing the issue of drugs, just as we might say "pit bulls and other dogs" or "trees, especially elms," an accurate way to combine these two words would be to refer to "alcohol and other drugs," or "drugs, especially alcohol." "Alcohol and other drugs" should not be thought of as a phrase that needs to be remembered, but rather a fundamental observation regarding structure and relationship that needs to be made and integrated.

You might think we are being nitpicky here, but the ways in which we pair words (and the ways in which we use words without inspecting meaning) can profoundly distort our perception of reality and lead to erroneous or even tragic consequences. Keep in mind that words are not the problem but rather a symptom of a problem. In this case, it's level confusion, something that contributes to a misapprehension of reality. In the confusion, alcohol is exempted (as are nicotine and caffeine) from some of the problems associated with drugs, and thus it is irrationally placed in a more legitimate category. What we see here is a situation in which we are collectively ignoring reality. Fundamental science and logic are being widely dismissed in the fog of a "war on drugs." The left brain, which readily accepts destructive processes, naturally supports war as a solution to a drug problem and is unconcerned with conventions of speech if they threaten to interfere with the war effort. The collective right brain, which sees no love or peace gained from locking up our children or other loved ones, sees the big picture but may be ignorant of the details, and in its lack of discrimination, it can take on the cultural baggage and belief systems (including belief in war) that our left-brain-dominant culture has created and promotes. Remember, the issue here is not our choice of words. The issue is integrity and correct perception, both individually and culturally. *Integrity*, for our purposes, means integrating the facts of the left brain (largely a function of science) and the wisdom of the right in an atmosphere of mutual respect for one another, something that is widely missing in our highly polarized cultural and political wars. Do we have accuracy and integrity or not? On this issue, the evidence suggests that as a culture we do not.

Naturally, certain individuals and cultures benefit from this confusion. Maintaining confusion in the minds of voters helps to maintain prohibitions against politically incorrect drugs while protecting politically correct drug freedoms and profits. And whether intentional or not, these efforts further suppress holistic perspectives and holistic processes. Both cannabis and psychedelics, for example—both the object of a war—are known to shift their consumers into a more holistic perspective and perception, something discovered in the hippie culture of the 1960s.

Paradoxically, the peaceful, cooperative side of holistic perception can get it into trouble. Its inherently noncritical, nonviolent quality allows it to be easily dominated by the dualistic forces of the left-brain culture, leading holistic individuals to go against their natural instincts. And so, although we might expect holistic-directed individuals to be inclusive and nonjudgmental, they often succumb to the left-brain urge to be separative and judge. In addition, the right brain must deal with two fierce competitors: the fears of its companion left brain, and the fears and objections of other people's left brains. Even if our left brain is not dominant, it can still exert a powerful influence on our perception.

Right-brain-dominant individuals as a whole are better at integrating their nondominant hemisphere than are left-brain dominants (integration is a right-brain process). However, under the influence of left-brain culture, right-brain dominants often abandon their strength, their holistic perspective, for the dualistic—as they do when they judge. And in such cases, they are more likely to make perceptual mistakes. An example of this can be seen in the broad-brushed judgments that right-brain dominants often make against left-brain qualities and influences. Recognizing the left brain's tendencies to selfishness, destructiveness, and linear thinking, they sometimes dismiss the value of the left brain altogether. (Paradoxically, when they engage in this judgmental behavior, they are abandoning their natural holistic perspective and succumbing to the very behavior—and left-brain responses—they so often despise in their left-brain counterparts.)

Add *competitive* to *judgmental*, and we create another problem that can negatively affect holistic individuals and cultures. When right-brain dominants judge the two perspectives (a left-brain act that is unnecessary except for purposes of study, since both perspectives are essential), the choices they find are rather simplistic: between color and black-and-white, between constructiveness and destructiveness, and between service and selfishness. From a right-brain perspective, the choices are all too obvious: "color," "constructiveness," and "service." Our dualistic left brain thinks that it sees the context—that it understands reality—and it does, but within narrow parameters that can create extreme distortions. The holistic perspective, on the other hand, is focused on the context. When someone *has* the context and is *given* the text, that person naturally has an advantage over those who are primarily text focused, all else being equal. As a right-brain-dominant individual, you enjoy an unlimited perspective, and when you look at the world, you can't help but see the limited nature of the left-brain perspective. You *know* it is limited. Some right-brain dominants develop a holier-than-thou attitude when they recognize this, creating even greater separation between the two ideological camps, in spite of the right brain's drive to manifest unity.

Potential Solutions to Partial Perception

Our attempt here is to come to an understanding of our perspectives and treat them with equal respect (though one perspective will still be dominant). In understanding and integrating them, we naturally create a more realistic, flexible, and powerful perception. While the two perspectives are vastly different, ultimately they are compatible and cooperative, not competitors. We need both the big picture supplied by the right brain and the details supplied by the left.

To enhance your perspective, seek to find a way to harness the power of each brain hemisphere to do what it was designed to do. Find a way to bring the extremes into harmony. Learn the two fundamental perspectives and their associated processes and perceptions well enough that you can start to see their influences on your actions. Developing a relationship between the two extremes establishes a fundamental matrix. It opens the field of opportunity. To engage your holistic brain, ask questions that only a holistic perspective is positioned to answer—questions that deal with the larger components of life, with higher issues, with the Now, with feeling, with constructive processes, with all of these.

To fully step into our role on the cosmic stage, it helps to accept that we are intimately and utterly connected to God, the Great Spirit, Oneness. This acceptance is like opening a door. It doesn't get us in, but it clears the way for a greater vision.

The belief or the acceptance that we can do or be a particular thing contains an energy capable of moving us along the path to success. But often that energy needs to be nourished, which we do by focusing our attention on it. We must also shape and guide that energy, which we appear to do through intention. Therefore, to be more holistic in perspective, we can focus more of our attention on relationships, with the intent of developing greater harmony, especially with respect to our beliefs. Success is also enhanced when we seek out and remove internal conflict from our beliefs and assumptions. As mental relationships are changed for the better, physical and spiritual relationships will also change for the better. Or focus on spiritual relationships and watch the physical respond. (Happiness promotes healing— as exemplified by the well-documented positive correlation between laughter and healing.)

Happiness is a companion of peace. Happiness is being at peace with what we have, at peace with who we are, and at peace with the Now. Happiness and peace are built on a foundation of giving and having freedom, which means not being at war with ourselves or others. The happiness that comes when we have the peace of freedom is a function of the relationships we develop—relationships that are both internal and external; are individual and collective; and are physical, mental, and spiritual in energy. It's a lot to manage, but the brain was designed for this job. Sometimes we just need to get out of its way. Often that's as simple as removing conflicting beliefs and other ideological barriers from our belief system.

Part Three

Application: Perspective's Influence on Culture

 Chapter Six

The Cultural Brain

Never trust anything that can think for itself, if you can't see where it keeps its brain.

— J. K. ROWLING, *HARRY POTTER AND THE CHAMBER OF SECRETS*

To this point, we have focused most of our attention on how our perspective affects our perception as individuals. In the remaining chapters of this book, we are going to shift our emphasis somewhat and look more at perspective's effect on our collective self and our collective perception. We will look at how some of the political, military, economic, and social spheres of our culture function, and observe how our perception and evaluation of them changes depending on which of the two fundamental perspectives we use in viewing them.

The Conservative Left Brain and Liberal Right Brain

In previous chapters, we have pointed out the inherently selfish, or self-protective, characteristics of the left brain. The social, cultural, and political vantage points of the left brain are essentially an extension of these characteristics, in which the "me" of selfishness is extended into the outer arena of "my" and "mine" —my family; the interests and groups with which I identify; and policies that protect my property rights, my lifestyle, and my freedom to be me. Another way of saying this is that left-brain dominants (and to some extent most of us, since we are all influenced by a left brain and a left-brain-dominant culture) are interested in preserving their own status quo from the disruptions of outside forces, including (especially) government. In other words, left-brain dominants tend to be conservative.

The idea of control over one's own choices and destiny is fundamental from a left-brain-directed perspective, as is the idea of securing (or conserving) one's hard-won advantages. The protection of that which is "mine" is perhaps most strongly reflected in the notion of property rights—hence the importance of home ownership ("my home is my castle") in the American Dream. It is also reflected in the sanctification of gun ownership and of the Second Amendment to the U.S. Constitution (interpreted as establishing the right to bear arms); both of these symbolize the protection of self, family, and property, even though these "protections" might come at the price of a more violent culture.

Self, family, and property—and the freedoms associated with them—represent the core values of the left brain as expressed in political and cultural spheres. Politically, that is consistent with the belief that control should remain in the hands of the individual and not be ceded to an outside entity. "Government" in such a view has come to represent control from outside.

Therefore, the most typical response of the left-brain-dominant individual is to believe in less government, especially in such areas as taxation (thus maximizing the freedom to use one's wealth as one sees fit). However, such an individual is likely to prefer *more* government in some areas—specifically, the elements of government that safeguard the individual exercise of rights, such as a strong military (which, at least theoretically, secures us from hostile influences and ideologies) and laws protecting property rights, gun ownership, and the like.

This focus on individual wants and needs forms the core of the agenda of political conservatives, and has (at least in theory) been the focus during a large part of America's history, although additions have expanded this agenda, and some policies of the political right tend to contradict these values. We will discuss the inconsistencies of conservative as well as liberal positions as we proceed.

It is also important to note that when we associate conservatism (or the political right) with left-brain dominance, this does not mean that all left-brain-dominant people are politically conservative—in fact, they range across the spectrum from extremely conservative to extremely liberal and all places in between. What it does mean is that the self-protective "me and mine" orientation of the left brain is reflected most consistently in the conservative political agenda—and in the United States, that usually means the agenda of the Republican Party.

In contrast to the tightly focused conservative political agenda, the liberal (or progressive) agenda appears to have a softer focus and more diversity. This reflects the difference between the limited but intense focus of the brain's left hemisphere and the broad, unlimited holistic focus of the right hemisphere. The right brain (the brain favored by the political left) is no less principled, but its focus is on inclusiveness, and therefore it tends to possess and project a relatively unstructured, "free-for-all" nature (much as we find in many fledgling democracies). In keeping with the great diversity of creation that right-brain dominants seek to understand, they have a wide range of interests, and liberals or progressives tend to include all of those interests. But beyond the diversity of individual interests, they also have a set of deep underlying principles. These include concern for elements like guaranteed education, universal health care, and the minimization of poverty that make for a healthy culture; concern for the environment as supporting health, well-being, and collective survival; and strong stances on civil rights. Note that the emphasis on rights among liberals tends toward civil rights—the rights of everyone to full participation in the benefits of society—whereas conservatives tend toward the right to be left alone and pursue happiness without interference. Obviously, both sides of the equation are necessary, but when one side is emphasized more, the other side tends to get squeezed out of consideration.

Of course, everyone has two brain hemispheres, and conservatives and liberals are fully capable of seeing the complementary nature of these sets of needs—even if this capability sometimes is buried by the agenda of their dominant side. Conservatives, because they tend to focus on personal issues, are somewhat naturally blind to the legitimate claims of the common good. Thus, conservatives sometimes take untenable positions such as those favoring the rights of giant corporations (which are fictitious entities) over the rights of people. Holistic ideas are sometimes viewed as inherently threatening in a polarity-based, individual-oriented culture. Conservatives tend to see the collective as aligned with big government against the individual. Lowering (or not raising) taxes is often viewed as sacrosanct, even when the collective need for tax dollars is dire, even when the very survival and well-being of certain individuals depends on sufficient collection of taxes to fund programs, and even when tax dollars fund programs to minimize fraud (an expenditure that actually saves them money). Liberals, on the other hand, perceiving reality from a largely holistic, collective perspective, see everyone as part of the whole that such government programs address—and so they do not see a conflict between their own interest and the larger good.

Cultural influences often alter our natural impulses, and can alter our perspective and our political response as well. As a result, we find many exceptions. Conservatives are not always conserving in their beliefs and actions, just as liberals are not always progressive. And we sometimes change. It's common to start out as a liberal and become more conservative as we age. We eventually recognize that our idealistic cultural energies are not sufficiently supportive: we share, for example, but people do not share with us, thus depleting our resources. In addition, we conclude that our idealistic ideas are not going to be accepted by society, and soon fear starts to work its way in. We start thinking that we will be out on the streets unless we shift to a more conserving mode. We start paying more attention to the alternative voice in our head. This process doesn't change our overall dominance, but it does shift our combined perspective and, consequently, our perception.

Nature, as well, seems to play a role in the shift from liberal to conservative—probably in order to expand our perception by diversifying our experience. As a rule, natural patterns, including energy, tend to follow a back-and-forth wave form (when viewed from the left brain), and thus we might reasonably assume that over a lifetime, our perceptual energies might shift from one side to the other. Naturally, we can also change from conservative to liberal—as one might do in response to "conservative" actions that employ violence, such as war. Whichever one of the two dominant perspectives we might have been born with, if we are reasonably critical, we are likely to find that the perceptions we derive from it have serious shortcomings (at least as practiced by the majority) and, in reaction, choose to shift toward the alternative.

Conservatives, being focused on survival, have the job of advancing and maintaining cultural forces that are inherently aggressive and destructive. Because the selective focus of the conservative agenda can be destructive, it is especially important that conservatives be true to their highest calling when choosing whether to resort to force. With so much of the world at war, it's clear that conservatives as a whole have not responded conservatively in this case. Liberals who support war provide us with another example of an exception. The brain hemisphere most often used by liberals is fundamentally opposed to war—it seeks to be harmonious and constructive rather than divisive and destructive—but the powerful influences of culture can often override our natural response.

The right hemisphere, being inherently holistic, *includes* the individual-based stance of the left hemisphere as part of the big picture. But because its main focus is on the collective, and because its holistic stance is an inherently inclusive one, it does not view freedom as being at odds with collective interests—or at odds with government. Consumer-protection laws, which are usually championed by liberals and often opposed by conservatives, are an example of a case where the holistic stance is friendlier to the rights and freedoms of individuals than is the dualistic, left-brained stance. In such a case, the freedoms gained by consumer protections—which involve protecting real people against corporate abuse—clearly outweigh the freedoms lost through some degree of government regulation of corporate life (in which the beneficiaries of this freedom are largely limited to stockholders and CEOs).

Some frequently held conservative positions reveal not merely myopic vision (as above) but blatant contradictions. Since conservatives are defenders of the individual's right to be left alone by government and to be responsible for his or her own path, gay rights and drug freedoms should be natural conservative causes. However, the self-protective tendencies of conservatives (and left-brain dominants) lead to such powerful identification with their own life that a kind of fortress mentality results, in which outside forces—from government to alternative lifestyles—all appear threatening. Thus, for much of the conservative rank and file, the primacy of one's life becomes confused with the primacy of one's lifestyle. Even if conservative politicians don't personally share these fears, political considerations make them reluctant to act in a way that is contrary to their most vocal constituencies. On the other hand, for the liberal (or holistic-minded) individual, the natural tendency to inclusion—as well as to viewing such issues through the lens of civil rights—makes such issues as gay rights and drug liberalization easier to espouse. Easier, but not always easy. These have become such hot-button issues that liberals often succumb to cultural pressures. (Consider the Clinton administration's strong posturing against marijuana decriminalization and the "Don't ask, don't tell" policy concerning gays in the military.)

Terry M. Clark, chairman of the journalism department at the University of Central Oklahoma, suggests that the words *conservative* and *liberal* are now so overused and abused that they've become mere labels—propaganda devices employed by politicians who are more interested in politics and profit than in principles. Labels, Clark says, are nothing but words that keep people from thinking. For example, he points out that *conserving* our resources is an inherently conservative act, yet those most interested in conservation are labeled "liberals." Because the so-called Patriot Act subverts our liberties, it should be consistent with conservatism to oppose this act in the name of individual rights, yet it was supported, drafted, and passed by "conservatives."[1]

Another example of the state of mental confusion in American culture is the conservative reaction to the notion of civil liberties—especially as embodied in the foremost watchdog of their protection, the American Civil Liberties Union (ACLU). Although it's "common knowledge" that the ACLU is a liberal organization, it can in fact be viewed as embodying core conservative principles, as Oklahoma State Senator Andrew Rice has pointed out.[2] What are these principles? Traditionally, and at their core, conservatives are the defenders of the individual and individual rights. Conservatives are engaged in battle against the more powerful collective for individual freedom. And fundamentally, that's what the ACLU does. *It protects individuals from collectives—from cultures, from their governments, and from other powerful organizations that usurp individual rights.*

Because the ACLU openly works to conserve individual rights, its efforts should be applauded by conservatives. Instead, the ACLU is widely viewed as an enemy. Perhaps that's because the ACLU respects and defends the rights of *all* individuals, not just conservatives, and this creates conflict in the conservative's dualistic brain, which sees things in terms of black or white, right or wrong, us versus them. The defensive/offensive left brain thinks something like: "The ACLU is assisting liberals, the enemy," and from that concludes, "The ACLU is my enemy." The response seeks to be logical, but it's nevertheless in error, having been made from an incomplete perspective. In any case, the ACLU simply advocates. It seeks freedom for people. Judges and juries, sometimes conservative, make the inflammatory decisions that have come to be negatively associated with the ACLU. Therefore, primary responsibility for unpopular decisions must reside with the law and the individuals judging it, not with those who advocate for one side or the other. Fundamentally, the ACLU is an organization that marries the advocacy of individual rights—a bedrock interest of true conservatives—with the liberal interest in universal justice.

Let's also not forget that we can be liberal with respect to certain belief positions and conservative where others are concerned. Depending on our experience, our focus, and our beliefs, we might see economic reality from a conservative perspective, and see social (spiritual) reality from a liberal perspective. Also, in a conservative culture we might be considered a liberal, and in a liberal culture we might be viewed as a conservative.

To bring greater clarity to our understanding of what it means to be conservative and liberal, let's consult the perspective of philosopher Ken Wilber. "The typical, well-meaning liberal approach to solving social tensions," Wilber says, "is to treat every value as equal, and then try to force a leveling or redistribution of resources (money, rights, goods, land) while leaving the values untouched. The typical conservative approach is to take its particular values and try to foist them on everybody else."[3] Liberals, Wilber observes, "believe primarily in objective causation of social ills (i.e., inequality is due to exterior, unfair social institutions); conservatives believe primarily in subjective causation (i.e., inequality is due to something in the character or the nature of individuals themselves)."[4] Conservatives, being so heavily focused on the individual, on personal responsibility, sometimes overlook issues involving the collective (the effect of violent video games on their kids, for example) or the effect of individuals on the collective (as when low individual tax rates starve essential collective/cultural needs that benefit them as well). Wilber also points out that liberals and conservatives "both have 'freedom' and 'order' wings, depending upon whether they value most the 'individual' . . . or the collective."[5]

Liberals, like conservatives, are torn between maintaining individual freedom and preserving collective order. Because we have both perspectives, we want both freedom and order. When we can't have both, brain dominance (nature) is likely to heavily influence our decision unless dominance has been overridden by cultural programming (nurture).

Because both perspective and perception are often heavily influenced by our cultural environment, our media possess enormous power. Naturally, the power of media to effect cultural change generates a great deal of emotion in a polarized political environment. Conservatives often protest that newsrooms are more liberal than the general public and complain that liberal views get more air time and more print. That is true, but it is no conspiracy. It is part of a natural process of human growth. In seeking to expand their understanding of events, reporters are engaged in holistic activities. As people come up through the various news organizations, regardless of their values or the values of their employers, they are exposed to a wide variety of people, perspectives, and perceptions. This has the inevitable effect of broadening and deepening their *personal* perspectives and perceptions—making them more complete and more holistic, whatever political convictions they might have started with. Although some reporters are naturally more open to change than others, as a reporter's understanding of life progresses, he or she naturally becomes more liberal or progressive. The spiral- or wave-based foundation of reality (explained by Don Beck, Christopher Cowan, and other theoreticians of "Spiral Dynamics"[6]) ensures that individuals and cultures swing back and forth, and so individuals and cultures may also grow more conservative at times. Nevertheless, as a whole, movement through time is experientially expansive, which means tending in a progressive or liberal direction. From a narrowly focused perspective, this might not seem so, based on the cycles of political elections and the ascendancy of many right-wing political groups in the United States and the world. But if we look at the broad trajectory of world history, then movement over time has clearly been toward the expansion of rights—as well as expansion of the *defi-*

nition of rights of minorities. We see this in the relaxation of marriage and divorce laws, the rights of the disabled, freedom of speech and religion, gay rights, the presumption of innocence of the accused, and a broad spectrum of human rights—a movement toward expansion and liberalization that is unmistakable. Even the most extreme reversals—such as the rise of Hitler and Nazism in Europe—created counterreactions that gave rise to sometimes unprecedented movement toward human rights, as embodied (for example) in the Nuremburg trials and the formation of the United Nations.

To maintain a conservative news organization, you need to somehow restrict this natural process. You have to screen people and hire only conservatives and in some way ensure that they remain conservative if they are to keep their job. But in that situation, you end up deliberately biasing the news.

Another complaint often made by conservatives involves the liberal "bias" of the entertainment industry. The nature of acting creates a veritable mother lode of liberals. As an actor takes on new roles, he or she takes on new lives along with new perspectives and new perceptions. Acting is perspective- and perception-expansive work. By expanding and accelerating an actor's understanding of life, theater creates an extraordinarily rich environment for mental and spiritual progress. All else being equal, the more enlightened and/or diverse the roles, the more progressive that actors become—assuming that they are learning from their new experiences. Of course, openness to change varies with actors as with everyone else.

Radio, on the other hand, is a friend of conservative cultures. Conservative talk radio is successful because it can and does focus almost solely on the dualistic perspective, which reflects the polarized, us-versus-them positions of left-brain-dominant culture as well as the positions of grassroots political and cultural conservatism. On conservative radio, life is polarized into black or white, good or bad, right or wrong—making it relatively easy for conservative listeners to find agreement and therefore bond. In this environment, the holistic liberal perspective becomes fodder for caricature—a situation that is hardly conducive to understanding. Liberal radio is less successful because liberals tend as a group to be less focused and less black-and-white in their outlook, as well as more diverse. Their holistic outlook cannot be easily fed from (or reduced to) a single perspective such as is common to conservative radio; rather, it is fed from a multitude of perspectives.

Perspective and Political Affiliation

In the United States, liberals, whose right-brain perspective offers a big-picture view that sees collective values and embraces the whole of diversity, tend to congregate in the Democratic Party, the more holistic of the two parties. From the holistic perspective and its external focus, we naturally look out for others. We have a perspective that sees oneness, and we feel a duty to help everyone, including the poor, the disadvantaged, and the uneducated. This of course is the stereotypical feminine response, reflecting what is common knowledge—that women often focus on helping others to the detriment of self. Their holistic view of reality perceives a world that thrives on cooperation. Helping others, they perceive, is what brings harmony, happiness, and holiness to the world.

These are, of course, generalizations, and there are many exceptions. The holistic attitude that tries to come through in the liberal, grassroots perspective of the Democratic Party is often distorted beyond recognition. Try to associate the Democratic Party with the holistic perspective and you soon come face to face with the *relative* nature of holistic perception and the aggressiveness and competitive drive of dualistic perception. Given the

strong emphasis on individual self-preservation that is characteristic of left-brain-directed males, the preponderance of males
leading the Democratic Party, and the competitive (dualistic)
nature of politics as a whole, the Democratic Party is holistic only
when compared with the Republican Party or with the general
population. Like most Republicans, most Democrats cooperate
with corporate lobbyists in order to obtain the money they need
to get reelected. This kind of activity puts self first, corporations
second, and country third. This is not a holistic response. Nor is
the Democratic response to the problem of drug use and abuse,
which is one of punishment and separation, the left-brain solution. Democrats also abandon the holistic when they allow
culture to drift along largely governed by market-oriented controls. Similarly, Democratic Party efforts to keep third parties off
the ballot are self-serving and hypocritical because they fly in the
face of the principles of democracy and freedom of speech.

Democrats, to the extent that they identify with holistic collective principles, are inclined to reach out to help others,
especially those who are socially and economically suffering.
Since helping others in a political context usually involves government programs that are paid for by tax dollars, Democrats,
whose focus is on assisting those in need, have earned the tax-
and-spend label. Republicans, since they are the party that
focuses on maintaining individual freedoms, especially economic
freedoms (even to the detriment of the collective good), naturally
work to lower taxes. Their intent, as pointed out above, is to
ensure their own and their family's wealth and survival. Peter G.
Peterson, lifelong Republican and former secretary of commerce,
explains the difference in perspective between the two political
parties and taxes like this: "Democrats push benefit hikes while
pretending that they're unrelated to a government that collects
taxes. And Republicans push tax cuts while pretending that
they're unrelated to a government that disburses benefits."[7]

The Republican Party, we find, is heavily dominated by conservatives. Conservative Republicans are sympathetic to the needs of others, but if they are going to help, the nature of the help needs to be consistent with their views of economic freedom (or nonintervention) and minimal government involvement. They don't want government giving away money. They know that government programs tend to be inefficient and often spiral out of control and cause problems. Republicans, being predominantly left-brain directed, are strongly opposed in principle to anything that interferes with individual control. They see an obligation to be conserving, especially of their money and their freedom. But of course, we always encounter exceptions.

Reflecting the seamlessness of diversity and the potential for cultural forces to override nature, we naturally find Republicans who are liberal and Democrats who are conservative. Prior to giving the keynote address at the Republican Convention of 2004, U.S. Senator Zell Miller was asked by Peter Jennings of ABC News to explain why he, a Democrat, was about to address Republicans. "I've been set in my ways for a long time because I'm a conservative Democrat, and there used to be a time when there was room for conservatives in the Democratic Party, but no more. But the main reason, of course, is because 9/11 changed everything. . . . I want a president who will grab [the terrorists] by the neck and not let 'em go to get a better grip. . . . When I hear a politician talk about seeing the complexities of things, that means it's a person that sees nothing but gray. They don't see black and white. They suffer from analysis paralysis, and they have a hard time making a decision."[8]

Here Miller demonstrates his left-brain dominance by expressing a desire to work with the party that will use the most force. Viewing reality from a dualistic perspective, Miller sees reality in terms of black and white (which is essential to the collective effort to understand reality accurately but is also limited).

To those who see only two fundamental options, the choice *is* clear. No wonder that Miller harbors doubts about people who can't make such a simple choice. But the situation is not that simple—which is why individuals whose perspective is holistic sometimes have a more difficult time making a decision.

Miller suggests that people who "see complexities" (see holistically) are unable to see black-and-white choices. The reality is, the holistic perspective encompasses the dualistic perspective, so both brain types can see black-and-white choices. Because this is more practiced in left-brain dominants, we might expect that it is more obvious to them than to right-brain dominants. On the other hand, living in a dualistic culture, holistically inclined individuals have been educated in the use of their dualistic perspective. In contrast, most left-brain dominants have been given comparatively little education in the use of the holistic perspective (artistic-oriented education being one exception). It's not that those who see a more complex world *fail* to see the black-and-white choice; rather, they are able to transcend the limitations of this choice and come to a more holistic, balanced conclusion.

There are, of course, other exceptions to the correlation between brain dominance and political affiliation. Through cultural forces such as programming, we are able to override our natural perspective to a degree; sometimes, programming alone is enough to shift us into one party or the other. Nature sets us up with hardware and basic programming and then allows us (individuals and cultures) to take over the job of programming. Most of us have been programmed directly and indirectly, to a large degree by our parents; therefore, in spite of our natural perspective, we often vote like our parents. Or, we may rebel and do the opposite of what our parents do. In either case, our parents are a strong influence—either to be emulated (through right-brain harmony) or to be avoided (using left-brain separation).

In both parties, selfish left-brain forces corrupt the political system and the politicians who populate it. Both parties give in to a variety of special-interest groups, fail to reflect their respective roots, and betray the fundamentals that they profess. Nevertheless, in 2008 we saw the Republican and Democratic parties reveal their hemispheric dominance in their approach to selecting candidates for their presidential primaries. Democrats, exhibiting their collective right brain's inclusive, unifying, holistic perspective, mandated that states assign proportional representation in selecting convention delegates, thus ensuring that more candidates would win delegates. Republicans, true to type, chose the left-brain-directed response: freedom of choice and a competitive focus on winners. Republicans let individual states choose their delegates on either a proportional or winner-take-all basis.

How Religion Affects Political Affiliation

Religious values, because they represent an especially strong case of "nurture," can also override hemispheric dominance. Members of sectarian religions often take on an us-versus-them mentality based on a rigid, exclusivist black-and-white theology. This, combined with a belief in scriptural inerrancy (or at least scriptural authority), often results in distrust of the outside world, including the findings of science. (The idea of evolution has long represented such a threat.) Similarly, secular government is often distrusted, leading many Christians, for example, to adopt largely conservative political views. Such polarized values may lead to a rigid conservatism that, ironically, is in direct contradiction to the teachings of Jesus.

Christianity is of special interest in our investigation, not only because the overwhelming majority of American are professing Christians, but also because the teachings of Jesus are so clearly holistic and "liberal," especially in the area of helping the poor. Indeed, Jesus's position concerning the poor and our obligation to help them is far more radical in spirit than even the most liberal political agenda of today. And yet, the exclusivist, sectarian nature of much religion has created a culture of left-brain dominants (even among many right-brain-dominant individuals) — and this sectarianism has trumped even the teachings of Jesus himself.

If we were to simply consider the peace-loving, people-serving, harmony-seeking, holistic teachings of Jesus, we might expect that Christians would identify with liberals, and that practicing American Christians would choose the Democratic Party, the more holistic of the two major political parties, the party of service to others.[9] But most practicing Christians in the United States are in fact self-identified conservatives and are members of the Republican Party. Although there is a large contingent of Christian liberals, and liberal activism has always had a strong Christian component, liberals are in the minority of practicing Christians.

Perspectives on Abortion

The dualistic perspective of our polarized and polarizing left brain separates everything that comes into its view, including *light*, *love*, and *relationship*, into seemingly opposite parts, based on the degree of wholeness or completion. If this is unclear, remember that a lack of wholeness in terms of light, for example, leads to darkness; in terms of love, leads to fear; and in terms of separation, leads us to overlook otherwise meaningful relationships. When examining the issue of abortion, the left-brain perspective experiences a similar pattern of polarization, and as a consequence gives the left-brain-directed viewer two basic responses. Thus, from a dualistic perspective, people are seen to either *support* the freedom of a woman to maintain control over her body (including abortion), or to *oppose* such freedom.

This polarization of the collective body is also extended to those who accept the idea of abortion as a choice. Since we are given only two primary choices by a dualistic perspective, we are more or less forced to take sides, and those who support a woman's freedom to choose an abortion are likely to be viewed as an accessory to murder, if not a murderer. Given the right brain's peaceful influence on our overall perception, the harshness of the dualistic response is often softened, but regardless, left-brain dominants tend to be guided by a perception that urges them to fight for the survival of the individual whole, and that can include the survival of individual beliefs as well as individual beings. The conservative brain's emphasis on survival of the individual, plus its willingness to fight in support of its beliefs, establishes a basis for war.

By itself, the left brain, with its dualistic perspective, has no intent, good or bad. (Intent is a choice we make that shows up later, in our perception.) The dualistic perspective simply shows us reality separated into two parts, a vision that depends on where we have positioned ourselves within our three-dimensional physical, mental, and spiritual world. Thus, our perception of good and bad often depends on how we manage our perspective. Because of the left brain's tendency to focus on a subject, unless we maintain awareness of the intensity (and the exclusionary nature) of our focus, we may sometimes rather easily overlook essential context. Consequently, when an issue is perceived as important enough, it tends to demand our full attention and can cause us to overlook other important issues. In the case of abortion, this context includes the rights of the mother and the delicate web of lives woven around the mother; it also includes the life that awaits an unwanted child. It is not that left-brain dominants don't care about context; in fact, they often care passionately when the context is within their focus. But when someone's focus is on a particular issue, or a passionately held belief, that focus becomes *the* defining issue. Because the sanctity of innocent life arouses such strong beliefs, adding more context is often mightily resisted. Taking the "lives" of "innocents" becomes the primary evil, even if the innocents cannot be shown to be separate beings who suffer. A mother, in contrast, can never be as innocent as an unborn child, because she can make decisions for herself (such as whether or not to have a child). *Innocent* then becomes almost synonymous with *unborn*, and with *helpless*. (For perhaps the same fundamental reason, conservatives have been up in arms about taking the life even of someone who is brain-dead.)

By observing the behavior of sports fans all over the world, we can see that the competitive polar left brain practically worships anything ranked number one—whether it's being number one in a sporting competition, the belief that there can be only one winner at anything (and everyone else is a loser), or, in the case of political issues, the belief that a single issue can trump all others. And what is more number one than life, especially *innocent* life?

As a consequence, when the survival of a defenseless individual is at stake, the focused left brain often ignores the context—which includes the collective and its opinions. Judging from the responses of people, we see that even the obvious and otherwise fundamental principle that there is nothing conservative about having big government dictate individual choices becomes meaningless when our separative perspective is focused on saving a life. Even a threat to the mother's life can be ignored. The left brain, being competitive and hierarchical, and associating effective and appropriate actions with black-and-white choices, tends to make choices based on narrow (though often important) principles. As valuable as this response is, it often excludes the broader (and even more important), more inclusive, holistic view.

Holistic liberals, because they so often fail to support the "conservative" solution, are sometimes characterized as uncaring, but in fact, they tend to care more; it is a care that is distributed over a broader area of life. Theirs is a caring that includes a broad focus on the collective good. Although the holistic perception is one that values the individual immensely, it is not willing to allow one individual, especially one yet to be born, to disrupt the harmony and freedom of the greater whole of the mother and those individuals who are emotionally connected to her. The loving, holistic brain comprehends complexity and thus understands the tradeoffs required to achieve the greatest good. It understands that to have freedom, we must give freedom.

The fact is, liberals share some conservative reservations about abortion, even including the idea that a life is (in some sense at least) being taken. What they don't share is the conservative solution, which is the use of *force* and *separation*—the forced (violent) separation of people from their freedom (prison-based solutions), from their families, and from their money (legal costs and loss of income). Although force often succeeds in conserving a fetus, it does little to conserve the greater collective of the mother, who is, remember, also a god, and those closely connected to her. When an individual tries to force his or her personal creative choices onto the collective, conflict is triggered.

According to *The Urantia Book*, the soul and its accompanying personality come into the body *after* birth, at the time when the child makes its first moral decision.[10] Should we accept this idea, it follows that abortion does not displace a soul. But even if the soul were to arrive prior to birth, the soul (which is spirit energy) is beyond being harmed by physical acts. Most spiritual traditions consider the physical body to be a temporary form for use during our sojourn here. Therefore, when a fetus is aborted, at worst, a spirit is displaced and denied the chance to come to this planet or is delayed. It's not an ideal result, but neither are force and punishment, fines and prison—which are the usual "conservative" solutions.

The choice of whether or not to abort is an issue most of us will never face, but we must make a sensitive and potentially damaging decision of our own. We must decide what to do with the women who refuse to manage *their* lives based on *our* beliefs. We must decide what kind of penalties we are going to impose, something we do through our support of certain legislators and laws. We must also decide what to do to those who support the women. Those acting on a perception derived from a dualistic perspective naturally tend to demonize those who offer assistance. It's a natural response of the left brain's polarizing you're-with-us-or-against-us attitude.

For years, a religious bookstore near my home displayed a large sign that included the request, "Pray to stop abortion." As I passed by this bookstore, I would think, "Pray to stop unwanted pregnancy" would accomplish the same goal—and it would be more acceptable to more people, as well as causing less harm to the community as a whole. When our perception is holistically oriented, we tend to respect both individual and collective rights. When it is dualistic, our tendency is to respect only individual rights, especially those that benefit us personally. The holistic perspective, like the dualistic, is pro-freedom, but the holistic perspective seeks freedom for *everyone*. From a holistic perspective, we see no gain in forcing women who do not wish to be mothers to spend much of their lifetime being one, especially when the result is an even more overcrowded planet. Holistically oriented people see motherhood as a voluntary choice and would never impose such an important and demanding role on an unwilling individual. If someone's rights are going to be supported, from a holistic perspective it makes more sense to support the established life, that of the mother, who is already a living strand in the great fabric of life, a fabric that would be stressed if she were hurt. A holistically oriented person recognizes that *our* responsibility, both as individuals and as a culture, is how *we* treat others, not how others treat others.

When our perception is holistic, we recognize that love and education offer a better solution than force, and we work to find ways to reduce the incidence of unwanted pregnancy through cooperative means. But education takes time. The left brain's solution, relying on aggressive (force-based, separation-based) processes such as prison and the threat of imprisonment to accomplish its goals, is a quick and relatively easy fix. All we have to do is convince a majority of voters and then let law enforcement do the painful dirty work (out of our sight). By criminalizing those we wish to control, we also create a comforting social and emotional buffer of separation between ourselves and our victims. And because they refuse to submit to our beliefs (harmonize with our values), we need no longer value them: "I am good," the polarized ego or left brain thinks; "those who are opposed to my beliefs must be bad."

The battle between the two brain perspectives retards the advancement of both sides of the culture war. It's a lose-lose situation. We need both perspectives and both processes to arrive at the truth—but we need them cooperating rather than fighting. When we fight rather than cooperate, we create conflict within ourselves, individually and culturally.

Trust and Perspective

Let's briefly explore the relationship between trust and the two fundamental perspectives.

The right hemisphere, being the hemisphere that perceives wholeness, is fearless and feels only love. The right's holistic perspective knows that ultimately there is nothing to lose, and therefore nothing to fear. Having nothing to fear, the right feels the deepest, all-pervasive, essential reality of the universe, which is love. Having nothing to fear, the right is the trusting hemisphere. Obviously, it's a perspective that ignores the world of things and physical survival; but that is why it's connected to the left hemisphere, whose job is to protect us when there is reason to be concerned for our lives, well-being, and property.

A staple of local news is the story of the elderly lady or gentleman who has trusted a con man and been robbed. Trust, we are often taught, is a Godlike quality to possess. As people age, they often focus ever more intently on spiritual goals, trust being one of them. This can make the elderly a soft target for scams that work on trust.

The right brain, which sees the big picture, recognizes that trust is only one of several factors to consider when making an important decision like trusting a stranger with your money. The right brain sees trust as part of a greater whole that also includes feeling, caution, logic, and experience.

The left brain's perspective, being the complement of the right, is naturally *distrusting*. Being responsible for our personal security and that of our family, the left brain has our skeptical perspective (the one that sees the glass as half empty). And being selfish, survival oriented, and competitive, the left brain is driven to do whatever it takes to win (although how this is acted out, if at all, is a matter of personality and perception, including education, morals, and the influence of the holistic right brain). Even so, as we have previously observed, the left brain can be fooled due to the narrowness of its perspective. When we separate trust from the greater whole, as we do when we focus on it, we can get lost in our focus and overlook holistic factors such as caution, experience, and advice, and consequently can be conned. We can even con ourselves. The holistic right brain usually comes in and saves us by moderating our left-brain perception, but this is an example of what can happen when we ignore the right brain's holistic insights and focus too heavily on a single element such as trust.

To achieve the harmony that is necessary to overcome polarization and allow us to act with a minimum of conflict, our trusting brain and our skeptical brain are able to talk back and forth and negotiate what is, in effect, a meeting of minds. We are thus able to perceive wholes as a single reality (without having to consciously connect inside and outside views) and process them (act) with a sense of security. Because both brain hemispheres feed into our perception, the difference between a right-brain-directed perception and a left-brain-directed perception ranges from subtle to extreme, depending on the degree of left- or right-hemispheric dominance (nature) as well as our cultural programming (nurture).

Cultural Polarization

In a healthy, holistic culture, right-brain attempts to achieve unity and harmony are appreciated and nourished along with left-brain attempts to protect individual rights. In a healthy, holistic culture, the cultural left brain (the voice of true conservatives) criticizes holistic perspectives and perceptions (those of liberals) in order to keep the liberal big-picture perspective sharp—and liberals appreciate the criticism and adjust accordingly. In a healthy culture, we find a center of power made up of left- and right-brain-directed individuals cooperating and competing in an environment of mutual respect. In this situation, ideological extremists are heard, but the power they exercise is mostly limited to the power of truth (since truth will always triumph, given sufficient time). In a holistic culture, we have a central core of stability, along with two enormously valuable but potentially dangerous extremes feeding new ideas into the center.

Such a scenario works. Here is what does not work: The center splits, and we are left with two relatively equal forces in a battle for control, each seeing the other as responsible for our cultural problems. When this happens, instead of the harmony of a whole regulated by the wisdom of the center, we have two polarized harmonies, disrespectful of each other, battling for supremacy. The result is a polarized culture, and a culture war.

When we lose our balance as a culture and lean excessively into a left-brain-directed perspective, then our entire culture becomes focused on details at the expense of the big picture, as was the case when we failed to protect the levees and marshland around New Orleans prior to Hurricane Katrina. When we lose our balance and tilt to the dualistic left side, we produce a culture that is *competitive* at the expense of being *cooperative*. Left-brain-directed government officials, with their primary focus on reelection, tend to allocate funds where they will be most politically effective. In effect, government held a competition for the money that could have secured the environment around New Orleans and prevented the flooding of Hurricane Katrina. Perhaps it went to Boston's Big Dig. The left brain's competitive, dominating drive also creates situations such as we find in the unwillingness of law enforcement organizations to share information that could save lives or prevent disasters like 9/11. The consequences of such competitive behavior can be, and often have been, disastrous.

Healthy, informed, holistic cultures recognize that we are living with two very different but complementary perspectives, and they are largely at peace with the differences. In contrast, dualistic cultures, with their polarizing perspective, tend to see our two fundamental perspectives as opposites. When we act based on intelligence derived solely from the dualistic left, we are prompted to fight to ensure that the dualistic perception dominates. Thus, left-brain dominants (directed by the left brain), along with right-brain dominants who have bought into the left brain's vision of things, view the more inclusive holistic vision as being in opposition to their cultural beliefs and values, and often respond by building walls of separation that effectively prohibit a unified perspective.

This is not to blame left-brain dominants, or the resulting political conservatism, for cultural polarization. The left brain is simply doing what it was designed to do, which is to seek separation from collective influences as a way of protecting individual freedom from the excesses of collective domination. Being protective, it seeks to conserve individual (including family) resources such as wealth. Being competitive, it challenges and motivates us and thus helps us to build our wealth (physical, mental, and spiritual). These are all essential functions—but the left brain, acting alone, sometimes goes too far in its responses (as does the right brain). Without the moderating influences of the right brain, the left brain lacks an efficient corrective mechanism. In addition, the cultural left brain ignores an important and fundamental idea: for all its strengths, a focused, dualistic perspective is no match for a holistic perspective when it comes to the broad and long-term view. One needs the holistic perspective for the big-picture decisions that will influence our lives for decades, centuries, and even eons to come.

Ultimately, if we are to blame someone for our cultural dilemma, for polarization, those most responsible are the ones we are least likely to question—the good, left *and* right. Just as we have corrupt cops in law enforcement because "good" cops fail to remove them, so too do we have corrupt politicians in both parties who are retained by the "good" in order to protect a voting bloc or some other vested interest—and they are there because of "good" voters who make bad decisions. Destructive elements are present in most cultures and must be dominated if there is to be peace. Unfortunately, the polarization of our culture into liberal and conservative camps has separated the good elements of society and weakened their influence. They now find themselves relatively powerless in an entrenched, tradition-dominated, dualistic political system determined to resist systemic change, a system in which independent thinkers are often coerced into following party goals by party enforcers.

If we are to become more holistic as a culture, we must deal with those at the extremes who resist being marginalized by a powerful center. We must have the courage to embrace their knowledge whenever they are in harmony with the truth, even though their contribution is radical. And at the same time we must have the discipline to act with sufficient care before embracing extreme ideas. The dualistic left brain is especially difficult to rein in once it gains control of culture because of its innate need for control and its willingness to use any tool available—including secrecy, deception, and violence—in the name of security, order, and its perception of individual and public interest.

Holistic cultures see oneness. Seeing oneness, holistic cultures see others as parts of the oneness. Holistic cultures understand that we hurt ourselves when we hurt others. The use of violence to solve a problem makes no sense to someone looking through the broad lens of a holistic brain. As a result, holistic individuals and cultures are naturally nonviolent. Nevertheless, holistic individuals and cultures have a fighting left brain. So although force goes against holistic principles, when threatened, feeling they have no other choice, most will fight.

Chapter Seven

The Military-Industrial-Congressional Complex

Fascism should more properly be called corporatism because it is the merger of state and corporate power.

— BENITO MUSSOLINI

In *Empire of Debt: The Rise of an Epic Financial Crisis*, William Bonner and Addison Wiggin analyze the dilemma of American empire and conclude, "All empires must pass away. All must find a way to destroy themselves. America found debt." The shift to decline began in the 1970s when the balance of trade turned negative and debt began to climb. "By the year Alan Greenspan took over at the Fed [1987], foreigners owned more U.S. assets than Americans owned foreign ones. . . . People chose to spend rather than to save. . . . They demanded bread and circuses."[1]

In *Wealth and Democracy: A Political History of the American Rich*, Kevin Phillips reports that "in just a little over two centuries the United States went from being a society born of revolution and touched by egalitarianism to being the country with the industrial world's biggest fortunes and its largest rich-poor gap. . . . Real disposable (after-tax) income for non-supervisory workers peaked in the late 1960s. Debt taken on by the bottom two-fifths of the population rose so sharply that by 1995 their inflation-adjusted net worths had fallen below 1973 levels."[2]

The weak go first. This should have been recognized as the canary in the coal mine, a warning to us all. With a more holistic attitude, we might have perceived that this change would move ever higher up the economic food chain and eventually reach all of us. Had we seen it coming, we might have prepared — some did. But from the separative perspective of the left brain, we are focused on our own financial survival and prosperity. Life is a collection of those things on which we focus, and our economic system is left for others to take care of. Systems management is a collective (right brain) issue and needs to be managed by people who are right-brain directed. Instead, it is managed by left-brainers focused on system parts and selfish goals. Instead of taking care of the system, they game the system. The left brain's job, remember, is to take care of us as individuals, including the things we hold dear, such as systems that support us.

Following the Money Trail

Empires must be financed. When managing the finances of an empire, it is helpful to understand financial fundamentals such as the directional flow of money within the system. As our government is managed now, Republicans craft plans based on wealth trickling down, and Democrats craft plans based on wealth flowing up. To switch back and forth between "theories" with every shift in party control is unnecessarily inefficient and wasteful. Perhaps we can clear up this discrepancy.

A farmer plants seeds and through the gift of Mother Earth harvests enough grain to sell. That grain is moved through a system that is designed to distribute it and its products to the consumer. We see the same flow pattern initiated by miners, fishermen, factory workers, oil workers, and others. Individuals create value through their efforts, harvesting the gifts of Mother Earth, and as their creations move to the consumer, others higher up the economic ladder take a piece of the action (in effect, enjoying a harvest of their own) in the form of a return on investment in such things as processing, transportation, warehousing, insurance, marketing, and/or finance.

It doesn't take a rocket scientist or an economist to see that wealth, as a whole, does not trickle down. Wealth begins with Mother Earth and the labor of the men and women who work with her gifts of food, fiber, minerals, metals, and other materials to create the things we want. That is not to say that all money moves upward. Some money does trickle down—donations for example, and incentives such as bonuses, prizes, kickbacks, hush money, and government payments just prior to an election. Whether we see money trickling up or down seems to depend on what we desire to see. As stated in A Course in Miracles, "Seeing adapts to wish, for sight is always secondary to desire."[3]

Like lemmings running toward a cliff, left-brain dominants and their cultures as a whole are focused on the short term. Nowhere is this more evident than in the influence of quarterly financial reports on stock prices. Managers run their companies focused on what the numbers are going to show in the next quarter, rather than on working for long-term success and stability.

In New World New Mind: Moving Toward Conscious Evolution, Robert Ornstein and Paul Ehrlich report, "Cultures did not spontaneously develop the ability to deal with long-term trends because they had no need to until very recently." They point out that politicians, who provide our leadership in the economic arena, "are the ultimate creatures of the moment," confronted with a "constant stream of problems that must be solved *now*. . . . At most their time horizons reach [no farther than] the next election, which in most Western democracies means a maximum of six years. . . . As a result politicians have little incentive to tackle or even to identify and analyze long-term trends."[4] I point this out so that everyone might recognize that long-term planning, which is vital, is almost always ignored by election-minded politicians and must be *forced* upon them by the electorate.

Progress is cumulative in medical science, Bonner and Wiggin remind us. What one generation learns is added to what previous generations have learned, and the sum of knowledge is passed on. In the world of finance, on the other hand, "progress is not cumulative, but cyclical. One generation learns. The next forgets. One makes money; the next loses it."[5] And when we are highly leveraged, we can lose a great deal of money very quickly. We can also lose money very slowly (as well as quickly), through inflation. Ernest Hemingway described it like this: "The first panacea for a mismanaged nation is inflation of the currency; the second is war. Both bring a temporary prosperity; both bring a permanent ruin. . . . Both are the refuge of political and economic opportunists."[6]

Under reasonable regulation, risks can be managed and losses kept under control, says nationally recognized consumer advocate Jamie Court, president of Consumer Watchdog (formerly the Foundation for Taxpayer and Consumer Rights), in his book *Corporateering: How Corporate Power Steals Your Personal Freedom and What You Can Do About It.* During President Reagan's leadership, corporate regulatory and tax structures were dismantled. This freed risk takers from their traditional oversight. President Clinton then followed up by championing governmental partnership with private industry and, with his permissive consolidation policies, concentrated power into the hands of a few big corporations.[7]

Left-brain-directed cultures are protective of individual freedom and feel oppressed by regulation. Intelligent regulation is holistic, because it exists to protect the whole from individual excesses. Paul Volcker, chairman of the Federal Reserve Board when Reagan took office, supported strong regulation. He was promptly replaced by Alan Greenspan, who supported deregulation and went on to preside over the inflation of a tech bubble that popped in 2000–2001, followed by housing and derivatives bubbles.

When we imagine an economic system in which debt is highly concentrated, highly leveraged, and managed with few regulations by left-brain-dominant (and therefore naturally competitive and destructive) young men on a long leash held by other left-brain-dominant men, we start to understand how empires managed with so little respect for the holistic perspective are ultimately doomed.

Congress: Ground Zero of the Crisis

"The crisis in American capitalism isn't just about the specific details—about tricky accounting, stock options, loans to executives, and so on," Paul Krugman observes in *The Great Unraveling: Losing Our Way in the New Century.* "It's about the way the game has been rigged on behalf of insiders."[8] Of course, rigging the game so that it benefits the individual instead of the collective is a left-brain response. As Kevin Phillips points out, wealth becomes more and more concentrated among ever fewer people "with the help of the corruption of politics on one hand and the persuasive efforts of market idolatry and economic Darwinism on the other."[9] The mechanism for rigging the economic game in the United States is, of course, the U.S. Congress.

Congress has a number of problems. It has lost sight of its most fundamental values. We see this when Congress makes decisions designed to strengthen the power of one's own political party or weaken the opposition, rather than basing decisions on the long-term welfare of the nation and its citizens. Congress has a *systemic* problem (which is a holistic problem). Rather than a well-thought-out system designed to manage a complex modern economy, the rules Congress has set for itself are a selfish patchwork based on protecting vested interests. We send good men and women to Congress, only to have their hands tied by the system in which they are forced to work. Take, for example, Senator Bernie Sanders (I-Vermont). Trying to find out how American tax dollars had been spent, Sanders asked Federal Reserve Chairman Ben Bernanke to tell the American people to whom he had lent $2.2 trillion of their dollars. Bernanke's simple answer: "No." Nor would Bernanke provide the information confidentially and off the record to Congress. As Washington's Blog explained it, "Congress doesn't run the country in the core areas of business, finance and the economy. The financial giants and their servants at the Fed and Treasury do."[10]

We see the dysfunctional attitude of Congress revealed in the fact that it doesn't even allow itself to read some of the bills on which it votes! Congress is in charge of the rules and the laws that guide the rules and could change this if it wished, but a quick vote allows language and terms to be inserted into bills that otherwise would not pass. Members of Congress get things for themselves, their party, their districts, and their friends. The country gets the bill. A system that does not allow bills to be examined by the public and *all* members of the deliberative body before being voted on comes from a selfish, separative left-brain-based power structure that has something to hide, a system that benefits the powerbrokers. We see this same left-brain influence in Congress's patchwork approach to improving or evolving the system. The system needs to make a quantum leap into something altogether more effective and responsive, but that would require a holistic approach—an approach that corporate interests seem determined to undermine. In fact, a dysfunctional or nonfunctioning government is very much in the interest of large corporations and many left-brain-directed politicians (if you are doing well, you want to keep things the way they are).

The two major political parties that dominate Congress are themselves dysfunctional. David Sirota (author of *Hostile Takeover*), writing in the *Washington Spectator* (September 1, 2006), affirms that the Democratic Party is split into two groups—one that represents citizens and one that represents corporate interests. As an example of the latter, he points to the Democratic Leadership Council (DLC), an organization funded by large corporate interests and supported by a number of high-ranking Democrats. Sirota, quoting the DLC's president, Al From, reports that From's goal is "to give Democrats 'a game plan to try to contain populism.'" "Populism," Sirota reminds us, "is defined as 'supporting the rights and powers of the common people in their struggle with the privileged elite.'" In other words, the DLC is attempting to "contain" a fundamental value of the Democratic Party—its focus on protecting and supporting holistic interests. The DLC, Sirota goes on to say, "bills itself as quasi grassroots, holding so-called 'national conversations' in an effort to create the impression that its corporate-written agenda has some semblance of public support." Nevertheless, Sirota reports that the *Rocky Mountain News* checked into one of the DLC's "national conversations" and found out that it was, "in fact, 'not open to the public.'"[11]

Congress, reflecting the national culture that elects it, is a culture dominated by separative, force-oriented, dualistic thinkers. As a result of this mindset, congressional actions, rather than being determined by a meeting of minds, are often based on what the strongest of the two sides wants. Most actions are determined by a majority vote rather than by a relatively harmonious agreement. The results are then imposed (a left-brain response) on the opposition: A *coalition of the most powerful decide; the rest are forced to go along.*

As a result of having only limited access to their holistic perspective, members of Congress as a whole do things that would surely embarrass them if they could see themselves from a more holistic perspective. We see ample evidence of Congress's selfishness and lack of concern for the average American where we find American schools that lack basic materials and children without access to the most basic health care, while members of Congress give themselves and their families everything they need and more—in spite of their doing what most Americans agree in poll after poll to be a below-average job of managing the country's assets. In 2009, with the economy clearly tanking and with record numbers of Americans losing their jobs, most members of Congress received a $4,700 pay raise. To try to separate themselves from any personal responsibility for this (a typical left-brain-directed response), they made pay raises automatic so that they would never have to vote on them. Now when they say to their constituents, "I was against a pay raise, but there was nothing I could do," they have cover.

Congress is sustained by (and sustains its supporters with) money. In his book *Perfectly Legal: The Covert Campaign to Rig Our Tax System to Benefit the Super Rich—and Cheat Everybody Else,* Pulitzer Prize–winning *New York Times* reporter David Cay Johnston explains, "When governments set tax rates, they are making decisions about who will prosper and by how much. A government that takes in 90 cents out of each dollar above a threshold, as the United States did in the Eisenhower years, is deciding to limit the wealth that people can accumulate from their earnings. Likewise, a government that taxes the poor on their first dollar of wages, as the United States does with the Social Security and Medicare taxes, is deciding to limit or eliminate the ability of those at the bottom of the income ladder to save money and improve their lot in life."[12]

Johnston reports that "some of the biggest tax breaks for the rich are not even in the tax code." He found that "the IRS was completely unaware of many widely used tax fraud schemes." What surprised him the most, he said, was "the realization that our tax system now levies the poor, the middle class and even the upper middle class to subsidize the rich."[13] This game-the-system attitude, which in effect steals from the vast majority of citizens in order to benefit a powerful few, reflects a pure, unfettered left-brain response.

From a business perspective, Kevin Phillips explains, the legislation that Congress enacts is viewed as an investment opportunity. To those with sufficient wealth, legislation is seen as just another investment—and often a very lucrative one. Through lobbyists, who are the corporations' version of stockbrokers, those with money are able to invest in laws with campaign contributions. Contributions buy access, and access gives you the opportunity to promote your ideas. If you manage the process well, if you contribute enough, a member of Congress will create a provision beneficial to your investments and insert it into some law that is about to be passed. And you can strike it rich. Phillips gives the example of a $30 million tobacco industry investment that produced $50 billion in revenue, for a return on investment of 167,000 percent; and a $5 million contribution made by the broadcast industry to secure free digital TV licenses worth $70 billion, a return on investment of

1,400,000 percent. And investment in legislation is not limited to big corporations. Big donors have similar opportunities. Phillips found that "some three-quarters of the individual money that fueled turn-of-the-century presidential and Congressional races came from donors with incomes over $200,000 a year."[14]

Phillips also reports that between 1993 and 1995, Congress enacted and implemented the first of the North American Free Trade Agreements (NAFTA) and made commitments to the World Trade Organization (WTO) that "seemed to push democratic precepts aside." Soon after, "the transnational deliberations of NAFTA, the WTO, and the European Union began to yield rulings that set aside local and national legislation and regulatory decisions." Phillips sums up the impact of the monumental agreement by remarking that "survival of the fittest had jumped onto an international stage."[15] In his book *Where the Right Went Wrong: How Neoconservatives Subverted the Reagan Revolution and Hijacked the Bush Presidency*, Patrick Buchanan says of the agreement, "Congress's surrender of its constitutional authority over trade has been total. In 1994, Congress was allowed only a yes or no vote on a twenty-three-thousand-page GATT treaty. No amendments were permitted. With its yes vote, Congress put the United States under the jurisdiction of an institution of world government, the World Trade Organization, whose dispute panels operate in secret. . . . The WTO was also granted power to . . . demand the repeal of American laws. And this it has repeatedly done."[16] Here again we see selfish left-brain perspectives and perceptions limiting the freedoms of the majority in order to concentrate power and promote the agendas of a relatively small power elite.

In addition to passing legislation crafted to favor larger companies—even transnational companies—over the average citizen, Congress directs its own corporations and passes laws that favor them. Through Federal Prison Industries, a massive "government-owned corporation" that does business "under the innocent name Unicor," Congress "monopolizes a huge share of government contracts," writes Jack Faris in an article in the *Alva Review Courier*. "This official arm of the government also exempts itself from regulatory mandates that legitimate businesses must accept, and Unicor is allowed to pay its labor force of prisoner-workers a sub-minimum wage of $1.23 an hour or less." Should it ever need cash, Unicor can simply go to the U.S. Treasury and borrow "up to $20 million at rates far below those available to even the largest commercial enterprise."[17] In the use of legislative force to deny small businesses a fair opportunity to compete, once again we see unmistakable left-brain footprints at the scene of a white-collar crime.

The Media: Controlling Information Flow

The industrial-congressional alliance naturally includes media. Powerful corporations, driven by forceful dominance-seeking males, go to great lengths to control what people see and hear. At the very least, they know that this gives them an economic advantage in a highly competitive marketplace.

In 1981, under the Reagan administration, media deregulation began in earnest, and wealthy and powerful interests quickly began an unprecedented power grab. Between 1981 and 1985, the number of TV stations any single entity could own grew from 7 to 12. In 1985, guidelines for minimum amounts of nonentertainment programming such as news and public affairs were abolished, and limits on the amount of advertising per hour were eliminated. In 1987, the Fairness Doctrine was eliminated. In 1996, under President Clinton, unprecedented consolidation took place in radio after a 40-station ownership cap was lifted. One company, Clear Channel Communications, eventually came to own 1,200 radio stations.[18]

But even big media can suffer setbacks. On January 18, 2002, a train derailment killed one person, spilling 210,000 gallons of anhydrous ammonia, and left a killer cloud threatening Minot, North Dakota. Time was of the essence. To quickly warn residents of the deadly toxic cloud, local authorities turned to Minot's seven commercial radio stations. But authorities were unable to contact six of them by phone—there was no answer (the six stations were part of the 1,200 owned by Clear Channel Communications). No one was on the air. Live people had been replaced with recorded programming.[19]

After that, many people, even some members of Congress, came to the conclusion that media deregulation might have some flaws. In response to what could have been a major disaster, Congress started questioning consolidation—but of course it eventually gave in to corporate pressure and in an omnibus spending bill raised the ownership cap enough to cover the giant media corporations that had already ignored the rules and exceeded the cap. By 2004, three-quarters of Americans watched channels that were owned by just six companies.[20]

Senator Bernie Sanders believes that media consolidation is *the* most important political issue we face. And he makes a strong case. "We're not going to be able to address the major economic and foreign policy problems facing this country," he reminds us, "unless the people have an opportunity to hear all points of view and learn the truth about what's going on in their country, and at the moment, they are not doing that."[21] Left-brain-directed cultures such as Congress and big business need to control the media if they are to keep people from knowing the truth about their activities. So far, they have been successful, but the holistic energy that springs from the Internet seems destined to change that. Nevertheless, keep in mind that a typical left-brain-directed response would be to attack and disable the Internet, and legislative attempts have already been made to diminish its power.

Congressional Betrayal

In the discussion of corporate influence (particularly that of multinationals) on government—as well as the related issue of Congress ceding to others its obligation to make tough decisions (with a resulting loss of accountability)—one of the strongest voices of criticism has come from the political right, in the voice of Patrick Buchanan. While he has often taken separative and divisive positions concerning cultural issues, in other areas, such as Congress's abdication of its traditional role, as well as the corporate oligarchy that this country has become, his unfiltered, no-holds-barred critiques are brilliant, and very much a service to the holistic perspective.

In his book *Where the Right Went Wrong*, Buchanan minces no words in condemning actions taken by his own political party in Congress, where he states, "The Republican Party, which had presided over America's rise to manufacturing pre-eminence, has acquiesced in the de-industrialization of the nation to gratify transnational corporations whose oligarchs are the party financiers. . . . The Republican Party has signed off on economic treason."[22]

Another area where, in Buchanan's view, Congress has passed the buck—and thus created an unaccountable system—is in the creation of money. "Congress is an institutional coward," Buchanan says. "The Constitution gives Congress the power to coin money, but in 1913, this power was transferred to a new Federal Reserve," a private bank that refuses to answer to Congress. (Or should we say the bank that Congress refuses to regulate?) Buchanan also points out that Congress has separated itself from responsibility in its central role—lawmaking. "Congress has, for half a century, been surrendering its lawmaking power to judges and justices. . . . Congress prefers to let . . . the courts make the decisions on issues that divide us deeply and emotionally." Reflecting its left-brain dominance, Congress prefers to let the judges take the heat. "The dirty little secret," as Buchanan sees it, "is that Congress no longer wants the accountability that goes with the exercise of power. It does not want to govern. Both parties prefer to make only those decisions that will be applauded by constituents and rewarded at the ballot box, and to pass on to others decisions that deeply divide or roil the public." As a result, "congressional powers granted in the Constitution [have] been seized and subdivided between presidents and a Supreme Court that is now the final and binding authority on what new laws Congress may enact and what Congress meant when it enacted the old laws."[23]

The next time you hear someone complain about liberal (or conservative) judges, remember that someone has to interpret the incomplete (nonholistic) laws that Congress passes. If the laws Congress gave us were reasonably complete and clear, there would be much less need for interpretation. If the public were able to see proposed laws online and comment on them before enactment, perhaps we might come up with more holistic (complete) laws and consequently have less fear of judicial discretion.

In trying to avoid personal responsibility for the problems of Congress, its members like to blame the other political party. In addition, congressional members will tell you that their hands are often tied, that the system is outdated. And it is. But the truth is that they don't want it fixed because the system in place provides them with security, something the left brain is designed to seek. Most members of Congress (regardless of party) — in spite of any patriotic rhetoric — are inclined to put self ahead of country. Examples of their selfish drive abound, and in many cases these examples are quite obvious. Other examples are less obvious to most people but telling nonetheless. One such example is the dismissive attitude toward the gold standard. Gold is a time-tested measure of wealth. Paper money can be kept honest by tying it to a standard value such as gold, or it can be set free and printed at will to provide goods and services to the voter without raising taxes—though that eventually creates inflation and punishes fixed-income retirees and those who save. Guess which option politicians favor. But to cover their attempts at deception, the standard that serves as a basis of comparison, usually gold, must be held in check at all costs—being the standard, it should not be changing. When people lose confidence in paper money, they seek the traditional store of value, gold, and it appreciates relative to paper "gold," paper money. When physical gold becomes more valuable than paper "gold," it suggests there is a problem with the paper. Howard Buffett (1903–1964), onetime securities trader from Omaha turned U.S. Representative (R-Nebraska), observed in a 1948 article titled "Human Freedom Rests on Gold Redeemable Money," "when you recall that one of the first moves by Lenin, Mussolini and Hitler was to outlaw individual ownership of gold, you begin to sense that there may be some connection between money, redeemable in gold, and the rare prize known as human liberty."[24]

The Culture of Big Business

In 1936, Standard Oil of California, Firestone Tire and Rubber Company, B. F. Phillips Petroleum, and Mac Manufacturing, under the leadership of General Motors, formed a holding company, National City Lines. National City then proceeded to buy electric trolley lines and tear up the tracks in cities all across the nation. In *Gangs of America: The Rise of Corporate Power and the Disabling of Democracy*, Ted Nace takes us through the unsavory details. "Each time it destroyed a local trolley system, National City would license the rights to operate a new system to a local franchisee, under the stipulation that they convert to diesel-powered General Motors busses. By 1949 more than one hundred electric transit systems in forty-five cities had been torn up and converted." Hit with antitrust actions in 1949, General Motors eventually paid a $1 fine, and the holding company paid a fine of $5,000 per company. "After the conviction, the companies [resumed activity]. By 1955, 88 percent of the country's electric streetcar network was gone."[25]

The power of big business to control our environment and shape culture is extraordinary. And naturally, what big business wants is a consumer culture. Thus, we find ourselves essentially led by a business system focused on moving product through our lives in order to enrich the (mostly) left-brain-directed guys running the system. Under this leadership, the pursuit of money and consumer goods becomes the fundamental goal of our culture. Corporations operate out of fifth-level consciousness, based on the eight-level system of Spiral Dynamics, formulated by Don Beck and Christopher Cowan.[26] Thus, from a cultural-consciousness standpoint, we have a fifth-level system trying to lead people at the sixth, seventh, and eighth levels of consciousness! It's cultural insanity. Quality, beauty, and goodness do sometimes come through to a substantial degree, as they always have (as a result of good, talented individuals working within the system), but the system's prime directive is to make money, to make the guys running the system rich—at the expense of the rest of us.

The indifference of the corporate culture to the human culture is "nowhere more evident than in the exporting of American jobs to cheap overseas labor markets," Lou Dobbs states in *Exporting America: Why Corporate Greed Is Shipping American Jobs Overseas*. "The rising debate over the outsourcing of hundreds of thousands of American jobs has revealed a fundamental imbalance in our economy and society."[27] On the other hand, corporate managers will tell you that if they don't go where the cost is lowest, they will become uncompetitive; they will be unable to sell their products and will be driven out of business. And they have a point. American consumers bear a much larger portion of responsibility for the loss of American jobs and its devastating effect on the economy than has generally been acknowledged (and don't overlook the security aspects of shipping our manufacturing overseas). When American consumers choose to focus on price exclusively (a left-brain-directed response), they are unwittingly *pushing* manufacturers into cheaper labor markets (which usually means overseas markets), and consequently pushing their neighbors out of their jobs while supporting foreign economies at the expense of their own, for personal gain—a left-brain goal.

Left-brain dominants, because they are focused on smaller wholes such as individuals, local cultures, and details, are keenly aware of the importance of economically supporting their neighbors. But left-brain dominants, as we know, are virtually hard-wired to focus on themselves and their families, so their natural tendency is to buy what best serves their personal needs, with little regard to its creator. Ultimately, the decision comes down to how they define *self*, as revealed by what they value (people, money, etc.)—something that can also be said of right-brain dominants.

Right-brain dominants too must contend with the power and determination of the left brain to get what it wants, and we see this in an indifference to the consequences of our consuming habits. We see this where caring right-brain dominants are lured by the self-satisfaction of quality and status away from more holistic economic and human values. Right-brain dominants, having a big-picture perspective, also tend to overlook the importance of smaller elements of the picture—details like someone's job (of course, when many people choose this way, it can mean many jobs). Whether we are left-brain directed or right-brain directed, our self-oriented left brain inevitably leads us to blame others for our troubles.

Marjorie Kelly, cofounder and editor of the journal *Business Ethics*, explains in *The Divine Right of Capital: Dethroning the Corporate Aristocracy* that corporations are dominated by an attitude of economic aristocracy that trumps the democratic principles on which the country was founded. "That more people own stock today has not changed the market's essentially aristocratic bias."[28] In the construct of a free market, "everyone scrambles to get what they can, and keep what they earn. In the construct of the corporation, one group gets what another earns."[29] Kelly points out that capitalism, as practiced by modern corporations, "embraces a predemocratic concept of liberty reserved for property holders, which thrives by restricting the liberty of employees and the community. . . . In the predemocratic mindset, people without property were not permitted to vote. And so it is with corporate employees today, for stockholders alone govern corporations. . . . The public corporation is a kind of inverted monarchy, with representatives of the share-owning aristocracy hiring and firing the CEO-king," she explains. "Stockholder privilege rests on the notion that corporations are not human communities but pieces of property, which means they can be owned and sold by the propertied class. . . . The free market reserves liberty for property holders, even as it denies liberty to employees and the community."[30]

In referring to corporations, we are referring to *large* corporations, and in particular, those that practice some of the invasive behaviors that are becoming increasingly troubling. Small corporations, we acknowledge, often struggle for survival along with individuals. Size matters. With size comes power. The growing power of the corporate system is allowing the corporate world to redefine the basic rules of society, law, and ethical customs to the detriment of traditional rights and individual freedoms. In his introduction to *Corporateering*, Jamie Court quotes the response of an editor to whom he was pitching his book prior to publication, who said, "Corporations are not just impacting culture, they *are* culture."[31]

Due to the size and influence of corporations, the rights of corporations frequently outweigh not only the rights of individuals, but also the rights of whole communities. Corporations have become "super-citizens" driven by competition to use their super-powers to try to influence political decisions that ultimately work against the good of the whole. Thomas Linzey, the attorney for a Pennsylvania group called FROST (Friends and Residents of St. Thomas Township), discovered this when he tried to stop the establishment of a limestone quarry near St. Thomas, a quarry that would have been located a thousand feet from an elementary school. "Decisions made by corporations and the corporate few that run them every day are trumping the rights of the majority at the local level to make decisions about what they want their communities to look like in 20, 40, or 50 years," Linzey concluded.[32]

Corporations dominate culture, Jamie Court suggests, by dominating the media. "By gaining power over what is and what is not told, media corporations can control what is sold both commercially and culturally. . . . [In recent years] corporations [have] become far more aggressive in making demands of the media and attacking it for coverage that is too critical of corporate interests." And if your only interest lies in maximizing corporate profits, why not? "The power to control the individual's and the public's perspective is the ultimate political power."[33] At the same time, "the majority of press releases and news pitches received by newsrooms across America come from public relations firms working for corporations that pitch their news all the time." And this is occurring in an environment in which newsrooms have been downsized, creating conditions that make reporters "more receptive to ready-made stories and satellite-fed video news releases."[34] Now, "instead of the media looking deeper into the corporation, the media corporation looks more deeply into the individual."[35]

When media corporations encounter subjects that conflict with their ideological goals, they sometimes attempt to suppress the news. When the ABC news program *Nightline* chose to honor those who had given their lives in the Iraq war by broadcasting their names and photos, Sinclair Broadcasting, which controlled or maintained 62 local television stations in 39 markets, made news of its own when it told its local ABC affiliates not to air the special broadcast.[36] Sinclair, being supportive of the war in Iraq and fearing that showing the war's true cost might diminish support for it, responded in typical left-brain fashion by withholding some of the facts.

As corporations have grown in size and gone transnational, we have seen a shift in the nature of the corporate structure. John C. Bogle, founder and retired CEO of the Vanguard Group, points out that as ownership has been diluted, owners have grown less and less powerful and less connected to their investment. Corporate leadership, Bogle says, has increasingly shifted to management, and now, instead of *owner*-based capitalism, we have *manager*-based capitalism. "The classic system — *owners* capitalism — had been based on a dedication to serving the interests of the corporation's owners, maximizing the return on their capital investment. But a new system developed — *managers* capitalism — in which [in the words of journalist William Pfaff] 'the corporation came to be run to profit its managers, in complicity if not conspiracy with accountants and the managers of other corporations.'"[37]

When Wall Street's corporate bears go hunting for meat, they head for Main Street, their claws being an economic system designed, Marjorie Kelly says, "to enrich a few at the expense of many." It is a system that exalts rising share price as the definition of corporate success, a system that tends to see culture as little more than a PR investment. Citing an egregious example of such abuse, Kelly asks whether achieving a 15 percent return for a billionaire is more important than paying employees a living wage.[38] For competitive left-brain dominants focused on money, it might be. As we've been pointing out, left-brain dominants manage their reality based on information filtered through a brain that is specialized to take care of them and their interests first. No amount of money is too much if you are highly competitive and those in similar positions make more money than you. The system eventually spirals out of control.

Stockholders, too, can be demanding, and like most of management, most stockholders are dominated by a dualistic perspective. In *Gangs of America*, Ted Nace describes how Henry Ford, in a holistic gesture, wanted to plow his company's retained earnings into building more factories to employ more people and "help them build up their lives and their homes." Shareholders took him to court and forced him to pay dividends. "Since Ford defended his reinvestment plans in terms of social goals rather than in terms of maximizing shareholder returns, he lost the case."[39]

Making a profit requires that corporations minimize their expenses. Nace, repeating an observation made by Ralph Estes in *The Tyranny of the Bottom Line*, warns that in corporate culture, "the goal of profit maximization requires corporations to off-load their negative impacts [onto society] wherever possible"—pollution being one of the most egregious examples.[40] Nace further points out that "particularly in the areas of labor law, pollution control, and government contracting, some corporations regard complying with the law to be more expensive than breaking it." Through their close partnership with Congress, corporations lobby to weaken laws that work against them so that when they break the law, penalties are minimal or eliminated. Nace explains that in contrast to citizens, who, if they have a felony conviction are prohibited from voting in certain states, corporations with a pattern of repeated legal violations are able to maintain their vote. They can still actively lobby Congress.[41]

When corporations can't weaken laws or get them crafted to their advantage, their employees, led by powerful legal teams, find other creative ways to boost the bottom line. When giant Texaco Oil Company was found to have underpaid for natural gas they had withdrawn from a section of land in which I held a mineral interest, Texaco refused to pay the mineral owners, citing statutes of limitations. The company claimed it owed us nothing based on the fact that we had not discovered this until more than two years after the gas was withdrawn. Later, in a separate incident, Burlington Northern Santa Fe (BNSF) resorted to this same law when I had a claim against them. To compensate for some property damage, the BNSF roadmaster in charge agreed to replace a fence, but instead, for more than two years, he delayed any action. Eventually a company claims representative refused to honor the agreement, citing statutes of limitations—knowing full well that company employees were responsible for the delay. Rather than accept responsibility and settle, the company offered me a small nuisance amount to try to keep out of small claims court.[42]

Consumer advocate Jamie Court reports that another disturbing corporate tactic is "the growth in deception by corporate groups who hide their identities from the public." Court says that, of the corporate-funded groups he battles, "all claim to represent individuals, not corporations." He cites as an example Citizens Against Lawsuit Abuse, a group that "fights to limit the individual's legal rights to challenge corporations in court. . . . It places letters to the editors in local newspapers and lobbies legislators under the banner of a 'citizen's' organization." Other examples he gives are Californians Against Higher Taxes and Higher Electric Rates, an organization operated by the utility companies with the goal of blocking deregulation, and the Civil Justice Association, whose "only goal is to limit liability for large corporations."[43]

Not only do some corporations practice deception in order to boost the bottom line, but some even claim the *right* to lie! Journalist Thom Hartmann reports that in response to a public relations blitz intended to quell consumer concerns about sub-contractor sweatshop practices, Nike was sued by a consumer advocate, Marc Kasky, who thought Nike had gone too far, "citing a California law that forbids corporations from intentionally deceiving people in their commercial statements. . . . Instead of refuting Kasky's charge by proving in court that they didn't lie, however, Nike instead chose to argue that corporations should enjoy the same 'free speech' right to deceive that . . . citizens have."[44]

Activities of the military-industrial-congressional complex are primarily the result of left-brain-directed perspectives and processes that can be summarized as follows: *Focus on self* (on what is good for the individual manager and his individual corporation). *Maximize profits and power* (at the expense of holistic goals such as the good of the community). *Offload negativity* (separate from it). We find a disturbing example of the effect of this level of thinking in the book *An Air That Kills: How the Asbestos Poisoning of Libby, Montana, Uncovered a National Scandal,* coauthored by Pulitzer Prize–winning journalists Andrew Schneider and David McCumber. They report a case in which W. R. Grace & Company managers discovered that the vermiculite ore they were mining and processing contained tremolite, an especially lethal type of cancer-causing asbestos, but kept on mining and processing it for years. No one knows how many hundreds or thousands have died or will die as a result of exposure. Several U.S. government agencies also knew of the problem and for years dragged their feet and failed to act.[45] Only left-brain dominants out of touch with their right brains are inclined to respond in such a blind, selfish way as to continue to produce a product that is killing their workers. From a pure left-brain perspective, if you have a problem, you get rid of it as best you can and keep working toward your goals. The holistic perspective, on the other hand, because it sees the whole, the integration, the harmony of everything, sees selfish actions like these as an infringement of the rights of others and is not inclined to participate.

The military-industrial-congressional complex we are examining not only creates problems for citizens of the United States, but it also creates international problems. And based on certain credible-sounding channeled writings, it appears to have even attracted intergalactic notice. From the celestial perspective of Arten, an individual identified as the former disciple of Jesus known as Thomas, speaking through Gary Renard in *The Disappearance of the Universe: Straight Talk about Illusions, Past Lives, Religion, Sex, Politics, and the Miracles of Forgiveness*, we are advised that "the government of the United States has become famous around the world in the last hundred years for propping up any government that will watch out for the best interests . . . of the American-based or U.S.-dominated multinational corporations [at he expense of the local people]. . . . Your country is hated in the Middle East by average people," Arten says, "not because you stand for freedom and democracy, but because you *don't* stand for freedom and democracy. You stand for whatever's best for American money."[46]

In 1999, after years of pressure from the World Bank, Bolivia's government agreed to privatize the public water system of Cochabamba, its third largest city. It was subsequently taken over by an international consortium led by the infamous Bechtel Corporation. Following the change, the cost of water rose substantially more than was promised. By some accounts, collecting rainwater in a tank required a permit. Owners of private wells were required to install a meter and pay. "These increases forced some of the poorest families in South America to literally choose between food or water. A popular uprising against the company, repressed violently by government troops, left one 17-year-old boy dead and more than a hundred people wounded."[47]

In 2002, the *Prestige*, a 26-year-old rusting, single-hulled tanker loaded with highly toxic number 4 crude oil, sank in an area off northwestern Spain that contains some of the world's richest fishing grounds. The spill, estimated at 20 million gallons, contaminated 350 miles of coastline, causing one of the worst oils spills in history. The *Prestige* spilled almost twice the amount of oil as in the *Exxon Valdez* spill of 1989. The subsequent investigation found that it had been known beforehand that the ship was not seaworthy. But when its captain had demanded repairs, the Greek owner found another captain — thus separating himself from a major repair bill. When the Spanish government tried to collect damages, they found that the ship was owned by a corporation that owned nothing else. A separate company had been set up to avoid any liability beyond the value of the ship — there was nothing in the company to collect.[48] A Spanish news organization reported that almost 7,000 fishermen (among others) developed respiratory damage within two years of helping to clean the region's beaches and waters. The cleanup masks given to the workers were inadequate.[49] The estimated cost to clean the Galician coast alone ranged as high as 2.5 billion Euros.[50]

As of late July 2010, a blown-out oil well in the Gulf of Mexico is setting new records for environmental disasters. And although evidence is still coming in, once again, it appears that the disaster is the result of ego-driven males operating in a competitive corporate culture, trying to increase the bottom line by cutting corners.

We find another example of the selfish and separative-oriented values of left-brained males and their corporations in a report on the pharmaceutical industry by renowned cell biologist Bruce Lipton. Based on his experience and study, Lipton concluded that the effects of mind on the business of medicine had been summarily dismissed, in part because of financial considerations. For example, Lipton found that drug companies were "studying patients who respond to sugar pills with the goal of *eliminating* them from early clinical trials." Citing Gary Greenberg in *Mother Jones*, Lipton explains that "in most . . . clinical trials the placebos, the 'fake' drugs, prove to be as effective as their engineered chemical cocktails." Lipton asks, "If the power of your mind can heal your sick body, why should you go to the doctor, and *more* importantly, why would you need to buy drugs?"[51] In order to separate you from more of your money and take it for themselves and their stockholders, some in the pharmaceutical industry would like to separate out those patients who respond to placebos and in the process make their drugs appear more effective than they are. The holistic perspective can be a threat to profits as well as a source of profits.

The Culture of the Military

In *Waking Up in Time: Finding Inner Peace in Times of Accelerating Change*, physicist, psychologist, and philosopher Peter Russell reminds us that "our cultural condition has trapped us in a materialist mindset . . . that says that if we are not happy, something in the world around us has to change."[52] That usually means *someone* has to change. Since most people don't like to change—or at least don't like to be forced to change to suit the whims of another—to get the change we seek, we often feel required to use force or a threat of force. In *Conversations with God: An Uncommon Dialogue, Book 3*, God tells Neale Donald

Walsch, "The problem right now in your whole society is that it is based on force." This includes "legal force (which you call the 'force of law') and, too often, physical force (which you call the world's 'armed forces')."[53]

The military, industry, and Congress form an interlocking, codependent whole that functions in the following way. The exercise of force requires offensive and defensive gear, and that requires the services of industry, which is all too happy to be of service to customers with a rich, gullible sugar daddy like the U.S. Congress. Money and the need to control others (for security purposes) are the forces around which the military-industrial-congressional complex comes together as one. Money men court military men in order to boost the bottom line. Working together, they court Congress to get preferential treatment for themselves and their organizations (more freedom, more money, and more power). And of course, Congress courts the military and industry in order to maintain its privileged position, and is rewarded in the form of election funding. By courting the military and the corporate world, members of Congress also gain a large voting bloc, thus further ensuring their security. Paramilitary organizations such as state and local law enforcement cultivate the same relationships with Congress and industry for the same reasons.

Taken as a whole, the military, like law enforcement and corporate leadership, tends to reward and promote the most aggressive (read forceful) and most focused behavior, all else (such as intelligence) being equal. As efficient and practical as this might seem from its point of view, when we have a more holistic perspective, this behavior can be seen to have negative, even catastrophic, side effects. Interventionism, a fancy word for applying force to make other people and countries do what we want, is dangerous, no matter how well intended. As Pat Buchanan has observed, "Interventionism is the incubator for terrorism."[54] People fight back. As a whole, left-brain-dominant managers apparently don't understand this or they would not have, for example, allowed behavior such as occurred at Abu Ghraib prison. Rather than help reduce terrorism, it increased it. Everyone involved was damaged. Yet, from the narrow perspective of the left brain, even these extremes of behavior can be seen as acceptable when used in defense of self and selfish interests, such as keeping your job and protecting your family and community. And, from that perspective, if an action helps you to achieve your objective, you go for it. Many Americans thought this was acceptable behavior because it took place in a state of war, and the only problem for many was that word (and photos) got out. The left brain's focus is on tactical success. Destruction of someone's dignity is not necessarily considered objectionable if the goal is sufficiently important and the negative impact falls on people outside your immediate whole—your sphere of protection.

Because left-brain dominants see themselves (along with their proprietary cultural sphere—family, home team, country, and the like) as separate from others, they feel relatively separate from any losses outside that sphere, including losses for which they are personally responsible. And remember, from that perspective, even the most extreme actions are done to achieve what is generally acknowledged as a noble, good objective: to take care of self and the self's family and country, and/or to serve the self's God. From that perspective, we are just defending our territory and other possessions. From that perspective, such acts are not mean-spirited. They are simply taking care of business, of self. But of course, this often gets out of hand—and sometimes *way* out of hand, as it did at Abu Ghraib.

This is not to say that military men and women don't appreciate the value of a holistic perspective. To understand the enemy, information must be gathered, put into context, and synthesized—a holistic process. The foundation of military success relies on the holistic principles of strength through size and cohesion. The holistic right brain also gives the military its strategic insight. Nevertheless, the military is mostly male, which means that most of its members perceive reality heavily filtered through a dualistic perspective. In addition, the military system itself has largely been designed by individuals whose orientation is dualistic. Add to all of this the fact that the military has long sought to discharge right-brain-directed males on the basis of sexual orientation, and the scene is set for a relatively weak overall holistic understanding. Nevertheless, because the right brain automatically responds when our question requires its perspective, military cultures often manage to be successful. Men don't have to be educated in the use of a holistic perspective, but education certainly helps.

A group of former military officers hired by the Pentagon to analyze the cost and effectiveness of weapons systems found that the Defense Department was spending more money for fewer weapons and underestimating their costs. They found that, rather than shifting the focus to the war on terror, the military was spending most of its money on legacy systems designed during the Cold War to deal with a massive national power. In an interview for the PBS series *Now*, Bill Moyers reported that one of the officers, Franklin C. "Chuck" Spinney, warned that the system was out of control, pointing to the Defense Department's own inspector general, who found that *the Pentagon could not account for more than $1 trillion*. The financial books bordered on pure fiction, Spinney told Moyers.[55] Catherine Austin Fitts, former assistant secretary of housing, now president of Solari and publisher of *The Solari Report*, a perspective on the global financial system, reports even more alarming figures. Fitts believes the amount (as of September 2000) was more like $3.3 trillion.[56]

Spinney reminds us of what most of us already know: "The Pentagon still spends more than the rest of the world's military spending combined. . . . Contractors funnel Pentagon dollars through a corrupt procurement process that kicks back a significant percentage to politicians who sign off on the spending and reward insiders with lucrative jobs in the defense industry the insiders are supposed to oversee."[57] A holistic approach would do what is best for the country as a whole, the military as a whole, and its soldiers as a whole, and it would seek to do this while respecting the rights of the hardworking individuals who must come up with the money to help fund the military. The separative approach used by left-brain-dominant individuals simply seeks what is best for those involved—the people managing and gaming the system—such as the members of Congress who push for weapons that the military does not need in order to create jobs in their districts and secure votes for their own reelection. Self-centered responses such as this weaken both the military and the country, but most of us have been so taken over by this prevailing mindset that we keep reelecting these people.

What We Can Do

How might we start to bring this dysfunctional system under control? To begin with, we might unify around fundamental principles upon which a large majority of Americans (even with our dualistic indoctrination) agree, such as transparency (which is clearly lacking) and responsibility (including demands that members of Congress be held accountable for such actions as buying weapons systems that the military itself does not want). The important thing is to acquire voter numbers by finding ideas around which a majority can coalesce.

Where do we start? When something does not work, the traditional, conservative approach is to try to repair it, especially when dealing with something that has historical value. Buckminster Fuller taught an alternative approach: "You never change things by fighting the existing reality. To change something, build a new model that makes the existing model obsolete."[58]

John C. Bogle, of the Vanguard Group, reminds us that, while most Americans think they live in a democracy—a government run by the people—what we actually have is a republic—a structure in which power is exercised through elected representatives. American corporations are also republics.[59] Whereas in government, Congress is supposed to represent the will of the people, in the corporate structure, the will of the stockholders is represented by a company's board of directors. Corporations, like individuals and governments, can be dysfunctional and need to be reined in at times. In both cases, we often fail to take action because of our polarized condition. We find ourselves separated into different camps in an environment in which, if we support the other side, we are considered a traitor and are subject to reprisals. This attitude limits communication and must be changed if we are to take holistic control—and by holistic, I mean take control as a whole, as stockholders in our company or our country. Obviously, if we are to return culture to truly holistic human control that synthesizes and integrates the best liberal and conservative ideas, we must do it through the existing, imperfect mechanism—a Congress that is dominated by personal interests as well as by corporate and military interests, with each of these interests dedicated to maximizing its own power.

How might we best respond to industry and the financial aristocracy that controls it? Marjorie Kelly writes in *The Divine Right of Capital*, "Civilization crossed a great divide into a new world of democracy in the twentieth century. But we have democratized only politics, not economics. . . . We can never really have political democracy without economic democracy."

She goes on to say that "wealth has not spread democratically in recent decades. It has concentrated in fewer hands. . . . This concentrated wealth controls not only corporations but also government. Rule by the financial aristocracy is the reality of life in America today. And Americans know how to combat aristocracy. We do it with democracy."[60]

In seeking to solve our problems with big business, Kelly suggests we keep in mind that "the problem is not with a free market, but rather with the design of the corporation" as chosen by the economic elite.[61] Knowing that, she counsels us to begin the process of change "with imagination. We begin by using the one territory that we the people still control: our own minds. We simply see that wealth supremacy is illegitimate. For once we see it and name it as illegitimate," she says, "we undermine the ground on which it stands and pave the way for its transformation."[62] In harmony with Buckminster Fuller's advice, Kelly emphasizes the need for systemic, profound change, and proposes we find alternatives that recognize that "the economic rights of the individual and the community are equal to those of capital owners." Since the corporation is made up of a community of humans, it should be governed democratically and not be given the rights of a person. Just "as it is the right of the people to alter or abolish government, it is the right of the people to alter or abolish the corporations that now govern the world."[63]

David Schweickart offers what might be another useful approach to the dominance of large corporations in his description of a scenario in which investor-owned corporations transition into employee-owned corporations when conditions leave a company struggling for survival. In *Gangs of America*, Ted Nace points out that Schweickart's idea leads to two other important ideas: "first, that the large investor-owned corporation can be replaced; second, that the [transition] can be smooth and orderly," and result in "a drastic broadening of ownership." Nace also suggests that smaller companies and individuals might organize and mobilize politically, and through their combined power challenge industry.[64] The power of unity is overwhelming. That's why corporations continue to grow. Unity can also be used to change corporate systems.

To begin to address the issue of congressional dysfunctionality, we might, for example, unify around common principles and ideas rather than working through the polarized political parties whose dedication to the voters and needs of the country always comes second to their own selfish left-brain-directed needs. We might come together outside the major parties (on the Internet, for example), make decisions that are acceptable to a majority, and then present our ideas, backed by a sufficient number of dedicated voters who are willing to demand change, and remove from office those who fail to support systemic change.

If we are to follow the advice of Buckminster Fuller and create a new system, we might want to recognize that the most harmonious way is also the most powerful way, since we gain strength through unity. We might start, for example, by demanding that Congress establish rules to ensure that new laws are published on the Internet for a minimum number of days before being voted upon—and that this occur without exception, although time frames might vary depending on circumstances. Most people would be in favor of that. We all are subject to, and pay for, the laws that are enacted. We should be able to see them before they are voted on so that we too might lobby our representatives to do our will. We might demand an end to the many special-interest projects that are inserted into legislation for the express purpose of obtaining votes to help support the politicians who submit such projects into law at taxpayer expense. We also need to recognize that the complexity of the system will surely require that change be addressed in steps, starting with the most fundamental aspects of the system, such as the procedural rules that Congress writes for itself to benefit itself and/or its political parties. Someone else must write the rules that govern the way Congress manages the nation's affairs, as it clearly is not capable of instituting real reforms on its own.

Chapter Eight

Perspective and War

The more prohibitions you have, the less virtuous people will be. The more weapons you have, the less secure people will be.

— *TAO TE CHING*, VERSE 57

W hy do we choose to create wars?
 The Urantia Book answers that, as gods, we possess free will in an environment where destruction is an option. When our will is geared toward destruction, we create oppression and conflict—which it describes as "a species of civil war in the personality"—and they lead to war and its evils.[1] The internal conflict of warring ideas that arises when we oppress others upsets our internal creative processes and creates mental stresses as well as spiritual depression or anxiety. Only by experiencing and transcending our destructive tendencies can we learn how to create and experience peace.

Why do we wage war? Greed. Revenge. Impatience. Desperation. Or because we seek to create a culture that supports our beliefs. There are many reasons. To understand why we choose war and how to stop it, it might help to also ask the question, where and when does war start? And where might we best focus our attention now, in order to find greater peace?

Perhaps war starts in the mind when we accept the idea that force is an acceptable way to solve our problems. Or perhaps it starts when we establish *intent* to use force (which means that we intend to deny someone his or her free will and substitute our own). At the very least, we are in a state of war by the time we *exercise* force—by the time we initiate action that interferes with someone's freedom.

War can start when someone tries to control us. War can start when we try to control someone. In either case, someone's freedom is threatened, and conflict is produced, and felt (in the physical, mental, and spiritual energy systems) in the form of tension, discord, and/or fear. (The energetic response and its feeling have many names.) The instant our energy body connects with conflict-based energy, the conflict *becomes* one with us—it dominates us and supplants our prior harmony. This shocks our system; the degree to which it actually changes us depends on the intensity of the conflict and factors such as our education and our skills in dealing with conflict (which includes our level of self-control).

Although we (being gods) are ultimately cooperative and gentle by nature, as a protective measure we have been given an aggressive left brain—and, being destructive and selfish in nature, the left brain is anything but gentle. Its complement, the cooperative right-brain persona, will often submit if that is what is required in order to achieve the peace and harmony it seeks. Nevertheless, remember that when we apply force (physical, mental, and/or spiritual) against another in order to obtain the outcome we desire, we are interfering with his or her creative freedom. Numerous spiritual texts and revelations state that such interference is a serious infraction of one of the universe's most fundamental rules: as gods, we are free to chart our own destiny.

In exploring the roots of war, we need to remember to always look in two directions. We must search *internally* for conflict within ourselves, a task that our left brain is designed to handle (under the influence of the right brain), and we must search *externally* for conflict with others, a task that we accomplish through right-brain consciousness supported and supplemented by left-brain consciousness.

To understand the full effect of war, it is also important to keep in mind the impact of *degree*, the measure we use to describe variance. War *varies* depending on the amount of energy behind it. This seems rather obvious, but the dualistic left brain by its nature tends to see war as all or nothing and can easily overlook variance. Thus, when the energy of war expresses itself in subtle ways, the effects of war can sometimes be overlooked yet cause serious problems. Like a low-level poison, this destructive energy can harm both our individual and our collective body, and possibly even kill given enough time. And when we ignore war—as when we fail to see it and acknowledge its impact—we naturally tend to ignore those who are promoting it, and ultimately we end up supporting them without being aware of our contribution.

In our role as creators, one of the things we can do to be more successful is to bring peace to our internal environment. Since we already have peace—it is our birthright—we do this by looking closely at ourselves and our relationships, and finding a way to eliminate any internal conflicts that might be present. But because of the chaos around us (if not in us), this can be challenging. Not only can internal conflict be difficult to detect, but external conflict can be difficult to keep out. And it's not always clear when we need to fight for our rights. We acknowledge that some wars must be fought—not everyone can escape every war—but most wars can be avoided through education, negotiation, and a respect for logic (except for a minority that benefits, the overall effects of war are almost always more harmful than beneficial). Since the subtleties of war can sometimes be overlooked, it is always wise to examine our individual (internal) and collective (external) relationships to see if we are supporting war to some degree.

Intent is another factor to keep in mind when seeking to understand war. We might refer to an aggressive attempt to impose our will on another as a harmless "nudge" or as a form of "encouragement," but in attempting to impose our values on another, we start down a path to conflict that will eventually lead to war unless someone submits or backs off—which is what usually happens and why war is usually avoided. Of course, people sometimes wish to get nudged or encouraged, especially when they can't decide. Parents, for example, sometimes need to help young children choose. Sometimes that requires a nudge and is an act of love. Obviously, these actions alone do not constitute war. The key to understanding war is intent. Is there selfish intent? Are you denying others their freedom in some (perhaps very subtle) way—physically, mentally, and/or spiritually—to support some goal of your own? What do you get out of your efforts to "help" someone?

Intent is not always clear. In Neale Donald Walsch's book *The New Revelations* (one of Walsch's continuing series *Conversations with God*), God says to Walsch,

> There is not a country and there is not a group of people on Earth that imagines itself to be an aggressor. Everyone who enters into war does so saying that *they are defending something*. . . . On your planet there are no "attackers," only "defenders." You achieve this interesting paradox by simply calling all attack a defense. In this way you are able to change your basic values from moment to moment as it suits you,

without seeming to change them at all. You get to kill people with impunity to obtain what you want by simply saying that you had no choice. You had to *defend* yourself.[2]

In *The Unfolding Self: Varieties of Transformative Experience*, Ralph Metzner, professor emeritus of psychology at California Institute of Integral Studies, looks at war and concludes that the conflict and destruction of war arise out of "a mixture of judgmentalism and violent rage." (Recall that judgment is one of our most fundamental acts.) When war is the product of judgment, Metzner found, it is because judgment "is expressed, acted upon, in a destructive and aggressive way. That which is judged to be bad is attacked and destroyed." Metzner suggests that, "for transformation to take place, we need to learn to become wise, impartial judges of ourselves, not punitive, vindictive judges." We start "by realizing that the opposing enemies are all within us: we are both judge and accused, both jailor and prisoner, both executioner and condemned."[3]

In seeking to explain our addiction to war, *A Course in Miracles* refers to an ego voice focused on the self and a nurturing voice focused on the greater collective good (which is a description of the functions of the left and right brain hemispheres). The Course explains that "the body exists in a world that seems to contain two voices fighting for its possession."[4] And further, "Every response to the ego is a call to war. . . . Those whom you perceive as opponents are part of your peace, which you are giving up by attacking them. How can you have what you give up?"[5]

We usually think of war as armed hostile conflict between nations or states. Although every such war has been justified (or rationalized as just) by its perpetrators, there is general agreement that such wars are inevitably destructive of innocent lives and of culture. When we speak of other kinds of wars—wars against disease, class wars, culture wars, the war on drugs—we often take the term *war* to be a generalized metaphor. And yet, when we look at some of these wars—in particular the war on drugs—these are true wars in just about every sense. In fact, the war on drugs (or "drug war") includes armed militias, many innocent civilian casualties, clearly unconstitutional procedures by law enforcement and courts, and more instances of incarceration in the United States than for all serious crimes combined—making our U.S. prison system a de facto prisoner-of-war camp for drug dealers, drug users, those living with or associated with drug users, and many innocent "collateral" cases in which an individual's only crime was to be in the wrong place at the wrong time. In fact, it can be said that the drug war is the most destructive war in which 21st-century America is engaged. It is being fought on our home turf, can potentially affect every family in this country (whether or not it includes illegal drug users), forces ordinary citizens to become informants (even against family members), and is (like many other wars) even based on a largely manufactured "problem."

For these reasons, we are devoting most of this chapter to an examination of the drug war in America. The lessons to be gained from this examination are instructive not only for what they say about *all* wars, but also for what they say about the kind of thinking that leads to such destructive, unholistic behavior. We will look at some of the creative choices we have made in trying to solve the problems of drug use, and then identify the hemispheric perspective from which they come. The extreme polarization of culture that we see in the issue of drug use, combined with the dramatic difference in the two perspectives (dualistic and holistic) on drugs and the drug war, make it relatively easy to identify the effects of perspective on our creative choices. But identification is not always easy. Remember, we are not always true to our dominant perspective. In addition, nearly all of us are influenced by the presence and dominance of our dualistic, left-brain cultural perspective.

Scientific Perspectives on the Drug War

For decades, we have been fed the prohibitionist perspective through corporate-owned media, law enforcement, and grass-roots "anti-drug" forces. In addition, governmental entities have been promoting this perspective by giving big bucks to big media. Although we will attempt to present a holistic, inclusive perspective, the prohibitionist perspective has enjoyed extensive and enduring coverage, so there is no point in going into detail on all the ways that drugs can destroy lives, especially the lives of children. It is beyond argument that *all* drugs should be kept away from children. Children should not be able to buy drugs, illegal or not, just as they are not allowed to buy guns. And, with a few exceptions involving strict adult control (often in consultation with a physician, preferably one who honors the body's natural healing processes), children should not *use* drugs, especially psychoactive ones and drugs that can cause harm. We allow adults to do many things that are harmful to children. Our discussion here will focus on adults. Nor will we discuss drug abuse generally. We all agree that illegal drugs, like legal drugs and almost everything else, can be harmful if used in an excessive or otherwise unwise manner. Our purpose here is to expand on our current understanding by looking at some of the things the military-industrial-congressional complex and its supporters have failed to tell us about the reasons for and consequences of this drug war. And although it is fiscally a very expensive war, costing many billions of dollars per year, the financial cost pales in comparison with the human cost. So, for the most part, we will focus on the human cost and ignore the financial.

Why do people use drugs? Ronald K. Siegel, an associate research professor at the University of California, Los Angeles (who has been referred to as the Leif Eriksson of psychopharmacology), has described our demand for drugs as the "fourth drive."

> History shows we have always used drugs. In every age, in every part of this planet, people have pursued intoxication with plant drugs, alcohol, and other mind-altering substances. . . . Almost every species of animal has engaged in the natural pursuit of intoxicants. This behavior has so much force and persistence that it functions like a drive, just like our drives of hunger, thirst, and sex. This "fourth drive" is a natural part of our biology, creating the irrepressible demand for drugs. In a sense, the war on drugs is a war against ourselves, a denial of our very nature.[6]

In his book *Waking Up in Time: Finding Inner Peace in Times of Accelerating Change,* Peter Russell says that people take drugs because "they want to feel better. They want to feel happy, high, relaxed, in control, free from fear, more in touch with life. In this respect, the drug user is seeking nothing different from anyone else—it is just the way in which he or she is doing it that contemporary society finds unacceptable."[7]

We face many of the same issues in our addictions to material things. In acquiring things, Russell explains, "we are trying to make ourselves feel better. But any happiness we get is usually only temporary, so as soon as one high wears off we go in search of another." We thus "become psychologically dependent on our favorite sources of pleasure."[8] These may include food, music, shopping, games, TV, violence, sex—we can become dependent on many things, and in the process harm ourselves and others.

Whatever our focus might be, we tend to seek to repeat responses we enjoy. Things that make us feel better can develop into an addiction in some people, spiral out of control into abuse, and give off ripples of negative energy that are absorbed by the collective. Consequently, culture (or the collective self) then feels abused and may respond, just as an individual would—first by requesting or demanding, and perhaps waiting patiently for a response, but soon moving toward use of force to bring the world back to our ideal—or at least back to what it was before the problems showed up. Eventually, we pass laws and hire people to enforce them in order to *force* compliance. Thus war is born. And as is so often said, the first casualty of war is truth.

Those of us who are left-brain dominant are at special risk when it comes to apprehending the truth, due to our tendency to home in on separate parts at the expense of the whole. In *Marihuana, the Forbidden Medicine*, Lester Grinspoon, M.D., describes how this separation from truth can play out in our lives. Grinspoon, being of the attitude that cannabis, or marijuana (its Spanish name), is a very harmful drug, set out in 1967 to define scientifically the nature and degree of its dangers. After three years of research, Grinspoon found that cannabis had "long been used as a medicine in India, China, the Middle East, Southeast Asia, South Africa, and South America," and that early "evidence for medicinal use of cannabis [includes] an herbal published during the reign of the Chinese Emperor Chen Nung five thousand years ago," as well as evidence of medical use in Europe. Grinspoon found that cannabis was considerably less harmful than tobacco and alcohol, and concluded that he, like many others, had been brainwashed. In 1971, Grinspoon predicted that cannabis would be legalized within a decade, based on the evidence he had discovered. Instead, he encountered a political climate in which it was difficult to discuss cannabis openly and freely. "It could almost be said that there is a climate of psychopharmacological McCarthyism," Grinspoon wrote.[9]

To understand the truth about the effect of cannabis on those who use it, how much more thorough and credible does the evidence have to be than this? In 1988, the Drug Enforcement Administration's (DEA's) own "administrative law judge, Francis Young, after taking medical testimony for 15 days and reviewing hundreds of DEA [and] NIDA [National Institute of Drug Abuse] documents posed against the evidence introduced by marijuana reform activists concluded . . . that 'marijuana is one of the safest therapeutically active substances known to man.'"[10] Granted, this didn't make many newspaper headlines, and perhaps many small newspapers failed to carry it since it wasn't what most of their readers wanted to see—but the information got out, and people who craft drug policy certainly noticed. Indeed, many must have been shocked. And most of the nation's legislators must have noticed. Considering that all of these groups have paid staff whose job it is to make such items known to them, these groups must have also been shocked in 1995 when the prestigious British medical journal the *Lancet*, in an editorial, observed: "The smoking of cannabis, even long term, is not harmful to health."[11]

They also must have noticed in 1994 when the *New York Times* published a comparison of six drugs based on the findings of Jack E. Henningfield, M.D., of the government-sponsored NIDA and Neal L. Benowitz, M.D., of the University of California, San Francisco. The two researchers, in independent studies, had compared nicotine, heroin, cocaine, alcohol, caffeine, and marijuana. Their studies focused on problems associated with withdrawal, reinforcement, tolerance, dependence, and intoxication. They evaluated the six drugs in terms of the five problems and assigned a numerical value to each problem, the values ranging from 1 to 6, with 1 being the most problematic. When we average Henningfield's results, we find caffeine and marijuana tied at 5.4, the highest score, meaning the *least* problematic of the six drugs. Benowitz's numbers show marijuana to be even *less* problematic than caffeine, caffeine earning 4.4 and marijuana 5.2. (As a comparison, Henningfield gave nicotine and cocaine equal ratings of 3.0, alcohol 2.4, and heroin 1.8. In Benowitz's study, nicotine averaged 3.6, alcohol 2.6, cocaine 2.2, and heroin 2.0.)[12]

Among other things, this information tells us that American drug laws are in conflict with science — so much so that they are nothing less than a deliberate flouting of facts arrived at through painstaking methodologies that should be beyond controversy. There are many among us who fear the truth. The truth can interfere with one's power, with one's love of wealth, and with the harmony of one's ideas (since the truth by its nature challenges any currently held ideas that deviate from truth). When we are guided by a dualistic perspective we find it difficult to accept facts that threaten our established beliefs. An example of this is found in the true story of a woman who had moved to the Solomon Islands to set up a business collecting old gold to resell. All of her life she had heard the phrase "passing the acid test," but it had been meaningless until she discovered that people would try to pass off brass as gold, and that nitric acid would reveal the truth. Her very first experience with pouring acid over brass took place in a room with 10 potential gold sellers. Naturally, upon contact with the acid, the brass immediately turned green and boiled up like a witch's cauldron, forcing everyone in the room to run for a door or window to escape the awful smell. Once the woman felt it was safe to breathe again, she looked over at the little man who had tried to pass off brass as gold and exclaimed, "That's not gold!" "Acid lie," the uneducated man replied, offering an excuse in a futile effort to hide his attempted deception.[13] Uneducated individuals and those in extreme denial of the implications of what they know still fail to appreciate the strength of science's contribution to truth and goodness. They still fail to recognize how transparent their ignorance and closed-mindedness is to those individuals who understand and accept science's role in keeping us informed and honest.

Antidrug warriors often contend that even if marijuana is not dangerous itself, it is dangerous in that it leads the user to try dangerous drugs. This is sometimes called the *gateway theory*. But just as "alcohol, tobacco, and caffeine do not cause people to use marijuana, [marijuana] does not cause people to use heroin, LSD, or cocaine," write Lynn Zimmer and John P. Morgan in *Marijuana Myths, Marijuana Facts: A Review of the Scientific Evidence*.[14] According to a review of scientific evidence by Zimmer and Morgan,

> In the end, the gateway theory is not a theory at all. It is a description of the typical sequence in which multiple-drug users initiate the use of high-prevalence and low-prevalence drugs. A similar statistical relationship exists between other kinds of common and uncommon related activities. For example, most people who ride a motorcycle (a fairly rare activity) have ridden a bicycle (a fairly common activity). . . . Bicycle riding does not cause motorcycle riding, and increases in the former will not lead automatically to increases in the latter.[15]

A quote from *A Course in Miracles* bears repeating here: "Seeing adapts to wish, for sight is always secondary to desire."[16] When we desire to believe the gateway theory to justify our support for the drug war, we find it easy to see as fact.

If the gateway theory is going to be used to guide our laws and behavior, then why not add caffeine? Roland Griffiths, a neuroscientist at the Johns Hopkins University School of Medicine, says that he is "concerned that impressionable adolescents exposed to marketing messages that promote caffeine as a performance enhancer will later turn to stronger drugs, like steroids, or Ritalin or cocaine."[17] And caffeine can have negative effects on brain function, brain scientist Daniel G. Amen, M.D., reports. Having studied the brain for at least 20 years, Amen says that "cerebral blood flow is essential to healthy brain function [and] caffeine restricts blood flow to the brain."[18] How would you feel if a member of your family got 20 years in prison for possession of a pound of coffee? If that sounds excessive, be advised that a pound of pot can get you more than that. And remember that Henningfield, a government scientist, found cannabis to be equal to caffeine in terms of the problems they cause society, while Benowitz, a nongovernment scientist, found caffeine to be *more* problematic than cannabis.

As justification for their violent response, supporters of the war on drugs often claim that illegal drugs cause behavioral changes in people. In *Saying Yes: In Defense of Drug Use*, Jacob Sullum states (and most experts agree) that "drugs do not cause behaviors or changes in behaviors. How a person acts after taking a drug is determined by a complex interaction of variables, a process in which the user's beliefs and choices play crucial roles."[19] He goes on to say that "alcohol is more strongly associated with violence than any illegal drug, but that does not mean it turns peaceful, law-abiding people into brutal criminals. The link between alcohol and violence depends upon the drinker's personality, values, expectations, and circumstances. The same is true of crimes committed by other drug users, with the added complication that black-market violence fostered by prohibition is often confused with violence caused by drugs."[20] Sullum explains that "just as drinkers do not typically become alcoholics, users of illegal drugs . . . do not typically become addicts," and cites University of California psychologists Jonathan Shedler and

Jack Block, who found that "problem drug use is a symptom, not a cause, of personal and social maladjustment."[21] Sullum also cites a government study by the National Institute on Drug Abuse that supports this conclusion. And he points out what should be obvious—that scientists who see drug use as anything other than a problem "are not likely to get funding from the government, which has no interest in raising questions about its war on drugs, or from academic institutions that rely on government money."[22]

"Outlawing drugs in order to solve the drug problem is much like outlawing sex in order to win the war against AIDS," Ronald Siegel says in *Intoxication: Life in Pursuit of Artificial Paradise*. "In order to solve the [problems that can accompany drug use] we must recognize that intoxicants are medicines, treatments for the human condition. Then we must make their use as safe and risk free and, yes, as healthy as possible."[23]

Is the "Drug War" Misnamed?

"The war on drugs" is much more than a war on drugs; it is a war on *people* and on *families*. *People* are forcibly detained and terrorized by the physical, mental, and spiritual violence of the process. *People* spend all their savings and more on lawyers to try to hold on to their freedom. *People* are wounded and killed—many of them adolescents. And *families* are traumatized: by being separated, by having their houses and cars seized, and by being forced into poverty. In almost every imaginable way, families are damaged. It would be a war on drugs if the result were simply to make drugs unavailable in order to "protect" individuals from their influence. But when the war on drugs takes aim at maximizing the suffering of the users (resulting in *far* more suffering than the drugs themselves usually cause) and destroying their freedoms—and when the result of all this is that the flow of drugs is undiminished or even increases—clearly it is a war against the users.

We might also ask if the so-called war on drugs is something any true conservative can possibly support in the form in which it is currently being waged. Even the most extreme social conservatives usually believe in the long-established American principle of the sanctity of one's home. Certainly, most of us in the United States grew up thinking we lived in a country where our homes were protective castles as far as the government was concerned. But that is certainly not true today. In a 2006 paper written for the Cato Institute, we are given a view of this issue from the perspective of Radley Balko, a former policy analyst with the Cato Institute and FoxNews.com columnist, and now a senior editor for *Reason* magazine who covers civil liberties issues.

> Over the last 25 years, America has seen a disturbing militarization of its civilian law enforcement, along with a dramatic and unsettling rise in the use of paramilitary police units for routine police work. The most common use of SWAT teams today is to serve narcotics warrants, usually with forced, unannounced entry into the home.
>
> These increasingly frequent raids, 40,000 per year by one estimate, are needlessly subjecting nonviolent drug offenders, bystanders, and wrongly targeted civilians to the terror of having their homes invaded while they're sleeping, usually by teams of heavily armed paramilitary units dressed not as police officers but as soldiers. These raids bring unnecessary violence and provocation to nonviolent drug offenders, many of whom were guilty of only misdemeanors. The raids terrorize innocents when police mistakenly target the wrong residence. And they have resulted in dozens of needless deaths and injuries, not only of drug offenders, but also of police officers, children, bystanders and innocent suspects.[24]

The castle walls, it appears, have been breached in pursuit of drugs, in the name of protecting us.

Ryan Frederick's nerves were a bit frazzled on January 17, 2008, when he went to bed in Chesapeake, Virginia, according to another report by Radley Balko. The 28-year-old man's house had been broken into earlier that week. Awakened by the fierce barking of his two dogs and the sound of someone trying to break down his front door, Frederick grabbed a gun he kept for defense and went to investigate. Seeing someone trying to squeeze through a busted panel in his door, thinking it was an intruder, Frederick fired. It was a drug SWAT team looking for a marijuana-growing operation. A team member was killed. "Neighbors described Frederick as shy, self-effacing, non-confrontational and hard-working. He had no prior criminal record." Police had acted on an informant's tip. They had no evidence that he was growing or distributing, and no marijuana plants were found.[25] Frederick was convicted of manslaughter and sent to prison.

Most raids take place under cover of darkness with no cameras. When things go wrong, the police almost always blame the occupants of the raided house for the results. Juries tend to believe whatever the police say. The infamous raid in Goose Creek, South Carolina, was all caught on surveillance cameras, and law enforcement had no cover. According to a report on StoptheDrugWar.org, "Tapes show students as young as 14 forced to the ground in handcuffs as officers in SWAT team uniforms and bulletproof vests aim guns at their heads and lead a drug dog to tear through their book bags." One of the students forced to kneel at gunpoint in the school hallway reported that "they hit that school like it was a crack house, like they knew that there were crack dealers in there armed with guns." The student's father, a local deputy sheriff who had served on SWAT teams, told reporters, "A school drug raid is not a SWAT situation, but that's how the Goose Creek police handled it." He referred to the police raid as unnecessarily dangerous, explaining, "It was a crossfire just waiting to happen. If one door slammed, one student dropped a book or screamed . . . those guns would have gone off all over the place." The raid, authorized by school principal George McCrackin, "came up empty. No weapons or drugs were found and none of the students were charged with any crime."[26]

Left-brain-directed government officials who promote and prosecute the drug war know about these atrocities. They know their laws and enforcement activities often inflict great harm on the community—including turning people against law enforcement—but they make a secure living from the war, and if the left brain has a number-one goal, it is self-security. In addition, left-brain-directed individuals have a difficult time taking responsibility for the suffering they cause, instead tending to separate from responsibility by blaming those upon whom they inflict suffering and labeling them "criminals." When our actions are based on good intentions—to bring "criminals" to justice—it becomes difficult for us to accept responsibility: "It's not our responsibility if people don't obey laws. We don't make the laws, we just enforce them," is the protest we often hear. The separation of law enactment from law enforcement gives law enforcement a solid excuse to accept whatever it is told to do. And law enforcement has little pressure to change. Most people seem to believe that the drug war is a necessary evil, and that as long as they don't do illegal drugs, they have nothing to fear from the police or the law; and so, even though they might not be comfortable with this war, they do nothing to oppose it.

We don't know if that's how 92-year-old Atlanta resident Katheryn Johnston felt or not. And it's too late to ask. She was killed after opening fire on a group of police officers who had forced their way into her home on December 1, 2006. Johnston reportedly was frightened of intruders and kept a gun for protection. The raid was based on a tip from an anonymous informant, who later recanted a statement that he had purchased drugs in

Johnston's house. From a police perspective, "no-knock" raids are necessary to prevent suspects from destroying evidence.[27] From a holistic perspective, the destruction of evidence in a few cases pales in comparison with the lives lost by this heavy-handed tactic and the destruction of the principle that our homes are off-limits to government intrusion. When you add to that the fact that the war effort as a whole is making no headway in combating the availability of illegal drugs, a case cannot possibly be made that this tactic is necessary in order to stem their flow, but in the absence of accountability for its actions, law enforcement has little pressure to change.

Commenting further on this case, Radley Balko tells us that

> the police alleged that they had paid an informant to buy drugs from Ms. Johnston's home. They said she fired at them first, and wounded two officers. And they alleged they found marijuana in her home. We now know that those were all lies. . . . The initial arrest of the ex-con [the informant] came via trumped-up charges. The police then invented an informant for the search warrant, and lied about overseeing a drug buy from Johnston's home. Ms. Johnston didn't actually wound any of the officers. They were wounded by fragments of ricochet from their own storm of bullets. And there was no marijuana. Once they realized their mistake, the officers handcuffed Ms. Johnston and left her to bleed and die on the floor of her own home while they planted marijuana in her basement.[28]

OK, you might say, but I don't do drugs. I don't even know anyone who does. I have nothing to fear from the American drug war. I don't even live in America. But consider the following.

Columnist Dave Kopel reports that on April 20, 2001, a Cessna owned by the Association of Baptists for World Evangelism, having filed a flight plan as required, took off on a return

trip from Islandia, Peru, on the Amazon River. Bound for Iqui-
tos, the plane carried missionaries James and Veronica Bowers;
their daughter, Charity; and their son, Cory. Just over an hour
into the flight, an A-37 interceptor aircraft, flying in a joint Peru-
vian-U.S. counternarcotics operation, fired 7.62-caliber slugs
into the plane, killing Veronica and Charity and wounding the
pilot, who was also with the missionary association. According
to the State Department, up to that time under the program,
some 39 aircraft had been shot or forced down.[29]

But, you might respond, at least the authorities would
have learned from their mistakes so that nothing like this would
happen again. In this case, however, learning from one's mistakes was apparently not an option. According to Kopel,

> the investigative team for the official report was specifically
> "not authorized" to either "question witnesses under oath or
> receive sworn testimony." Nor were they to "examine miscon-
> duct or fix blame." In other words, the investigators were
> prevented from conducting a real investigation. While for-
> mally barred from assigning responsibility . . . the investigators
> still attempted to scapegoat missionary pilot Kevin Donald-
> son—even though his only mistake was to occupy airspace
> where government agents had been given a license to kill. . . .
> Nor were the accident investigators merely forbidden to
> assign blame. They were also barred from making "a recom-
> mendation or determination with regard to the suspension or
> start up of counternarcotics aerial intercept operation in
> Peru."

Kopel's conclusion: "The message is clear: Legal accountability for killings has been eliminated, lest it hinder the work
of drug warriors."[30]

Wonder how an operation like this gets created? Kopel
thinks he knows. One reason for the policy, he suggests, is that

Bill Clinton was gearing up for his re-election campaign. "His advisors worried that Republicans would raise 'the character issue.' Clinton needed to prove his stern morality on drugs, and so he began ramping up spending for the drug war—especially military spending. Veronica and Charity Bowers, then, join the long list of females who had to be destroyed, one way or another, to make the world safe for Bill Clinton."[31]

"The war on drugs has turned into a war on minority communities and a war on the poor," says Fatema Gunja, director of the Drug Policy Forum of Massachusetts. "The punitive nature of our drug laws stems from a basic premise that links drug use with morality: those who use drugs commit immoral acts and, therefore, should not be granted the same privileges afforded to those who choose to abstain. . . . In 1996, Congress passed the Welfare Reform Act. . . . Introduced and ratified in just two minutes with bipartisan support, Section 115 . . . made felony drug offenders, including nonviolent drug offenders, ineligible for welfare benefits and food stamps. No other crime, *including murder or rape*, results in the loss of such benefits [emphasis added]." Subsequently, the same punitive measures were extended to public housing, higher education, adoption, and foster care. "In theory, these laws are justified mostly on punitive or deterrent grounds. In reality, their effects delay successful reintegration of ex-drug offenders into society, leading many back to prison."[32]

Before cell phones, drug dealers often relied on pay phones to receive messages. To discourage this activity, pay phones were changed so that incoming calls were blocked. Of course, this also prevented everyone who could not afford a phone from receiving calls. Imagine how you would feel if you couldn't receive calls. What problems would that introduce into your life? The situation has changed, but the phones have not. Once the typically separative male with his destruction-based "solutions" focuses on an important issue, such as "stopping drug traffic," his competitive brain demands that success be achieved, *whatever it takes*—including going to war if necessary.

Until about 1965, the drug war was focused mostly on minorities. In 1965, according to estimates by the National Organization for Reform of Marijuana Laws (NORML), approximately two people per hour were arrested for marijuana possession. And though the sentences were sufficiently harsh to act as a deterrent, they failed to produce the desired results—people didn't stop using drugs just because the "moral" majority wanted them to. As a result, year after year, new and more punishing laws were passed, and more and more people were dragged into the system. By 1992, for example, the arrest rate had escalated to more than 39 arrests per hour and was making headlines in the heartland: "Drug Sentencing Questioned," the *Daily Oklahoman* told its readers. "Prosecutors and drug agents say the punishment fits the crime. Defense attorneys and, privately, some judges call it draconian." The newspaper's front page article reported that "more than 90% of the convictions on drug offenses in the U.S. Western District of Oklahoma carry more than a ten year sentence. . . . Many defendants get sentences of 20 to 30 years, and in the last month in Oklahoma City federal court, four individuals were sentenced to life, including a 25-year-old woman with no prior convictions."[33]

According to the FBI, 829,625 persons were arrested for marijuana violations in the United States in 2006, breaking a record for the largest total number of arrests in one year. This brought the rate up to 95 arrests per hour.[34] The year 2007 set another record with 872,721 arrests, an increase of 5.2 percent over the previous year, bringing the arrest rate up to 99.6 per hour. Compare that with 597,447 arrests nationwide for *all violent crimes combined*, which includes murder, non-negligent manslaughter, forcible rape, robbery, and aggravated assault.[35]

The latest statistics available, those for 2008, show a slight decrease in the rate of arrests but bring the total number of arrests for marijuana violation as of January 1, 2010, to over 21 million![36]

Legendary reporter and news anchor Walter Cronkite discovered that almost 80 percent of incarcerated women are in prison for drug offenses, and as a result, the increase in the number of female prisoners far outstrips that of male prisoners (although in absolute numbers, the overwhelming majority of prisoners are still male). "The deep perversity of the system," Cronkite explained, "lies in the fact that women with the least culpability often get the harshest sentences. Unlike the guilty drug dealer, they often have no information to trade for a better deal from prosecutors and might end up with a harsher sentence than the dealer gets." Cronkite pointed out that many of the women are mothers of young children. "Those children left without motherly care are the most innocent victims of the drug war and the reason some call it a 'war on families' as well as on drugs."[37]

From the experienced holistic perspective of U.S. District Judge John L. Kane, we see that a broad and sometimes surprising range of people suffer as a result of the drug war.

> They are those people and businesses who can't get into court to have their cases heard. They are the victims of traditional crimes such as burglary, rape, and robbery who can't get justice because the police are tied up with drug cases. They are merchants [bankrupted] because the police no longer have time to investigate or prosecute bad check cases. They are the battered spouses whose mates are not sent to jail because there's room there only for pot smokers. They are the physicians and other medical care providers who cannot treat their patients according to conscience and the discipline of their profession. They are the sick and dying who endure unnecessary pain. They are the children whose parents are taken from them. They are the police who have given up honorable

and challenging work investigating and detecting crime because they have become addicted to and dependent upon an informant-based system. They are the families forced to select one member to plead guilty lest the entire family be charged. They are the prosecutors and defense attorneys who have turned the temples of justice into plea-bargaining bazaars. They are, most painful to me, judges who let this happen and don't say a word. . . . Our national drug policy is inconsistent with the nature of justice, abusive of the nature of authority, and ignorant of the compelling force of forgiveness. Our drug laws, indeed, are more mocked than feared.[38]

Contrast Kane's holistic perspective taken from the front lines of drug-war reality with the simplistic and dualistic perspective we so often hear: "The drug war is the price we must pay to protect our kids." Of course, the latter perspective totally ignores the damage that *war* does to kids, and only makes sense if drug use is considered the worst of all possible evils in every circumstance. It also ignores a crucial set of facts: Young people are instinctively driven to experiment, and they are inexperienced in dealing with law enforcement, a deadly combination that leads large numbers of them to be caught up in the war, unjustly punished, and alienated from society just as they are beginning their independent lives.

The drug war is a war on freedom, and it affects us all. *International Living* magazine prepared a "Quality of Life Index" in 2008 in which it rated the various countries around the planet based on nine criteria, one of which was freedom. In terms of freedom, a number of countries earned a 100, including Canada and most European countries. Team USA earned a 92.[39] Although these numbers reflect factors beyond our number-one ranking in terms of the percentage of our citizens that we incarcerate (or the effect of the drug war on such statistics), there can be no doubt that a major reason for the lower standing of the

United States in this index is the drug war. In any case, the limits imposed on our freedom by the drug war go far beyond the issue of imprisonment. These limits also extend to several other areas — including our ability to heal ourselves and alleviate pain with natural, whole medicines.

We have already mentioned the fact that cannabis has long been used by various cultures for healing a wide range of health problems. Psychedelics are another group of drugs that have shown tremendous potential for healing and learning. According to a report written by David Jay Brown for *Scientific American*, prior to 1972 when psychedelic drugs could be studied, "research suggested that psychedelics offered significant [healing] benefits: they helped recovering alcoholics abstain, soothed the anxieties of terminal cancer patients, and eased the symptoms of many difficult-to-treat psychiatric illnesses, such as obsessive-compulsive disorder. For example, between 1967 and 1972 studies in terminal cancer patients by psychiatrist Stanislav Grof and his colleagues at Spring Grove State Hospital in Baltimore showed that LSD combined with psychotherapy could alleviate symptoms of depression, tension, anxiety, sleep disturbances, psychological withdrawal, and even severe physical pain. Other investigators during this era found that LSD may have some interesting potential as a means to facilitate creative problem solving." As a result of the poisoned political climate, after 1972 there were no human studies of psychedelic drugs in the United States until 1990. Since then, limited research has resumed, focusing on "cluster headaches, depression, obsessive-compulsive disorder (OCD), severe anxiety in terminal cancer patients, post-traumatic stress disorder (PTSD), alcoholism and opiate addiction." Brown goes on to say that "psychedelic drugs affect all mental functions: perception, emotion, cognition, body awareness and one's sense of self. Unlike every other class of drugs, psychedelic drug effects depend heavily on the environment [in which they are experienced] and on the expectations of the subject, which is why combining them with psychotherapy is so vital."[40]

A highly disturbing recent trend that goes even beyond the criminalization of drug use is the criminalization of *pain relief* and of the doctors who provide it. Reporting for the *Washington Post*, Mark Kaufman explains that the drug war now threatens our access to *legal* drugs, especially drugs for pain control. "Official rhetoric has escalated to the point where federal and state prosecutors often accuse arrested doctors of being no better than drug kingpins or crack dealers." Quoting one of the fathers of modern pain management, Russell K. Portenoy, "Treating people in pain isn't easy, and . . . now . . . medical ambiguity is being turned into allegations of criminal behavior." Pain specialist Rebecca J. Patchin adds, "Doctors hear what's happening to other physicians, and that makes them very reluctant to prescribe opioids that patients might well need."[41]

In addition to interfering with our freedom to seek individual means of physical and mental healing, the drug war limits the options we have in our spiritual search. In other words, it directly abridges our religious freedom. In a spiritual quest, as native peoples have used them for centuries, psychedelics are referred to as *entheogens*—which literally means that which generates God ("theo"), or the Divine within. Entheogens help us draw closer to our God nature. But positive news of any kind undermines and threatens the prohibitionist perspective and all those individuals and businesses that benefit from it. As a result, permission to scientifically study cannabis and psychedelics, and opportunities to prove their benefits to humankind for physical, mental, or spiritual healing, are very hard to come by.

By prosecuting a war on the very people it seeks to serve (many of whom help pay their salaries through taxes), law enforcement becomes less and less respected among large segments of the population, making the job even more difficult. As one Colorado district attorney remarked about the war against marijuana, it is "the single most destructive force in society, in terms of turning our children against the system."[42] From a holistic standpoint, hearing something like that would cause us to pay close attention and investigate. Because young people have a tendency to do the opposite of what they are told, it only makes sense that drug prohibition might even be *encouraging* a segment of our youth to experiment with illegal drugs. But from our usual dualistic perspective, we see ideas like this as a threat to our war effort, and it frightens us. And since the left brain is survival oriented, we become defensive and typically respond with an attack—we attack people's motives and morals, rather than examining their ideas impartially with an interest in discovering truth.

The Effects of Prohibition

Albert Einstein, speaking of alcohol prohibition in *My First Impression of the U.S.A.*, remarked that

> the prestige of government had undoubtedly been lowered considerably by the prohibition law. For nothing is more destructive of respect for the government and the law of the land than passing laws which cannot be enforced. It is an open secret that the dangerous increase of crime in this country is closely connected with this.[43]

No doubt Einstein would have said the same thing about today's *drug* prohibition laws—and he would not be alone. In an interview conducted for public television, Nobel Prize–winning economist Milton Friedman said, "The case for prohibiting drugs is exactly as strong and as weak as the case for prohibiting people from overeating. We all know that overeating causes more deaths than drugs do. If it's in principle OK for the government to say you must not consume drugs because they'll do you harm, why isn't it all right to say you must not eat too much because you'll do harm? Why isn't it all right to say you must not . . . go . . . skydiving?"[44]

It doesn't take a rocket scientist or Nobel Prize winner to understand the effects of prohibition; nevertheless, considering that the majority of voters still support prohibition in the case of certain drugs, perhaps we should remind ourselves of what is at stake. The mother of former Minnesota governor and professional wrestler Jesse Ventura lived through the alcohol-prohibition era, and has a perspective that includes the benefit of hindsight. As she sees it, there are obvious similarities between alcohol then and illegal drugs today: in both cases, the gangsters get rich while the government wastes money fighting a losing battle.[45]

So far, we have looked at what people *think* about prohibition, but remember, we are *feeling* beings. What we think is extremely important, but what we feel reflects who we are. How does prohibition feel? Let's take the perspective of Tracy Ingle of North Little Rock, Arkansas, as again reported by Radley Balko, a senior editor at *Reason* magazine and Reason.com. This account comes from the blog, "Hit & Run."[46]

Imagine waking in the middle of the night on January 7, 2008, to the sound of someone trying to break into your house. Someone is pounding on the front door, and you hear your bedroom window shatter. Thinking robbers are entering, you grab a broken gun to try to bluff them into thinking you might be a threat. As you grab the gun, you are fired upon, and your thigh bone shatters, your lower leg nearly severed. You don't know it yet, but it's a drug raid, and hearing the first shot, other officers open up on you, hitting you four more times. One bullet lodges just above your heart.

Police take you to intensive care, where you remain for a week and a half. Upon release—still in your pajamas—you are taken to the police station and questioned for five hours. You are not allowed to speak with your family. Police then take you to jail, where the pain medication and antibiotics you have been prescribed are withheld from you. Though you have been instructed to clean your wounds every four to six hours, your jailer changes them only twice in the four days that they keep you in jail, and your wounds become infected. But your troubles are only starting.

Police find *no* drugs, and you have *no* drug-related prior arrests, but your sister, a former sheriff's deputy, had stored some common jewelry-making equipment at your house that included a scale and some plastic bags. Based on this, police charge you with running a drug enterprise and set your bail at $250,000—a high amount because you "engaged in a shootout with police"—never mind that you thought they were robbers and that you were knowingly using a broken gun that was incapable of firing a shot. Having to sell your car to make bail, you walk two miles to your hearing on crutches with an infected leg.

Lucky for you, your neighbor had a direct line of sight into the bedroom and saw the entire raid. Unlucky for you, the North Little Rock Police don't question him until a month later. And when they do, they question him for four hours, alone, refusing to let his wife come home or to allow anyone else to see him. After the "interview," your neighbor reports that the police told him that he did not see what he thought he saw. This experience has resulted in your neighbor's being afraid to speak to the media. You have no health insurance, and no money to pay for medication or to otherwise treat your injuries. In April 2009, a Pulaski County jury finds you guilty of felony assault for pointing your nonfunctional pistol at the officers who entered your home. They also convict you of maintaining a drug house, as well as possession of drug paraphernalia. You are sentenced to 18 years in prison and fined $18,000.[47]

How does that feel?

You are a paraplegic living in Sayre, Oklahoma. Confined to a wheelchair, you suffer from chronic antibiotic-resistant infections in your lower body. Staying in a rehabilitation clinic, you hear about cannabis's success in treating people with spinal cord injuries, relieving pain and spasm in their paralyzed limbs; and so, in spite of your disability, with the help of cannabis you are able to support yourself as an auto mechanic. Unfortunately, you get caught with two ounces of marijuana in the back of your wheelchair—arrested by a lawman named Lawless (who was later charged with embezzling from the police property room). The cannabis was for your personal use, but at the trial, another officer claims that he has never seen anyone with two ounces who was not a major dealer. The jury believes him and gives you, a first offender, the maximum sentence for each charge, amounting to life plus 16 years and a $31,000 fine, later reduced by the judge to 10 years and $20,000. Law enforcement then attempts to seize the house in which you live, a house that belongs to your elderly mother, further increasing your legal burden. After a year in prison and nearly dying twice because of the failure of the state of Oklahoma to provide adequate treatment for the highly communicable infections, and being a medical threat to other prisoners, you are released on an appeals bond. The Oklahoma Court of Criminal Appeals affirms the distribution conviction and sentence based solely on one officer's testimony.[48]

The "justice" imposed on you is so outrageous that your story is included in an ABC News report. But before it runs and you can see it, you are reimprisoned, frequently placed in solitary confinement, and handcuffed to a prison bed without adequate medical treatment for the antibiotic-resistant infections in your lower body. After a public outcry, you are released on medical parole, which is officially protested by the district attorney. You later lose a leg from an ulcerated bedsore developed in prison.[49]

How does that feel?

Events like these don't simply happen. We create them when we support prohibition with our silence and with our energy (such as our vote and our moral and financial support of prohibition-oriented organizations and policies).

Ironically, under American "justice," *evidence* of a sale is not required in order to convict someone of drug trafficking (selling)—if "evidence" is taken to mean any proof that a sale has taken place. As Jimmy Montgomery, profiled in the above story, discovered, you can go to prison for life based on nothing more than the *suspicion* of law enforcement and the quantity in your possession, an amount that can be as little as two ounces (as if no one ever bought or stored more than one ounce at a time). I've even seen reports of trafficking convictions for less than one ounce based on such "evidence."

The Drug War Creates More Problems Than It Solves

In the 1980s, with the drug war still not working—drug usage climbing along with drug-war budgets and violence—many with the pro-drug-war mindset thought that the sentences being given out by some liberal judges were too soft and were undermining the system. Oblivious to Einstein's definition of insanity as doing the same thing over and over again and each time expecting different results, they continued to pursue their original policy of the application of pain as a deterrent, accompanied by ever greater infringements on personal liberty. In a get-even-tougher mentality, mandatory-minimum sentences were passed in the Drug Abuse Act of 1986. Sentencing discretion was taken from federal judges and replaced by a schedule of minimum prison sentences for drug cases based on the type and quantity of drug involved.

Sheila Devereux, a mother of three, devoted her time to caring for her kids and earning a business degree. After a bitter divorce and custody battle, she turned to drugs to ease the pain—a common response in our culture. After an accidental overdose of cocaine, Sheila was taken straight from the hospital to jail and charged with felony possession. Several years later, her truck broke down and police found a marijuana cigarette in it, her second felony. For a second time, she was given probation. According to FAMM (Families Against Mandatory Minimums), in 2005 Sheila's ex-husband had custody of their children, and Sheila was spending a few days with a new acquaintance until she could move into a house near her children. About a week and a half after she moved in, police burst into the house, and the resident, a man named Allen, turned over six grams of crack. According to the FAMM account,

> Though Sheila had no drugs in her possession and was not a resident of the house, she was held accountable for Allen's crack. Oklahoma law requires that if over five grams of crack is found, everyone involved is considered a drug trafficker. At trial, the police testified they had never seen Sheila participate in any illegal activities, nor was she intoxicated when they searched the house. Allen admitted that the drugs were his and Sheila knew nothing about them. However, because of Sheila's two prior felonies, she was charged under Oklahoma's three strikes law and sentenced to mandatory life in prison without the possibility of parole. Allen received 13 years.[50]

Actions like this are automatic in many states as well as in the federal system under this still-widespread type of law. Of course, the use of mandatory sentencing totally disregards the

fundamental holistic, realistic, justice-oriented intent of allowing judges to use their discretion based on the variable nature
of circumstances. But this is war, and justice is always put aside
in wartime. Mandatory sentencing is a response to war—and,
by definition, sentencing that allows for no leniency, no variabil-
ity, no respect for human factors, *cannot* be just. Mandatory
sentencing effectively dispenses with the fundamental role of
the judiciary and turns judges into high-paid law clerks. This is
a pure left-brain, male, aggressive, separative, destruction-ori-
ented, single-purpose, truth-suppressing response.

Naturally, mandatory minimums increase the size of our
prison populations. A 2009 report ranks Oklahoma number one
among all states for the percentage of its women that it imprisons
(half of whom are mothers with small children). Oklahoma's
incarceration rate for women is nearly double the national
average.[51] According to research by the National Council on
Crime and Delinquency, the United States, which has an incarceration rate that is four times the world average and incarcerates
more people than any other country in the world, also incarcerates more women than any other country (over three times more
than any other nation, Russia coming in second). Thus, based
on reported data, as a percentage of its population, Oklahoma
imprisons more women than any country on the planet![52]

But mandatory minimums don't deter illegal drug activity,
so another get-tough attitude idea that prohibitionists came up
with was to create drug-free zones around schools, parks,
churches, housing projects, and other public areas, where extra
penalties were added. In some cities, that covered most of the territory. In New Jersey, a commission found that "instead of
declining, drug arrests in the zones rose steadily after the law took
effect in 1987." It also found that "96 percent of offenders jailed
for zone violations were black or Hispanic." Only 2 percent of
the cases they studied involved students. "A former assistant attor-

ney general in Massachusetts reviewed hundreds of drug-free-zone cases, and found that less than one percent involved drug sales to youths."[53] Thus, the well-intentioned goal of deterring drugs from being peddled around schools has led to disastrous results. Rather than helping students, this law has instead become just another tool of punishment, another opportunity for prosecutors to add prison time or a fine to someone's sentence and to further crowd our prisons. An Alva, Oklahoma, man experienced the consequences of this law when cops found illegal drugs at an isolated bar that he operated on the edge of town. Although it was far from an actual school, because it was near school-owned *farmland*, he was charged with violating drug-zone statutes.[54]

Another reflection of government's desperate get-tough attitude was to start going through people's trash. "By a six-to-two vote, the U.S. Supreme Court ruled that police may freely rummage through ordinary household trash left at curbside without obtaining a search warrant."[55] In Alva, Oklahoma, they search trash. When residue was found in the trash of two men, although there was no evidence that they had any connection with a nearby school, they were charged with felony possession of marijuana within 1,000 feet of a school, a charge calling for imprisonment of up to two years and a fine of $2,000.[56] That would, of course, be on top of the other drug-related charges.

Trash searches can get you killed. In Beaver Dam, Wisconsin, police searched Scott Bryant's garbage for cannabis residue for several days before getting a no-knock warrant. According to news and eyewitness reports, the four sheriff's deputies storming the residence made no effort to identify themselves prior to smashing in the door, and shot the unarmed Bryant immediately. Bryant made no attempt to resist and was killed in front of his seven-year-old son. Police later reported finding less than three grams of cannabis.[57]

Another major tool of drug-law enforcement is forfeiture. Glenn Greenwald, a former civil rights litigator, explains:

> Unlike English common law, which required conviction prior to seizure, American forfeiture dispenses with the need for proving the property owner guilty of anything. All that is necessary is for the state to claim a connection between the things seized and drugs, whereupon the government may confiscate the property. It is then up to the owner to prove (at their own expense . . .) that the property is "innocent." Critically, **the proceeds from the seizures go into the budget of the state or federal law enforcement agencies and prosecutors offices,** creating a horrible incentive for officers to go after seizures solely for the purpose of enriching their units with a swell new fleet of fully loaded police cruisers, or lovely new desks for the DAs.[58]

We see clear evidence of the incentive nature of forfeiture in the fact that "as part of training for ATF [Alcohol, Tobacco and Firearms] agents and state and local task force officers, ATF purchased a number of Leatherman tool kits engraved with the words, 'ATF Asset Forfeiture' and 'Always Think Forfeiture' for distribution to the participants."[59] We see evidence of the effect of incentive in the attitude of Oklahoma City police. After seizing $1.3 million in a suspected drug bust, although no drugs were found, they kept the money anyway because of traces of cocaine found on the bills—despite the fact that it has long been common knowledge that used bills often contain traces of cocaine due to the widespread use of the drug.[60] Due to contamination by counting machines and other factors, approximately four of every five bills in circulation carry trace amounts of cocaine![61]

Not only is the war on drugs failing to solve many of the problems associated with drug abuse, but as we have been see-

ing, it *creates* a multitude of problems. From the perspective of
Eric E. Sterling, president of the Criminal Justice Policy Foundation and former counsel to the U.S. House of Representatives
Committee on the Judiciary from 1979 until 1989, we see that
"the strategy to reduce supply by arresting participants in the distribution [of illegal drugs] actually has a positive, strengthening
effect on the illegal drug market. . . . Drug enforcement weeds
out the less effective, less ingenious participants and encourages
the more ruthless and the more cunning."[62]

One of the greatest and most widespread of the many problems created by the drug war is the damage it does to everyone
by supporting international terrorism. Former Secretary of State,
Secretary of Labor, and Secretary of the Treasury George Shultz
warned us way back in 1984 that "money from drug smuggling
supports terrorists."[63] We were warned again in 1994 by Inter-
pol's chief drug-enforcement officer, who reported that "drugs
have taken over as a chief means of supporting terrorism."[64] Our
lawmakers know that they are aiding terrorist activity. Sheldon
Richman, writing for the Future of Freedom Foundation, quotes
former Republican House Speaker Dennis Hastert as saying,
"The illegal drug trade is the financial engine that fuels many
terrorist organizations around the world, including Osama bin
Laden." Richman points out that even former drug czar William
Bennett (notwithstanding his intransigent drug-war advocacy)
owns up to this fact. Referring to the editorial page of the *Wall
Street Journal*, Richman quotes Bennett as saying, "We have
learned a great deal about the connection between terrorism
and illegal drugs, including the fact that our enemies in
Afghanistan have derived considerable sustenance and resources
from the drug trade."[65]

"Prohibition forces drugs into an underground, unregu-
lated market which creates a highly lucrative source of funding
and personnel in the armed and violent actions against civilians

and governments around the world," warns the Drug Policy Alliance.[66] If all drugs were legal, prices would drop dramatically, depriving terrorists of a major source of much-needed funding. If government officials know of this, then why do most support something that aids terrorists? The self-protective left brain hemisphere dictates it; officials have higher priorities than stopping terrorism—such as keeping their jobs—and before we reach the end of this chapter, we will discover other powerful reasons why they support the drug war. (Hint: They involve the subject of the previous chapter.) Meanwhile, government drug warriors, using taxpayer money, run Super Bowl ads that seek to blame drug users for supporting terrorists. The ads have stopped running—perhaps because they were causing the government's own actions to come under scrutiny—but the attitudes behind the ads remain.

According to a report in a conservative Oklahoma newspaper, U.S. drug agents were alleged to have "kidnapped, raped and tortured Bolivians while trying to build a drug case." The story reported, "Twenty-nine Bolivians allege in sworn declarations that the Drug Enforcement Administration and Bolivian army used brutal methods . . . while seeking information." A woman claimed to have been "blindfolded, interrogated, given electric shocks and raped. Others alleged they were beaten with rifle butts. One man claimed agents pulled out one of his toenails."[67] Nor is government-sponsored terrorism limited to the federal level. In Oklahoma, a plot to kidnap and torture a suspected north Texas drug dealer was uncovered when Marietta police Lieutenant Tom Hankins notified the FBI in response to a request by Love County Sheriff Wesley Liddell Jr. to participate in the kidnapping. Liddell confessed to the FBI after he was arrested. According to FBI spokesman Dan Vogel, Liddell told the FBI in a recorded conversation that he and his brother-in-law, a Marietta, Oklahoma, police officer, planned to use "a heated curling iron [as] the instrument of torture because it could be applied to certain parts of the body and would not leave any marks."[68] "Sometimes you got to break the law to help the law," Liddell was heard saying in one recording. In another recording, the sheriff's son-in-law, Roger Ray Hilton, can be heard talking about getting rid of the man they planned to kidnap, saying that "if for some reason something goes wrong and somebody is going to have to kill him, I'd just as soon Junior (Liddell) did it."[69]

Commenting on the local community's attitude—one of rousing support of the pair—an Oklahoma City columnist expressed concern. "The attitude which some of these people have taken is that it doesn't really matter if Liddell and Hilton are guilty. They support the pair, not because they think they are innocent, but because the two were trying to fight the war on drugs."[70] In court, the pair claimed they were not planning to carry out the planned act and were acquitted.

Local attitudes tend to reflect national attitudes: do whatever it takes to win, even if that means ignoring the facts of science, the justice of law, and the will of the people. In what was described as a "desperate and transparent" attempt by Congress to support the federal government's drug policies by prohibiting changes to drug policy, Congress barred the District of Columbia from spending any money to count the votes on Initiative 59, a medical marijuana measure on the November 1998 ballot. "Exit polls showed that the measure was being approved by a vote of 69 to 31 percent,"[71] reports former California Superior Court Judge James P. Gray in *Why Our Drug Laws Have Failed and What We Can Do About It: A Judicial Indictment of the War on Drugs*. Congress must have been surprised by the response. "All over the country, newspapers wrote editorials denouncing Congress's act, saying such things as, 'It is hard to imagine that in the history of American elections—or of American democracy—there is precedent for stifling the legally expressed will of the people by denying the money necessary to count their ballots.'"[72] Yet Congress was unbowed. The separatist response of the left brain often allows left-brain dominants to mentally evade their critics.

In war, winning is everything. In war, justice, or the will of the people, has little if any value. You use the laws that benefit you and ignore the ones that do not. The same goes for the facts. And blue ribbon commissions? Likewise—unless they support you, you ignore them. After annual increases in penalties, and seeing that marijuana use was still increasing among middle-class youth, President Richard Nixon set up the Shafer Commission to study the issue. "In 1972, after reviewing the scientific evidence, [the commission concluded] it was 'of the unanimous opinion that marihuana use is not such a grave problem that individuals who smoke marihuana, and possess it for that purpose, should be subject to criminal prosecution,'" write Lynn Zimmer and John P. Morgan in *Marijuana Myths, Marijuana Facts*. Unhappy with the findings, Nixon ignored the report, but "between 1969 and 1977, government-appointed commissions in Canada, England, Australia, and the Netherlands all issued reports that agreed with the Shafer Commission's conclusions. All found that marijuana's dangers had been greatly exaggerated."[73]

A rare few members of Congress truly respect the will of the people. One is U.S. Representative Ron Paul (R-Texas), one of the few conservatives who has fairly consistently recognized what should be a bedrock conservative principle: that one cannot be a true defender of liberty while ignoring or opposing individual freedom in *any* sphere. Explaining why conservatives should oppose the drug war, Paul points out, "Government intervention in *social* matters [produces] the same unintended consequences, distortions, and inefficiencies as government intervention in *economic* matters [emphasis added]." Paul believes that, "although

. . . philosophical questions rarely surface in the drug debate, they are critically important. When we fail to adopt a consistent guiding philosophy, we allow emotions rather than principles to frame the debate. . . . In America, the overriding principle should be that human freedom is our greatest priority."[74]

Ron Paul reminds us that the drug war ramped up

in a decade when conservative, limited-government thinking was otherwise ascendant. . . . President Reagan famously told the nation that government was the problem, not the solution. Reagan conservatives argued that individual initiative and personal responsibility . . . were the keys to a better life for Americans. Yet the war on drugs turned the idea of personal responsibility upside down, placing the blame for personal moral failure on drugs rather than the individuals abusing them. Drugs became a national boogeyman, while individuals were reduced to helpless victims. In this sense the war on drugs mirrored the gun-control movement's [liberal] push to ban firearms, as both attempted to blame inanimate objects for the misdeeds of individuals.[75]

The drug war has contributed to the polarization of America. "The addict belongs in the hospital, not in the prison," wrote Alfred R. Lindesmith, a professor of sociology at Indiana University, in the *Nation*. Referring to Congress's escalation of the use of mandatory minimums, Lindesmith described its legislation as reflecting "conceptions of justice and penology which can only be adequately described as *medieval* and *sadistic*."[76] A prominent viewpoint from the prohibitionist side—that of former drug czar William Bennett—certainly lends credence to Lindesmith's strong characterizations. Bennett believes that even drug *users* belong in prison. Speaking at W. R. Thomas Middle School in Miami, Bennett encouraged youngsters to turn in their relatives and friends if they used drugs.[77] When asked on a television program why we don't behead drug dealers as they do in Middle Eastern countries, Bennett responded, "Morally, I don't have any problem with that at all."[78] Here Bennett shows us a pure left-brain separate-and-destroy-the-threat attitude toward problem solving.

Even if you don't do drugs and face no threat from drug-funded terrorism because you don't travel or you live in an isolated area of the country, if you live in the United States, you still face substantial risks as a result of the drug war. Law enforcement, like every other organization on the planet, makes mistakes. For example, they sometimes go to the wrong address in their attempts to root out drugs. Because of that one fact, every day many of us play Russian roulette with our lives and those of our family and pets.

If a clean-living city mayor can be threatened, so can you. Such was the case with the mayor of Berwyn Heights, Maryland. On the basis of a package of marijuana delivered to the mayor's house on July 29, 2008, a SWAT team broke down his front door and shot his two Labrador retrievers. The mayor and his mother-in-law were kept bound for nearly two hours next to the two pets and interrogated while blood pooled on the floor. Although authorities initially claimed to have been operating under a "no-knock" warrant, it later came out that the police did not have, nor did they even seek, such a warrant. A Maryland state senator who represented the district said it was just another example of frequent police action in minority communities. But this time, it drew far more attention because it involved a mayor. The mayor believes his dogs were executed the very second the SWAT team entered. And law enforcement's attitude toward the mayor? Separate from responsibility by focusing the attention on someone else. The sheriff said the dogs' deaths were justified—the officers felt threatened. The county police chief portrayed the mayor as the victim of a local drug ring.[79]

We have already seen that law enforcement officers sometimes ignore the law altogether and can place people's lives in
great peril in the process—as, for example, in the story of the
Love County Sheriff and his policeman brother-in-law. Another
such example is the case of Rachel Hoffman, a 23-year-old col-
lege graduate who occasionally used marijuana. After a
Tallahassee, Florida, police raid found some marijuana in her
home, she faced five years in prison and a fine. According to
Paul Armentano, NORML (National Organization for Reform
of Marijuana Laws) deputy director, Hoffman was threatened
with jail and told that if she cooperated by helping with a drug
operation, the police would not file charges. Untrained and
unsupervised, and in flagrant violation of Tallahassee Police
Department protocol, she was instructed to meet with two men
whom she had never met and purchase a large quantity of
cocaine and ecstasy, and a handgun. Since Hoffman was already
enrolled in a drug court program from a prior marijuana possession charge, cooperating with Tallahassee police would have
been in violation of her probation, and police were required to
first gain formal approval from the state prosecutor's office.
"Knowing that the office would likely not sign off on their
deal . . . police simply decided to move forward with their infor-
mal arrangement and not tell anybody." As Armentano put it,
"Rachel became the bait; the Tallahassee police force went
trolling for sharks." On May 12, 2008, Hoffman was shot and
killed by the two men.[80]

We are engaged in a war that creates terrible conflict in the
lives of millions of our brothers, sisters, parents, and children,
and costs billions of dollars every year, yet as a culture we have
never openly and freely discussed it. Because there has never
been an open and honest discussion, it is often difficult for people to get the facts, sort out the fundamentals, and find the
truth—or even recognize the irony of their words and actions.

The Real Reason Why Cannabis Is Illegal

According to most scientific findings, the psychoactive component of cannabis is one of the safest of common drugs, if not *the* safest in many respects. (Unlike most drugs, cannabis has never caused anyone to die from an overdose.) At the very least, considered as a whole, it is no more of a problem than caffeine. Yet federal laws treat cannabis as a *very* dangerous drug. The objection to cannabis seems to be that people use it to get high, to alter their consciousness—and in the minds of many people, it is a bad thing to alter your consciousness. But what if you could grow cannabis that would not make you high? Well, you can. Cannabis has long been used for its strong fibers. In fact, "the first laws addressing any of the currently illicit substances were passed during colonial times, and they *required* the various townships to grow a certain amount of cannabis sativa, or hemp [emphasis added]."[81] Yet laws treat this otherwise commercially valuable plant as a harmful psychoactive drug. The discrepancy between science and American drug policy with respect to hemp is rather strange, don't you think?

James P. Gray reports that prior to the Harrison Narcotic Act of 1914, other than "a couple of state and local statutes . . . there were no illegal drugs in the United States."[82] And no drug war. The fibers of the cannabis plant were widely used as rope by the U.S. Navy, farmers, and fishermen, for example. "Several drafts of the Declaration of Independence were printed on parchment made from the same natural substance. . . . [Hemp paper] was even used as money from 1631 until the early 1800s. George Washington, Thomas Jefferson, and a large number of other famous planters in the colonial period all grew large crops of hemp."[83] In *Intoxication: Life in Pursuit of Artificial Paradise*, Ronald K. Siegel explains that "the Harrison act was widely interpreted as national prohibition of . . . opium, morphine, heroin, coca, and cocaine . . . but it was merely a law for the orderly marketing of these drugs in small quantities over-the-counter and in larger quantities on a physician's prescription. Marijuana was not included because of strong lobbying by the pharmaceutical industry."[84]

The next round in drug prohibition was instituted by moralist idealists and was aimed at alcohol. Started in 1920, it was a disastrous war that officially ended on December 5, 1933. During this period, "the United States saw a material increase in death from poisoned liquor, crime, violence, and corruption," writes James P. Gray in *Why Our Drug Laws Have Failed and What We Can Do About It*. "It also saw a higher consumption per capita of stronger beverages like whiskey than of weaker beverages like beer, in accordance with a cardinal rule of prohibition: there is always more money to be made in pushing the more concentrated substances. In many cities there were actually more 'speakeasies' during Alcohol Prohibition than there previously had been saloons."[85]

Next to become a prohibitionist target was cannabis. This time, however, the lead was taken by corporate interests whose goal was not so much to combat drug usage, which was minimal at the time, as to eliminate economic competition from hemp, a strong but soft and versatile fiber. As Jack Herer, a best-selling author and political activist, explains in *Hemp & The Marijuana Conspiracy: The Emperor Wears No Clothes*, "When mechanical hemp fiber stripping machines and machines to conserve hemp's high-cellulose pulp finally became state-of-the-art, available and affordable in the mid-1930's, the enormous timber acreage and business of the Hearst Paper Manufacturing Division, Kimberly Clark (USA), St. Regis— and virtually all other timber, paper and large newspaper holding companies—stood to lose billions of dollars and perhaps go bankrupt."[86]

The rise of hemp also threatened another powerful corporation. "In 1937 DuPont had just patented processes to make plastics from oil and coal, as well as new sulfate/sulfite processes to make paper from wood pulp which would, according to their own corporate records and historians, account for over 80% of all its railroad car-loadings for the next 50 years." Herer concludes that "if hemp had not been made illegal, 80% of DuPont's business would never have come to be."[87]

Jack Herer has extraordinary backing for his claims. In Neale Donald Walsch's *Conversations with God: An Uncommon Dialogue, Book 2*, God says to Walsch,

> If it were grown, half the cotton growers, nylon and rayon manufacturers, and timber products people in the world would go out of business. Hemp happens to be one of the most useful, strongest, toughest, longest-lasting materials on your planet. You cannot produce a better fiber for clothes, a stronger substance for ropes, an easier-to-grow-and-harvest source for pulp. You cut down hundreds of thousands of trees per year to give yourself Sunday papers, so that you can read about the decimation of the world's forests. Hemp could provide you with millions of Sunday papers without cutting down one tree. Indeed, it could substitute for so many resource materials, at one-tenth the cost. And *that is the catch*. Somebody *loses money* if this miraculous plant—which also has extraordinary medicinal properties, incidentally—is allowed to be grown. And *that* is why marijuana is illegal in your country.[88]

By threatening DuPont's business, hemp also threatened DuPont's chief financial backer, Andrew Mellon, who, in his role as secretary of the treasury, appointed his future nephew-in-law, Harry J. Anslinger, to be head of the newly reorganized Federal Bureau of Narcotics and Dangerous Drugs, the predecessor of the DEA (Drug Enforcement Administration). Jack Herer explains, "Testimony before Congress in 1937 for the purpose of outlawing hemp consisted almost entirely of Hearst's and other sensational and racist newspaper articles read aloud by . . . Anslinger." Anslinger testified that "marijuana is the most violence causing drug in the history of mankind." Preying on racial fears, he testified that about half "of all violent crimes committed in the U.S. were committed by Spaniards, Mexican-Americans, Latin Americans, Filipinos, Negroes, and Greeks, and these crimes could be traced directly to Marijuana." American Medical Association (AMA) doctors, upon learning of the bill two days prior to the vote, protested that Congress was about to outlaw a "benign substance used in scores of illnesses, for 100 years in America, with perfect safety," and that the law had been prepared in secret over a span of two years without the medical profession having been consulted. But it was too late. And when a member of Congress asked, before voting, if anyone had consulted with the AMA on the bill, he was falsely told that the AMA had been consulted and was in complete agreement.[89]

In 1970, Congress provisionally categorized cannabis as a Schedule 1 drug, a drug with a high tendency for abuse and no accepted medical use. Schedule 1 drugs cannot be prescribed. If you can't prescribe it, there can be no legal medical demand for it. If there is no legal demand for it, there is no need for anyone to produce it—*and that seems to be the key*. If there were a legal demand, people would need to farm cannabis for its medicinal purposes. And that would create a serious problem for some powerful individuals. If farmers were allowed to grow cannabis for its medicinal value, what would stop them from growing it for its fiber, or for one of its other commercially valuable properties?

And then there's the CIA's connection with drugs, which Michael C. Ruppert, a former Los Angeles narcotics detective, has studied for more than 25 years. Ruppert values the CIA's cut of the illegal drug trade at around $600 billion per year.[90] According to Ruppert, "The CIA has been dealing drugs since before it was the CIA," starting back in World War II when it was the OSS. "The use of the drug trade to secure economic advantage . . . is at least as old as the British East India Company's smuggling of opium from India into China in the late 1600s."[91]

According to Jim Willie CB (editor of the *Hat Trick Letter*, a subscription publication that discusses currencies, the world economy, and other related topics), "The irony is that the US agencies known as the Central Intelligence Agency (CIA) and the Drug Enforcement Agency (DEA) act precisely as drug cartels . . . but under the aegis of the U.S. Government. . . . The DEA has long acted as the private security force for the CIA syndicated operations, turning over seized narcotics to syndicate inventory, and killing competitors. In fact, the inside joke among US Government agencies unsympathetic to the cause is their name of Cocaine Importing Agency. Confirmation is easy," Willie reports. "To me it came from three military contacts and a defense industry consultant. That consultant, formerly an employee at Northrop Grumman, claims that defense contractors earn considerable profit by using private corporate jets for narcotic shipments on a routine regular basis, with no customs inspections."[92] The CIA connection to drug running gained widespread public attention in the mid-1980s after an insider confession that linked CIA drug activity to an airport at Mena, Arkansas.

Once you head down this road, it is difficult to turn back. And any activities that interfere with these profits must be prohibited at all costs, even if it means ignoring science and incarcerating people—which in turn means separating them from their families. This might even include killing disabled war veterans.

Gary Shepherd of Kentucky, a shotgun-carrying 45-year-old

disabled war veteran, smoked pot to ease the pain from his war-incurred injuries. When Kentucky police and National Guard troops went to his property to cut down and burn his 55 marijuana plants, Shepherd refused to let them. Like the heroic man in Tiananmen Square who stopped a column of tanks, Shepherd stood his ground. After a seven-hour standoff, police ordered Shepherd to lower his shotgun. As he complied, he was shot and killed, his four-year-old son standing beside him. Shepherd's wife, with hands up, was shot in the head but miraculously survived. Shepherd never fired. Following the shooting, a member of the assembled force was heard to remark, "We've killed Jesus!" "Jesus" was the police code name for the long-haired Shepherd.[93]

But perhaps there is another sense in which they "killed" Jesus. It has often been said that we "crucify" Jesus when we turn our back on his teachings and example, and refuse the lessons that he came here to teach — to love your neighbor as yourself, to treat others as you would have them treat you, to be a peacemaker, to practice unconditional love. Which of these teachings are being held up in the war on drugs as it is being waged today? What would Jesus say and do about all of this?

A Spirit-Based Perspective on Drugs

Most American antidrug crusaders are Christian. So what can we glean from the Bible that might help Christians to understand Jesus's attitude toward drugs and drug users? The book of John (John 2: 1–11) says Jesus went to a wedding party where they served wine, and that the wine ran out. It also says that the house where the wedding party took place had six stone jars, each capable of holding 20 to 30 gallons (76–114 liters), and Jesus asked that they be filled to the brim with water, which Jesus then turned into wine.[94] Was there a greater crowd than expected? Was there heavy drinking? On these matters we can't know for sure, but with that much wine we can make a pretty good guess that at least some people drank heavily. We do know without a doubt that the alcohol in wine is a powerful drug and that the amount created was 120 to 180 gallons—and that it was *in addition* to the wine provided by the host. It therefore seems reasonable to assume that Jesus tolerated the liberal use of alcoholic intoxicants. (Of course, we recognize that people were not driving automobiles then, but try telling a judge or a jury that you should not be convicted of a drug-related charge because no one was going to drive after consuming the drugs.)

Would Jesus have been tolerant of other intoxicants? Jesus's comments recorded in the Gospel of Mark (Mark 7:15) suggest a "yes" answer and, at the very least, leave an opening: "Nothing that goes into a man from outside can defile him; no, it is the things that come out of him that defile a man."[95] Might not those things that come out of a person and be defiling include votes and other acts that support legislators, law enforcement, and judges who wage war on otherwise peaceful people for selling and possessing relatively safe intoxicants?

What would Jesus do? Assuming that Jesus respected the truth—a more-than-reasonable assumption—we would expect him to respect the findings of science unless he knew science to be wrong (I refer to *knowledge* here, not simply an opinion based on political propaganda). As far as we know, he never opted for ignorance or narrow-mindedness or rigid thought of any kind— in fact, given the radical nature of his teachings, it is safe to say the opposite is true. His positions always seemed to challenge and contradict those who feared the mind and avoided the heart. In other words, he was both passionate and rational, both loving and respectful of reality—in short, he seemed to epitomize the integration of the left and right brain. Given his acceptance of wine, reason and logic would suggest that less powerful and less harmful intoxicants (as we know cannabis and caffeine to be) would also be acceptable for adult use. The conservative side of his nature would probably support conservative use while cautioning us to take care of ourselves. The liberal side of his nature would consider the whole of the issue—something today's liberal leaders fail to do when they ignore the enormous human and financial costs of war. His liberal nature would (and in fact did) lead him to extend mercy rather than impose force.

Jesus was a *peacemaker*. It's hard to imagine that Jesus would declare war on anyone over his or her choice of intoxicant, or especially on young people, whose natural tendency is to experiment and ignore authority. That's not to say Jesus would not try to talk someone out of using, especially young people—or to say he would not act to help people deal with any problems that might come up as the result of drug use. But it is consistent with everything we know about him to say that his actions would not be warlike—that he would not act against another's will, unlike the tendency of so many of today's spiritual teachers and their followers.

Jesus was a *healer*. The compassionate right brain of Jesus would allow people to have the medicines of their choice. The realistic, rational left brain of Jesus would recognize that differences in individuals are sometimes best served with different intoxicants. For example, certain individuals and groups such as American Indians have a natural chemistry that does not harmonize well with alcohol. Jesus would probably think it cruel to force people like American Indians to endure a system wherein the only legal intoxicants were alcohol, tobacco, and caffeine.

Jesus was a *teacher*. Had he thought people needed to do something other than what they were doing, he would have sought educational means, rather than force, to effect change. *A Course in Miracles* quotes Jesus as saying, "You must change your mind, not your behavior, and this *is* a matter of willingness.

You do not need guidance except at the mind level. Correction belongs only at the level where change is possible. Change does not mean anything at the symptom level, where it cannot work."[96] Of course, most American cultures are focused at the symptom level.

What about other great teachers? What, for example, would the Buddha do? The Buddha, according to His Holiness the Dalai Lama, would encourage us to "explore for ourselves ways of training and educating the mind, developing the emotions, becoming aware of ourselves, managing our negative habits, and detoxifying ourselves from our mental toxins."[97] According to Professor Ron Epstein, lecturer for the Global Peace Studies Program at San Francisco State University, "The Buddha taught that peaceful minds lead to peaceful speech and peaceful actions. If the minds of living beings are at peace, the world will be at peace."[98] Knowing this, do you think the Buddha would support a war on his brothers and sisters simply because they chose a different intoxicant than the majority of their culture?

What would most great spiritual leaders, whose wisdom has stood the test of time, do? Great spiritual leaders achieve their lofty status because of having been able to transcend the fears of their fellow humans, transcend the urge to control them, and come to understand that love and freedom go hand in hand. We can expect that most great spiritual leaders would be in harmony with the Buddha and Jesus.

A Solution

The issue of how to deal with drugs is a very serious one, and we would not wish to ignore the advice of seasoned veterans who have experienced the front lines of the drug war. One such individual is Edward Ellison, who spent years in Scotland Yard organizing its antidrug squad and fighting drug use. His conclusions are not unique; in fact, Ellison's advice is pretty much the same advice you would get if you asked a number of other individuals, including former U.S. Secretary of State George Shultz, former Attorney General Gustave de Greiff of Colombia, the late author and syndicated columnist William F. Buckley Jr., former New Mexico Governor Gary Johnson, U.S. District Court Judge Robert Sweet (New York), former federal prosecutor and Superior Court Judge James P. Gray (Orange County, California), and—for that matter—Dear Abby.[99] But Ellison's conclusions are those of an insider—one whose passion is born of deep knowledge and personal experience. Ellison says:

> As a former drugs squad chief, I've seen too many youngsters die. I'm determined my children don't get hooked—which is why I want all drugs legalized. Seventeen years of my life was spent in Scotland Yard's anti-drugs squad, four as its head. I saw the misery that drug abuse can cause. I saw first-hand the squalor, the wrecked lives, the deaths. And I saw, and arrested when I could, the people who do so well out of drugs: the dealers, the importers, the organizers. I saw the immense profits they were making out of human misery, the money laundering, the crime syndicates they financed. We have attempted prohibition. All that happened was that courts became clogged with thousands of cases of small, individual users, and a generation of young people came to think of the police as their enemies. There were no resources left to fight other crime. I say legalize drugs because I want to see less drug abuse, not more. And I say legalize drugs because I want to see the criminals put out of business.[100]

In the fight for freedom, a fight that pits individuals against a massive militarized industrial-congressional complex, individuals have received limited support from philanthropic organizations. Writing for the *Drug Policy Letter*, David C. Condliffe, former executive director of the Drug Policy Foundation, reminds us that "for too long, mainstream philanthropy has been timid and halfhearted in the field of drug policy reform."[101] And we need to act quickly. U.S. Supreme Court Justice William O. Douglas (1898–1980) warned us that "the privacy and dignity of our citizens is being whittled away by sometimes imperceptible steps. Taken individually, each step may be of little consequence. But when viewed as a whole, there begins to emerge a society quite unlike any we have seen—a society in which government may intrude into the secret regions of a person's life."[102] Obviously, this has already happened, but it is not too late to reverse the trend.

Reflecting a perspective that incorporates both foresight and hindsight, James P. Gray suggests that "we will look back in astonishment that we allowed our former policy to persist for so long, much as we look back now at slavery, or Jim Crow laws, or the days when women were prohibited from voting—and we will wish fervently that we had not waited so long to abandon these failed and destructive policies."[103]

Remember, as individuals, our creative responsibility is always to focus on our own creative processes, on our own actions, not the actions of others. What am *I* creating? What am *I* doing that negatively affects the lives of others? We much prefer to focus on what others are doing, because we like to think that others bear the ultimate responsibility for our lives and are to blame when things go wrong. It is also easier and less uncomfortable to focus on others' deficiencies than to have to face our own.

As creators, we play a dual role. We are responsible both as individual creators and as collective creators. In the former role, our creations are often public. Voting, on the other hand, is an example of collective creation, and it is done in private. When acting through the anonymity of the voting booth, it is tempting to take out our cultural frustrations on others; it is easy to become ballot-box bullies. Perhaps among the questions we need to ask ourselves are: Do I truly escape responsibility when I vote for violent actions sight unseen, effectively voting to have a representative administer the violence, rather than engaging in such actions personally and openly? Do I escape responsibility for the sometimes-violent actions of legislators and law-enforcement officials as they carry out my instructions, even though I don't specifically authorize individual acts of violence or hear the cries of pain? Do I manage my own life so well that I am qualified to manage the lives (and choices) of people I have never even met, let alone understand? Do I really want to take on the enormous task of dictating the life choices of others by taking away their ability to make their own choices?

Of course, whether we are acting as individuals (directly) or as collectives (allied with others, which often means acting indirectly), we have two defining fundamental choices based on what we perceive from our two fundamental perspectives, the dualistic and the holistic.

When we view our creative choices from a *dualistic* perspective, we protect ourselves either by separating from perceived danger (by *escaping* the threat) or by separating the danger from ourselves and our loved ones (by *removing* the threat—typically, through the use of hired professionals and tools such as imprisonment and execution). But the dualistic perspective is a balancing act. On one hand, we champion individual rights. We believe that people should have the freedom to make their own choices, take responsibility for them, and learn from them. Having this self-protective perspective, we are focused on keeping government and its inefficiencies out of our lives as much as possible. And being rational, we know that people must create an environment for freedom in order to receive freedom. On the other hand, in our narrow focus on correcting and controlling others as a way of ensuring our security, we often overlook the controls we impose on ourselves and our families. The drug war that conservatives so often support (and many liberals acquiesce to) does not distinguish between one's own family, which one tries to protect, and the family across town, which one is willing to sacrifice for the sake of one's own family. In addition, we face the power of fear to stir our emotions, a power that can easily trump not only rational thought, but also our professed conservative principles. Ironically, conservatives, who are so often derisive of liberal methods, have adopted the worst features of liberalism when they allow the collective to choose for the individual.

When we view our creative choices from a *holistic* perspective, we are well aware of the options perceived by the dualistic brain, but we perceive them in a broader context, and this added context results in different choices. From a holistic perspective, we are more aware of the great diversity of God's creation, and that naturally allows us to give others greater latitude in their behavioral choices. From a holistic perspective, we see others as part of ourselves, and assuming that we would not put ourselves or our children in prison for drug use, we are unwilling to put others in prison for drug use. From a holistic perspective, we see that force is a short-term fix and understand that correction can be accomplished only at the level of mind, which means that we tend to choose education over force to solve problems involving drug use and abuse.

On the other hand, the right brain's focus on the collective can have its own drawbacks; along with its holistic inclusiveness is a tendency to ignore and curtail individual freedoms if we think they are harming the collective. And remember, even though we might perceive reality from a right-brain-directed perspective, we are still subject to powerful left-brain fears, still capable of being duped by incomplete information or subjective biases, and still influenced by cultural forces to make a decision based on a dualistic, left-brain model—which helps explain why so many right-brain-directed individuals support the drug war. Having lost sight of (or suspended) our holistic principles, having succumbed to the power of fear, nudged by a right-brain desire to cooperate with the majority, and desiring a quick fix, we sometimes take the easy way out. We turn to force.

The drug war is unusual in that it is overwhelmingly one-sided. One group attacks aided by the full force of the law and backed by a powerful military-industrial-congressional complex, sophisticated modern technology, and largely supportive media; the other, lacking the support of law enforcement or the community, mostly hides. In the middle is a large group that neither actively wages war nor actively works for peace or justice, a group of people who are often fearful or simply in denial. And like those who are the objects of war, many who look on are often afraid to object, or afraid to see what is really happening.

To obtain peace, we must work for peace through good thinking, good feeling, and good action. *Doing nothing is doing something.* In the face of an unjust war, doing nothing is supporting unjust war. Gandhi reminded us that noncooperation with evil is as much a duty as is cooperation with good.[104] Sometimes silence is not golden; it is yellow.

 Chapter Nine

Peace

The choice is no longer between violence and non-violence;
it is between violence and non-existence.

— MARTIN LUTHER KING JR.

Is the United States a peace-loving nation? Based on an annual comprehensive survey of the world's nations, apparently not. A worldwide team of experts organized by analysts from the highly respected Economist Intelligence Unit (an economic forecasting agency) have created the Global Peace Index, the first such survey ever created to measure the world's nations by their peacefulness. Nations are ranked by 24 indicators, which include internal factors such as transparency and human rights, as well as external factors such as war and relations with other nations. The 2008 survey showed that the United States ranked 96th out of 121 countries, with Norway in first place and Iraq last.[1] By the 2009 survey, the United States had moved up to 83rd place but remained far down in the bottom half of the list as New Zealand took over the top spot and Iraq remained mired in last place.[2] Public opinion seems to confirm this perception. In a 2006 survey carried out by newspapers in Britain, Canada, Israel, and Mexico using professional polling sources, 69 percent of the British believed that U.S. policy had made the world less safe, and 62 percent of Canadians, 36 percent of Israelis, and 57 percent of Mexicans agreed.[3]

Peace, as the Global Peace Index acknowledges, can be internal to a country as well as external. Democracy, governmental transparency, and a system that applies justice equally and fairly are all indicators of peace. But in addition to these quantifiable outward signs, peace is an energy. Without peaceful energy, there is no peace. And peaceful energy begins within each individual. In this chapter, we will look at peace from all of these aspects, with an emphasis on inner peace (the peace that we can create inside ourselves). So, unless otherwise indicated, by *peace* I mean *inner* peace. Inner peace is a reflection of *individual* peace. Outer peace, which reflects *collective* peace, is achieved or created when enough individuals have inner peace. We bring peace to the world by changing ourselves and, once we have peace, by helping others to change themselves. We can teach others peace, but only they can change themselves.

In *The Way: Using the Wisdom of Kabbalah for Spiritual Transformation and Fulfillment*, Michael Berg, codirector of the Kabbalah Centre, stresses that it is conflict at the personal level that really counts in our lives—such as how we interact with family and friends. "When sages speak of [attaining] peace through study, they refer to peace within ourselves. When each of us is at peace with the person we see when we look in the mirror, strife between nations will cease."[4]

Paramahansa Yogananda, the famous Indian yogi and guru who introduced many in the Western world to yoga and meditation through his best-selling book *Autobiography of a Yogi*, understood and taught that "peace in the world starts with peace in individual hearts."[5] In *Inner Peace: How to Be Calmly Active and Actively Calm*, Yogananda states that "peace emanates from the soul, and is the sacred inner environment in which true happiness unfolds."[6]

In our quest for peace, we face a number of problems, one of the most serious coming from the institution that is arguably the most responsible for bringing it about — religion. As Nobel Peace Prize winner Mairead Corrigan Maguire points out, "There can be no world peace until the great religions make peace with one another."[7] However, keep in mind that when Maguire refers to religion as a barrier to peace, she is referring to *external* peace — that is, to collective peace, a peaceful environment. As individuals, we can always have *internal* peace, irrespective of our external environment or what the religions of the world do.

Religion, *the foremost barrier to peace?* Ironic, isn't it? For many religious people, that must be difficult to accept. But consider the following: Of the major religions most involved in world warfare, three "share" common holy ground. They also share the fact of having organizational structures dominated by males who have largely excluded holistic women from scriptural interpretation and leadership roles, except at relatively low levels. And as we have seen, males, being left-brain dominant, tend to be separation oriented rather than unification oriented, selfish rather than sharing, competitive rather than cooperative, and prone to the use of force to get what they want. Since religion is largely directed by left-brain-dominant males — especially at the higher and more competitive levels — this means that religion is directed by individuals who, as a whole, are poorly equipped to share, poorly equipped to cooperate, and poorly equipped to maintain peace. To that, add the salient fact that this shared holy ground lies in an area that has a long history of extreme violence—something we might expect, since it lies in close proximity to what is thought to be the cradle of civilization.

As early populations grew, those inclined to fight in order to remain where they were born would have stayed in the area, reproduced, and passed on their violent values. Peaceful individuals born into this environment, reluctant to fight, would naturally have been inclined to leave, preferring the security of colder climes to war, and in the process creating an ever-intensifying concentration of individuals with violent tendencies. The more peaceful you were, the farther you would have had to travel in order to escape the violence. Thus, centuries later, we see peace awards being handed out in cold, peaceful Sweden and in neighboring Norway, which ranked as the world's most peaceful country in the 2008 survey previously mentioned. Four Scandinavian countries—Denmark, Norway, Finland, and Sweden—all made it into the top 10 in both the 2008 and 2009 surveys. Coming in dead last in both peace surveys we find a country (Iraq) from the heart of a region of endless fighting— which is also the region where the three great monotheistic religions were birthed; while its neighbor Israel (although a democracy) was two positions from the bottom in 2008, and three in 2009. When you pass your revenge on from generation to generation, it never ends. The deception of hate will not allow it (hate blinds, and blinded, we are more easily deceived). You live with hate or you leave.

Because so much of the violence on the world stage radiates outward from the cradle of western civilization, let's survey that locale for a moment from the perception of an Israeli theoretical physicist (and chair of the Davidson Institute of Science Education), Haim Harari, whose family has lived in the region for almost 200 years. Providing what he calls the views of the "proverbial taxi driver," Harari reminds us that the ongoing

Arab-Israeli conflict is far from the only source of strife in this part of the world. In fact, his blunt assessment is that "this entire . . . region [stretching from Morocco to Pakistan] is totally dysfunctional." He cites the war in Sudan, where Arabs slaughter black Christians; the on-and-off violence in Algeria; Iraq's invasion of Kuwait and its war with Iran; the elder Assad of Syria, who killed tens of thousands of his own citizens in one week; the Taliban in Afghanistan. Harari mentions the Saudi role in 9/11 and other acts of force, often directed toward women who come into conflict with rules severely restricting their rights, noting that the social status of women in the Arab world is "far below what it was in the Western world 150 years ago." And the dysfunctionality of this region goes well beyond the issue of women's rights or sectarian struggles, Harari points out. "According to a report prepared by a committee of Arab intellectuals and published under the auspices of the U.N., the number of books translated by the entire Arab world is much smaller than what little Greece alone translates." The region's poverty and general state of cultural decline, he suggests, create a "breeding ground for cruel dictators, terror networks, [and] fanaticism." Harari acknowledges that most Muslims are not part of the violence that we find in this region, but neither do they actively oppose it. Afraid to express their views, they become double victims — victims of their own environment and victims of an outside world that has developed Islamophobia.[8]

How does one calm the agitated head and bring peace to the heart? Yogananda suggests an approach long advocated by wise men and women — meditation. "When . . . human knowing and feeling [is] calmed by meditation," he explains, "the ordinary agitated ego gives way to the blessed calmness of soul perception."[9] Once one has filled one's reservoir with peace, he says, this calmness then "pours out freely to one's family, friends, community, nation, and the world. If everyone lived the ideals exemplified in the life of Jesus, having made those qualities a part of their own selves through meditation, a millennium of peace and brotherhood would come on earth."[10]

In *Change Your Thoughts—Change Your Life: Living the Wisdom of the Tao*, Wayne W. Dyer, internationally renowned author and speaker in the field of self-development, reminds us of the wisdom traditionally attributed to the Chinese Taoist philosopher Lao-tzu (sixth century BCE), who wrote or inspired the Tao Te Ching. This seminal work of Taoism taught a path to peace that comes from living without force. "Force creates a counterforce, and this exchange goes on and on until all-out war is in progress," in the words of Dyer. He quotes from and then expands on the Tao Te Ching, which states, "You must never think of conquering others by force. Whatever strains with force will soon decay. It is not attuned to the Way." The Tao Te Ching, Dyer says, encourages us to look for alternatives to force when we need to settle a dispute. Moreover, it suggests that if we can find no other option, we need to abandon any reference to ourselves as winners or conquerors. "The Great Way of Tao," Dyer explains, "is that of cooperation, not competition."[11] And, of course, as we know, the way of cooperation is the way of the right brain; the way of competition is the way of the left brain.

A discussion of peace is useful, but keep in mind that words are instruments through which we seek to express feeling. Want peace? Seek the *feeling* of peace. When seeking peace, monitor your feelings for guidance. Those of us who are left-brain dominant tend to focus on thoughts and are relatively separated from our feelings (compared with right-brain dominants)—at least until our feelings overwhelm us or otherwise demand our attention. Thoughts, and the energies they create, can help orient us toward peace, but remember that peace is a *felt* experience. By changing our external environment (escaping its irritants), we can often lessen feelings of conflict, but to have real peace, we have to change internally—which means that our personal attitudes, actions, and feelings must change.

To move in the direction of peace, imagine the feeling of love, the feeling of peace, and the feeling of freedom as being connected parts of a whole rather than separated out. *Be love, peace, and freedom*, and know that your peace is only as strong as the weakest of these three. Now, having established your internal environment, turn outward and imagine a peaceful environment. And be there now without regret of the past or stress over the future. For a moment, let every thought and every action go, and just be and feel peace. When you strip away all your attachments, what you are left with is your essential self, which is now and always at peace. Even if, a moment later, life rushes back in, be grateful for the present moment and recognize that, with practice, a moment can grow into seconds, seconds into minutes, and minutes into hours and days. When you want to reward yourself for some reason, instead of turning outward to your favorite addiction for a feeling of satisfaction, consider turning inward and rewarding yourself with a peaceful moment.

Peace, Like Nonattachment, Is a Choice

Because we are gods, our default setting is peace. Spirit, unless it chooses to experience something other than the default, experiences the peace of harmony continually. But once we give it up, as we do when we live on this planet, it is not easy to regain, given the programming we acquire as we grow up (mental attachments in the form of beliefs). Peace is a function of our beliefs, as we see in the fact that the beliefs of a terrorist are what create a terrorist. And since we have the freedom to choose our beliefs, peace becomes a function of the choice of beliefs that we make. Jeshua (Jesus), a spirit-presence who identifies himself as the author of *A Course in Miracles*, speaks the following to Brent Haskell in *Journey Beyond Words: A Companion to the Workbook of the Course*:

> All it takes to walk this earth in peace
> Is to know that as Spirit
> You are the creative source —
> And nothing can ever happen to you
> That is not totally your own choice.
> And all it takes to walk this earth in peace
> Is to know that God, and you,
> Are love,
> And freedom,
> And peace,
> And joy.[12]

If we are truly gods, and if our lives are ours to control, why then do so few of us have peace?

An entire book could be written in answer to this question, but it's fair to say that we are immersed in war, because war is so much a part of our cultural expression — our cultural self is at war. As a result, we have few peaceful role models to help guide us out of war, and without such role models it often becomes difficult to see our alternatives, difficult to understand who we are, and difficult to recognize how powerful we are when we use peaceful means to solve our problems. And challenging problems come up; impatience overcomes us; and to create the circumstances we think we need in order to succeed, we resort to the ubiquitous cultural left brain's solution — force. This creates conflict and blurs (if not obscures) the internal harmony that is our guide to peace and its freedom. Force, we quickly learn, gives us leverage. Even the threat of force often produces wanted results. Culturally, we have a long tradition of using force to get what we want, force being a default response of left-brain dominants.

When we do manage to find our way to peace—when we at last still the voice within that is constantly demanding an attachment to certain things and relationships (a list that for many of us seems to be never-ending)—we inevitably find that our peace is difficult to maintain. We are constantly bombarded with reasons to fight.

Why is it that our attachments lead to war? To find out, let's examine the nature of attachments. The object of our attachment can be physical (perhaps some big new, shiny purchase), mental (beliefs that give us comfort), spiritual (relationships and feelings), or a combination of these elements, such as physical and spiritual (sex being one example, emotions being another). Most attachments involve all three of these to some degree, though we often focus on only one of the three. Left-brain dominants (most men) tend to focus on the physical—cars, games, or things like work and investments that translate into prosperity and represent success. Right-brain dominants tend to focus on and associate with spiritual things, such as personal relationships, and feelings or emotions. Viewing life from the timelessness of an eternal perspective, right-brain dominants intuitively (but usually unconsciously) recognize that the spiritual energy system is the only real energy system because it involves things that do not disappear or disintegrate over time. Spiritual values, when attended to, remain and strengthen, whereas physical stuff tends to dissipate. Left-brain dominants can see this if they look, but are not inclined to look.

If we believe (are attached to the idea) that we must have a new car or a certain brand of clothing to be happy, to be at peace with our desire to acquire, we have created a situation in which our beliefs determine whether or not we can be happy and at peace. Material things can never truly bring us peace, but not having them can get in the way of our peace if we believe they are essential to our happiness. We feel a temporary sense of peace when we get (attach to) the things we believe we need, yet it is a sense that quickly dissipates once the new distraction is no longer new and no longer distracts. It is a system that must be fed.

Introduce people and accidents into this equation and the situation becomes explosive. Someone damages our valued possession (or terminates a relationship), and suddenly our attachment is damaged. Typically, we immediately abandon our peace (to the degree that we had it). We become upset! *We feel emotionally harmed.* Yet we have not been forced to feel harmed. People can't dictate how we feel; it's impossible. Feeling is an internal mental and spiritual response that only we are capable of controlling. If we feel bad about an external event, we *choose* to feel bad at some level of consciousness. This choice is not a rational one; it does not involve thought or deliberation. Instead, we simply react. Notice that the damage is not decreased or stabilized by our typical response; rather, it is increased. A response that is always harmful, but that we nevertheless continue to make, is really an insane choice. But this is how we've been taught to respond: someone hurts something of ours that we value (or apparently "hurts" us), and we respond by becoming upset, by hurting ourselves, and sometimes others.

So how do we detach? Must we detach from everything to have peace? In his book *Waking Up in Time: Finding Inner Peace in Times of Accelerating Change*, Peter Russell offers some clarification. Russell describes peace as "an intrinsic quality of life itself, not something that can be created or destroyed," but acknowledges that it can be eluded through attachment, and in explaining attachment, he starts by explaining what it is not. Sometimes nonattachment is misinterpreted as a withdrawal from life, such as "a lack of concern, a lack of responsibility, or a lack of feeling." But, says Russell, true nonattachment is when we are "no longer attached to the need for things or for events to be a certain way." The peace we seek comes when we "let go of the belief that what goes on around [us] determines whether or not [we are] content."[13]

The energetic link between physical reality (things) and spiritual reality (feelings) is, as we have said, mind—specifically, the beliefs we harbor in our mind. As a consequence, once we arrive at a state of consciousness that allows us to understand that physical reality is a creation of spiritual reality, we have an opportunity to disconnect from the drama. Knowing that only spiritual feeling is of real value, and that physical things are just tools and toys of spirit, we can simply take an adult attitude and avoid emotional fights over our tools and toys. If we feel it necessary to defend our territory (and it might sometimes be), we can still defend it, but then we can do so with an elevated attitude and with more positive physical and spiritual feelings. In essence, the emotional connection between things and feelings exists in potential—and through our intent, we can either actualize the connection or not. This is part of our creative choice. Beliefs, mobilized by intent and directed by attention, direct energy. Observe that when we experience a negative response to some damaging incident, our feelings correspond with our *beliefs* regarding the damage, not the damage itself. We can *believe* that we have been hurt by someone's actions, and consequently *feel* hurt, even though there was no hurtful action.

To escape the traditional response—that of choosing to be emotionally (internally) hurt by external events—we need to first acknowledge that being hurt is a choice. This acknowledgment may not come easy. For most of us, the choice to be hurt has become so habitual with lifelong repetition that it doesn't seem to be a choice at all. Add to that the fact that nearly everyone else seems to be responding in the same way, and that they expect us to respond in like manner, and we can see how our beliefs—and our choice to be hurt—are self-reinforcing.

Once we get past these barriers and decide to change our old response to damaging encounters, we must choose a replacement response. We must choose how to react to damage (physical, spiritual, and/or to our belief system). At this point—having made the choice to respond peacefully— the follow-up step is, of course, practice. Habitual patterns resist change.

The reality is that other people are able to manipulate our internal environment only when we let them—when we cooperate with them. We can learn to avoid stepping *out* of our peace—and learn to step back *into* it. It is not easy for most people to do, but people have been doing it for centuries, so it's not beyond our reach. Peace (internal peace) might be more easily attained than you think. As God reminds Neale Donald Walsch in *Conversations with God: An Uncommon Dialogue, Book 1,* "It is much easier to change what you are doing than to change what another is doing."[14]

What are some creative options we have for advancing peace? Following are some suggestions.

Seek harmony.

To create a greater experience of peace, cultivate harmony within yourself. As a start, bring the two polarized perspectives (the dualistic and the holistic) together so that they can take part in the same dance of life, rather than living in a struggle with one another. Let them fall in love with one another, and send your light of peace out into the universe. We have been taught that the two perspectives (and their typical counterparts in the political and social/cultural spheres, conservatism and liberalism) are opposites, one of which is bad, and that we must fight to defend our dominant perspective. We often encounter this attitude in social and political conservatives due to the strong drive for survival that comes with left-brain dominance, and commonly see this in the vigor with which they attack holistic ideas and perceptions, especially liberal ideology.

The fast track to peace, to spiritual harmony and its healing effects, shows up when we find ways to *appreciate* those who see reality from the opposite perspective—those we often view as the enemy. *Appreciation* is an extraordinarily potent spiritual energy. If you identify with conservatives and feel threatened by liberals, learning to appreciate their responses will result in being able to grow and be more creative in your own responses. If you identify with liberals and are uncomfortable with conservatives, learning to appreciate the opposing side will make them seem less of a threat to you and will make it easier to expand the scope of your holistic thinking and actions. None of this means that you must like or embrace opposing ideas—or even the sometimes ignorant people who espouse them; it simply means that they are no longer perceived as a threat. It means that you are at least open to considering those ideas and trying to see how they might benefit you and your culture.

To enhance your inner peace, harmonize your *ideas*; bring them to a state of peace with one another. One way to do this is to look for errors within your belief system by seeking conflict. Although truth is internally harmonious—and harmony is what we are after—it is perhaps best achieved by finding and removing conflict. Therefore, as an exercise in creating a harmony of belief, search for ideological conflict (such as we see, for example, in simultaneously harboring the belief that God is the essence of love and mercy along with the belief that God sends people to everlasting hell—a common but profoundly illogical combination) and find ways to resolve it. This process can take many forms. It might involve reconciling opposing points of view by recognizing common features and strengths on both sides. Or it might be much more complex, involving whole new ways of seeing things (for example, learning how to perceive and think holistically, or learning how to recognize arbitrary cultural pressures). Or the issues themselves might be of such complexity that we need to learn the art of critical observation. We also need to recognize that, to the extent that we use critical observation, we often use it as a weapon to attack ideas we don't like. Yet at the same time, *we often fail to apply this same process to our own ideas*. Becoming intelligently critical of our own ideas and being willing to change them is a fundamental benchmark for attaining truth.

To acquire internal peace, remember to *be* peace. The removal of conflict from among our ideas and our relationships frees up our natural internal peace and moves us toward hemispheric harmony. Harmony does not require us to balance the two hemispheres; rather, it requires that any conflict between the two be removed so that each accepts the other as a beloved teammate. It means that ideological territory is defended firmly, though not angrily, as when two good friends wrestle for fun. One friend—or one position—might be large enough to dominate, but will be smart enough to exercise restraint. Your dominant side will remain dominant, but with full respect for and appreciation of the nondominant side. If your dominant perspective is dualistic, make peace with holistic perspectives and processes, the beliefs they create and support, and the people who are guided by them, even those perceived as extremists. Acknowledge their value to you (for one thing, they tend to show you the context of your ideas and can help you refine them and make them stronger). If your dominant perspective is holistic, make peace with dualistic perspectives, processes, and beliefs. Understand that they bring you clarity, even if their wisdom is born out of conflict and out of details that seem unimportant from your holistic perspective.

Though we might think or speak of creating peace, remember that we don't actually *create* peace; it's already there. Instead, we have to get rid of the conflict that infects and thus distorts the harmony of peace.

Practice peace.

Consciousness wants to evolve. Writing in *Peace Is the Way: Bringing War and Violence to an End*, Deepak Chopra, bestselling author and lecturer on spirituality and mind-body medicine, describes military and industrial consciousness as forms of frozen consciousness, "emblems of the old order." Yet in spite of the considerable power of the military-industrial complex to affect our daily lives, he says, we are still in control: "The reins of change lie in our hands."[15] Chopra shares the reins by giving his readers seven practices to enhance peace, one for each day.

Expand your perspective.

To expand the scope of our peace, we can expand the scope of our perspective. When we expand our perspective, we enlarge our context, which means that we enlarge our body of information. This in turn expands our perception. With our perception sufficiently expanded, we are better able to understand the universe, and our fears and conflicts start to melt away—as we can see in this excerpt from *The Urantia Book*:

> In the mind's eye conjure up a picture of one of your primitive ancestors of cave-dwelling times—a short, misshapen, filthy, snarling hulk of a man standing, legs spread, club upraised, breathing hate and animosity as he looks fiercely just ahead. Such a picture hardly depicts the divine dignity of man. But allow us to enlarge the picture. In front of this animated human crouches a saber-toothed tiger. Behind him, a woman and two children. Immediately you recognize that such a picture stands for the beginnings of much that is fine and noble in the human race, but the man is the same in both pictures. Only in the second sketch you are favored with a widened horizon. You therein discern the motivation of this evolving mortal. His attitude becomes praiseworthy because you understand him. If you could only fathom the motives of

your associates, how much better you would understand them. If you could only know your fellows, you would eventually fall in love with them.[16]

With true love comes true peace.

Read about peace.

I will not attempt to provide a comprehensive list of books about peace here. The best result would come from your allowing your peaceful inner voice to lead you. However, if you have yet to recognize your inner voice, I offer three possibilities here for a start. The first is a powerful soul-oriented book and perhaps the easiest to read and understand, as well as the most directly associated with inner peace. The second is more philosophically oriented: because it helps the mind understand life and its structure, it can also help to dispel fear, and therefore it can help return us to a state of peace. Both of these books are relatively short and powerful, and focused (relatively) on individual actions that can be taken. The third suggestion offers a road map toward achieving collective peace—peace in the outer world, but from a distinctly spiritual perspective.

My first suggestion is a book recommended by His Holiness the Dalai Lama. *Peace Is Every Step: The Path of Mindfulness in Everyday Life* is written by Thich Nhat Hanh, expatriate Vietnamese Zen Buddhist master, poet, and peace activist. The Dalai Lama states in the book's foreword that "love, compassion, and altruism are the fundamental basis for peace," and he summarizes the importance of this book as follows: "Thich Nhat Hanh begins by teaching mindfulness of breathing and awareness of the small acts of our daily lives, then shows us how to use the benefits of mindfulness and concentration to transform and heal difficult psychological states. Finally he shows us the connection between personal, inner peace and peace on Earth."[17]

As we have stated, peace appears to start in the mind with our beliefs. For a more mind-based approach to the development of inner peace (and a more challenging—but also entertaining—read), I recommend *The Integral Vision: A Very Short Introduction to the Revolutionary Integral Approach to Life, God, the Universe, and Everything,* by philosopher Ken Wilber (Shambhala, 2007). Unlike the other books mentioned, this one does not deal explicitly with peace. Yet the integral, holistic vision it lays out can have a highly liberating effect on our mind and bring it to a state of profound inner peace; and Wilber's approach can greatly assist our understanding and appreciation of *all* points of view, which is a critical prerequisite to the achievement of outer peace as well. A master at crossing disciplines and showing how everything relates to everything else, Wilber uses left-brain analytical tools to open the mind of soul to a right-brain holistic perspective. It is this inclusiveness that brings peace.

With his integral vision, Wilber looks at the various world cultures and systems of thought to see what they reveal about human potential, and identifies the patterns that connect their knowledge. From this he creates an all-inclusive map (an "Integral Operating System"). By giving us a comprehensive description of the fundamental nature of our environment, Wilber's map works to help us better understand who and where we are, and thus it dispels fear and allows our peace to be felt.

For a greater understanding of collective peace, I recommend Adi Da's *Not-Two Is Peace: The Ordinary People's Way of Global Cooperative Order.* Adi Da (an American spiritual master whose work gave birth to the Global Cooperation Project) says that if we are to have peace, the people of the planet will have to band together as one and wrest control from power- and money-oriented organizations through a global cooperative forum—in other words, unify and draw on the power of unity, and thus manage our affairs from a position of strength. "Virtually every kind of human collective—a household, a family, a village, a country, and so on—is made subject to agreements, limits, laws, rules, and means of keeping it straight, productive, and positive. The totality of the human world is an exception to this. Humankind as a whole is not managing itself. Instead, it is managing all of its separate, 'tribalized' elements. There is no instrument of order applied to the whole." But he warns us that this will not be easy and explains why. "There is terrific political resistance to the notion of a true global cooperative. However, what must be understood is that a true global cooperative order is <u>not</u> a globally-extended super-state (which would be a kind of totalitarian power), but a global cooperative order in which all freely participate. The globally-extended super-state," Adi Da says, "is what the big warrior-states are moving toward" and must be stopped. For Adi Da's vision to be achieved, a way must be found to connect the people of the planet, to harness their inherent unity (or "prior unity," as he calls it). "That means that the total human collective, or everybody-all-at-once, must become conscious of itself," something that has never before been done.[18]

Traditional Paths to Peace

Although the dualistic, separative perspective (which has dominated the male outlook throughout history) is reflected in much of the history of religions, including the founding scriptures, all traditional religions have at their core a strong message of peace. Ironically, this message can be found most explicitly and radically in the teachings of Jesus himself—I say "ironically" because the Christian tradition throughout its long history has been anything but peaceful. The teachings of the Buddha (Siddhartha Gautama), although different in emphasis, lead to similarly radical conclusions (such as the belief that we are gods, and therefore we have everything and are service oriented, rather than self oriented). Below is a small but instructive sampling of such radical traditional teachings.

The Christian Mind on Peace

The Jewish/Christian Old Testament reflects a collective culture dominated by males whose lives and beliefs are largely restricted to a focused, separative, linear, dualistic perspective due to their brain dominance. The God we see from this perspective is separate from man. The New Testament offers a more holistic perspective. In Mark 9:38–41, for example, we see the disciple John and others encounter a man who is healing in the name of Jesus, one with whom they are unfamiliar. Having yet to shed their dualistic attitudes, and seeing the man as separate from them, the disciples try to stop him. Their response reflects a typical left-brain attitude that dislikes someone infringing on one's territory. Unable to mentally bridge the distance between Jesus's work and the man trying to do good in Jesus's name, they view the man as being separate from the ministry of Jesus and a competitor. The response of Jesus when they tell him of the incident is one of inclusion, a holistic response: Don't try to stop him. Don't give in to your left brain's force-based response. Leave him alone (let him keep his freedom to follow his heart). Let him help us (reflecting the right brain's inclusiveness). "He that is not against us is for us," he says (referencing a dualistic perspective, but informed by a broad, holistic view). When Jesus comes upon a woman caught in adultery who is about to be stoned according to Old Testament law (John 8:1–11), he responds in a similar way. He comes to her rescue with his inclusive perspective. In effect, he is saying that whatever choices she has made, she is still one of us. She is an individual and deserving of our love and her freedom. Be forgiving. Don't judge. In trying to maintain the peace, Jesus embodies the holistic (liberal) stance, which embraces but transcends the dualistic (conservative) stance.

Buddha Mind on Peace

People tend to view Buddhism as a religion, but according to Robert Thurman, professor of Indo-Tibetan Buddhist Studies at Columbia University, "The Buddha founded an educational movement rather than a religion. His vision was to bring out our own wisdom rather than to assert the truth. . . . In that sense, the Buddha was a scientist—a noetic scientist. He understood that the most important factor in the quality of life for a human being is how the person's mind is managed." The Buddha therefore focused on human beings, on the transformation of human consciousness, rather than on God.[19] Having said that, I do not wish to leave the impression that the Buddha did not believe in God, as some have concluded. As Thurman explains, "Buddha was not a religious prophet, but he was not an atheist either. He actually was said to have met the Hindu god Brahma during his transformative experience."[20]

Ron Epstein, research professor at the Institute for World Religions in Berkeley, California, explains, "Buddhists believe that the minds of all living beings are totally interconnected and interrelated, whether they are consciously aware of it or not." Like a combined radio station and radio, mind constantly transmits and receives. "Even the most insignificant thoughts in our minds have some effect on all other beings. . . . Each thought in the mind of each and every one of us brings the world either a little closer to the brink of global disaster or helps to move the world a little farther away from the brink," Epstein tells us.[21] "Buddhism teaches that whether we have global peace or global war is up to us at every moment. . . . Peace or war is our decision. The fundamental goal of Buddhism is peace. . . . The Buddha taught that peaceful minds lead to peaceful speech and peaceful actions."[22]

Control of Our Thoughts and Creations

Consider the perspective of a collective known as the Hathors, a group of ascended beings who claim to have energetically worked with Tibetan lamas in the formative period of Tibetan Buddhism, as well as with the ancient Egyptians and others.[23] (Hathor likenesses—now associated with the goddess Hator—are prominently located in several ancient Egyptian temples.) Masters of love and sound (vibration), the Hathors currently work through a number of individuals. One who has written a book about his experiences is the scientist, sound healer, shaman, psychotherapist, and musician Tom Kenyon. In *The Hathor Material*, the collective advises, "Nothing can be done without the power of God because the power of One is what sustains, creates and continues all realms. Yet one has free will to do certain types of actions within whatever level one has achieved or entered. Ultimately it is God that does it all. However, within each realm where beings have choice, they experience the results of their creation, whether it be positive or negative. *One must experience the results of one's own creation* [emphasis added]."[24]

Our interactions with life energies have consequences, physical, mental, and spiritual. Thoughts, words, and deeds move energy toward peace or toward war. In *Peace Is Every Step: The Path of Mindfulness in Everyday Life*, Thich Nhat Hanh advises us of the importance of being mindful of the *quality* of the energy flows to which we attach. That naturally includes the energies we attach to when we create our entertainment—and they are not always helpful, which is why we need to be mindful. "Our senses are our windows to the world," he says, "and sometimes the wind blows through our openings and disturbs everything within us. Some of us leave our windows open all of the time, allowing the sights and sounds of the world to invade us. . . . Do you ever find yourself watching an awful TV program, unable to turn it off?"

he asks. "Why do you torture yourself in this way? . . . Watching a bad TV program, we become the TV program." To expose ourselves like this is "leaving our fate in the hands of others who may not be acting responsibly. We must be aware of which programs do harm to our nervous systems, minds, and hearts, and which programs benefit us." And, he adds, "I am not talking only about television"; we are in fact surrounded by many lures, and we must constantly be mindful of protecting our peace.[25]

In *Conversations with God: An Uncommon Dialogue, Book 3*, we are given similar advice:

> Thought control is the highest form of prayer. Therefore, think only on good things, and righteous. Dwell not in negativity and darkness. And even in moments when things look bleak—especially in those moments—see only perfection, express only gratefulness, and then imagine only what manifestation of perfection you choose next. In this formula is found tranquility. In this process is found peace. In this awareness is found joy. . . . When you leave the body, it will . . . be a big surprise to see the instant and obvious connection between your thoughts and your creations. It will be a shocking surprise at first, and then a very pleasant one, as you begin to remember that you are at cause in the creation of your experience, not at the effect of it.[26]

If this advice to "think only on good things" and "see only perfection" seems impossible to fulfill, remember that *we are gods*, capable of immense acts of creativity—in fact, we perform such creative acts every moment of our lives. And the most truly creative act of all is, first, to recognize the relationship between our thoughts and our creations, and then to control our own thought forms in the manner described above. This will bring an indescribable peace and joy that radiate outward into the world, transforming our individual and collective lives.

Remember also that all of us (whatever our hemispheric dominance) have been given a right brain hemisphere that is already intimately familiar with this creative process. Many of us (even right-brain-dominant people) are unaware of what our right brain already knows, because we have been so thoroughly trained to disregard its input. It has been a primary purpose of this book to assist in breaking down these barriers in order to release more of our own creativity and our own magnificence.

As a final reminder of how our right brain functions, *and how we can use it to achieve inner and outer peace,* we return to the invaluable insights of Jill Bolte Taylor, the brain scientist who—as a result a massive hemorrhagic stroke in her left brain hemisphere—was able to observe firsthand (with all her scientific curiosity intact) the workings and experiences of the right brain hemisphere unmediated by the left. She describes that experience as "nirvana," and in the following words (from a talk given in Monterey, California, in 2008), she unequivocally states that such an experience of peace and joy is available to all of us.

> We have the power to choose, moment by moment, who and how we want to be in the world. Right here, right now, I can step into the consciousness of my right hemisphere, where we are—I am—the life-force power of the universe . . . at one with all that is. Or, I can choose to step into the consciousness of my left hemisphere, where I become a single individual, a solid—separate from the flow, separate from you. . . . Which would you choose? Which *do* you choose—and when? I believe that the more time we spend choosing to run the deep inner-peace circuitry of our right hemisphere, the more peace we will project into the world, and the more peaceful our planet will be.[27]

Peace.

Acknowledgments

The project that evolved into this book began about 30 years ago. Due to the time involved, it is no longer possible to remember some of the smaller contributions, but to all who have had a part in bringing this work to print I offer my deepest appreciation.

Among those whose contribution cannot possibly be forgotten, first and foremost I acknowledge that of my late friend David "Buddha" Ashbaucher. Not only did Buddha challenge me to think on a deeper level that could be accomplished only through the discipline of writing, but he also gave me a copy of *Zen and the Art of Motorcycle Maintenance*. Perhaps more than any other factor, this book inspired me to write a book of my own. And Buddha introduced me to *The Urantia Book* through a copy loaned to him by the late Berkeley Elliot. Although several years passed before I acquired my own copy of the book and read it, ultimately it was through Buddha that I first became aware of the existence of modern revelation.

Other friends who failed to live long enough to see this project to completion include Georgia Parks, who guided me as I struggled to learn how to put my ideas into written form, and author Mike McQuay, who gave me writing lessons and inspiration to help me transition the early difficult days. Most of all I thank my loving parents, Miles and Nellie Olson, for their generosity in providing me with the financial, educational, and spiritual resources I required in order to survive the years of work that it took to produce this book.

Lawrence "Scotty" Schkade introduced me to the subject of brain lateralization and gave me valuable guidance on a couple of occasions, and for this I am eternally grateful. Had I not attended one of his weekend workshops, during which I had my brain mapped, this book would have taken a substantially different form.

I deeply appreciate the many authors whose contributions have enriched this book. Special thanks to Robert Ornstein for his insights into the workings of the brain, to Ken Wilber for his discoveries and writings on the fundamental nature of wholes, to Neale Donald Walsch for publishing his enlightening conversations with God, and to Drunvalo Melchizedek, Tom Kenyon, and Judi Sion for their introductions to sacred geometry.

Thanks to David Muir for introducing me to the *Conversations with God* series, Steven Danford for suggesting that I look into the work of Adi Da, and Mike Bridenstine for assistance with the author photograph and early consultation on cover design.

To my editors and publisher I extend my profound gratitude. Vesela Simic was the first editor to see the manuscript and helped grind off some of the rough edges. Larry Boggs was next to work on it, spent the most time and effort, and was the most instrumental in shaping it into a readable work. Elissa Rabellino then took over and helped polish the manuscript and bring it into its final form. Finally, thanks to my publisher, Byron Belitsos, whose wisdom and guidance was of immense assistance in bringing this project to fruition.

Notes

Chapter 1

1. JewishEncyclopedia.com, s.v. "Pharisees," http://www.jewishencyclopedia.com/view.jsp?artid=252&letter=P (accessed April 7, 2010).

2. *Eight Translation New Testament* (Wheaton, IL: Tyndale House, 1974), 558–59. *King James Bible, Living Bible, Today's English Version*, and *New International Version* all translate this statement "is within you." *Phillips Modern English* translates this "is inside you"; the *Revised Standard Version* "in the midst of you"; *Jerusalem Bible* and *New English Bible* "is among you."

3. Thich Nhat Hanh, *Living Buddha, Living Christ* (New York: Riverhead Books, 1995), 37–38.

4. Nithyananda, *You Are God: Discourse on Bhagavad Gita, Chapter 2* (Bangalore: Nithyananda Foundation, 2006), 210.

5. Paramahansa Yogananda, *The Second Coming of Christ: The Resurrection of the Christ Within You*, vol. 1 (Los Angeles: Self-Realization Fellowship, 2004), xxv.

6. *A Course in Miracles—Text*, 2nd ed. (Glen Ellen, CA: Foundation for Inner Peace, 1992), 5.

7. Brent Haskell, *Journey Beyond Words: A Companion to the Workbook of the Course* (Marina del Rey, CA: DeVorss & Co., 1994), 81.

8. Ibid., 30.

9. *The Urantia Book* (Chicago: Urantia Foundation, 1955), 10, 1260–67.

10. Ibid., 1273, 1278, 1458.

11. Neale Donald Walsch, *The New Revelations: A Conversation with God* (New York: Atria Books, 2002), 269.

12. Neale Donald Walsch, *Conversations with God: An Uncommon Dialogue, Book 3* (Charlottesville, VA: Hampton Roads, 1998), 140, 172–73.

13. Ibid., 200.

14. Neale Donald Walsch, *Friendship with God: An Uncommon Dialogue* (New York: G. P. Putnam's Sons, 1999), 183.

15. Neale Donald Walsch, *Tomorrow's God: Our Greatest Spiritual Challenge* (New York: Atria Books, 2004), 142.

Chapter 2

1. Walsch, *Conversations with God, Book 3*, 155.

2. *The Urantia Book*, 43.

3. Ken Wilber, *The Collected Works of Ken Wilber*, vol. 7, *A Brief History of Everything* (Boston: Shambhala, 2000), 70.

4. *A Course in Miracles—Text*, 155.

5. Bruce H. Lipton, *The Biology of Belief: Unleashing the Power of Consciousness, Matter and Miracles* (Santa Rosa, CA: Mountain of Love/Elite, 2005), 27.

6. Three Initiates, *The Kybalion, by Three Initiates: The Hermetic Philosophy* (Charleston, SC: Forgotten Books, 2008), 75.

7. Jeffrey Satinover, Scene 11, Disk 1, *What the Bleep!? Down the Rabbit Hole*, Quantum ed. DVD. (2004 Captured Light & Lord of the Wind Films; Beverly Hills: Twentieth Century Fox Home Entertainment, 2006.)

8. Bruce H. Lipton, "The Biology of Perception, the Psychology of Change, Retreat" (lecture and conversation), Breckenridge, CO, August 2007, http://www.spirit2000.com/docs/2007brochure.pdf.

9. *A Course in Miracles: Workbook for Students*, 2nd ed. (Glen Ellen, CA: Foundation for Inner Peace, 1992), 257–58.

10. Wilber, *The Collected Works of Ken Wilber*, 77.

Chapter 3

1. Ned Herrmann, *The Whole Brain Business Book: Unlocking the Power of Whole Brain Thinking in Organizations and Individuals* (New York: McGraw-Hill, 1996), 12–16.

2. Lawrence Schkade, e-mail message to author, May 24, 2007.

3. Sally P. Springer and Georg Deutsch, *Left Brain, Right Brain: Perspectives from Cognitive Neuroscience*, 5th ed. (New York: W. H. Freeman/Worth, 1998), 40.

4. Bruce H. Lipton, *The Biology of Belief: Unleashing the Power of Consciousness, Matter, and Miracles* (Santa Rosa, CA: Mountain of Love/Elite, 2005), 80.

5. Herrmann, *The Whole Brain Business Book*, 16–17.

6. Robert Ornstein, *The Right Mind: Making Sense of the Hemispheres* (New York: Harcourt Brace, 1997), 17, 18.

7. Herrmann, *The Whole Brain Business Book*, 17.

8. Fritjof Capra, *The Tao of Physics: An Exploration of the Parallels between Modern Physics and Eastern Mysticism*, 3rd ed. (Boston: Shambhala, 1991), 27.

9. Ornstein, *The Right Mind*, 157.

10. Ibid., 152

11. Ibid., 153–54.

12. It makes a lot of sense to state the situation this way: Disassembly does simplify and inform. However, one might legitimately claim that this approach leads us *away* from reality, since the truth (or reality) is holistic and unified and needs to be understood holistically. Only by *assembling* the components of reality do we eventually arrive at the truth. Nevertheless, to understand how to assemble them, it sometimes helps to first disassemble them.

13. Right-brain-dominant males exhibit this pattern of seeking multiple partners as well, but keep in mind that they also have a left brain that demands variety. Even when the left brain is subservient to the right, it still can be extraordinarily powerful,

especially when combined with male sex hormones. In fact, it's probably accurate to say that the effect of hormones simply overpowers brain perspective in many males.

14. Lipton, *The Biology of Belief*, 52.

15. *American Heritage Dictionary of the English Language*, 3rd ed., s.v. "continuum" (Boston: Houghton Mifflin, 1992).

16. This and much of the following discussion of sacred geometry and spheres can be found in Drunvalo Melchizedek, *2012: The Prophecies from the Heart* (DVD) (Santa Monica, CA: Arthouse, 2009).

17. Andrew Newberg and Mark Robert Waldman, *Why We Believe What We Believe: Uncovering Our Biological Need for Meaning, Spirituality, and Truth* (New York: Free Press, 2006), 94.

18. Ibid., 67.

19. Rita Carter, *Mapping the Mind* (Berkeley: University of California Press, 1998), 39.

Chapter 4

1. Carter, *Mapping the Mind*, 71.

2. William J. Sabol, Heather C. West, and Matthew Cooper, "Prisoners in 2008," *Bureau of Justice Statistics Bulletin*, http://bjs.ojp.usdoj.gov/index.cfm?ty=pbdetail&iid=1763 (accessed April 22, 2010). At the end of 2008, females made up 7 percent of the prison population.

3. Only God knows the score here, but total up the work of people like Joseph Stalin, Pol Pot, Mao Zedong, and Adolf Hitler, and it's clear that males have an overwhelming lead. If we ignore war and look at murder in the United States, we find, for example, that in 2005 (the most recent year for which government statistics are available), males were almost 10 times more likely than females to commit murder, according to the table "Homicide Trends in the U.S. (Trends by gender)," on the U.S. Department of Justice, Bureau of Justice Statistics site, http://bjs.ojp.usdoj.gov/content/homicide/gender.cfm (accessed April 22, 2010). I suspect that the ratio of men to women is even higher with respect

to the use of torture, but of course there are always exceptions, as suggested in this story in the *Daily Mail* (and *Mail Online*): "Dick Cheney and Condoleezza Rice 'authorised waterboarding torture of Al Qaeda prisoners,'" William Lowther), April 11, 2008, http://www.dailymail.co.uk/pages/live/ articles/news/news.html?in_article_id=558812&in_page_id=177 0 (accessed April 22, 2010). See also the *New York Times* Editorial Board blog (the Board) of April 23, 2008: "Condoleezza Rice: Teflon No More?" http://theboard.blogs.nytimes.com/ 2008/04/23/condoleezza rice teflon-no-more/?scp=1&sq=condoleezza%20Teflon&st=cse (accessed April 22, 2010); Jan Crawford Greenburg, Howard L. Rosenberg, and Ariane de Vogue, "Sources: Top Bush Advisors Approved 'Enhanced Interrogation,'" ABCNews.com, April 9, 2008, http://abcnews.go. com/TheLaw/LawPolitics/story?id=4583256&page=1 (accessed April 22, 20010); and Digby, "Torture Nation," *Hullabaloo*, April 13, 2008, http://digbysblog.blogspot.com/2008/04/torture-nation-by-digby-in-keeping-with.html (accessed April 22, 2010).

4. Mark Mazzetti, "Spy Agencies Say Iraq War Worsens Terrorism Threat," *New York Times*, September 24, 2006, http://www.nytimes.com/2006/09/24/world/middleeast/24terror.html (accessed April 22, 2010).

5. Gary R. Renard, *The Disappearance of the Universe: Straight Talk About Illusions, Past Lives, Religion, Sex, Politics, and the Miracles of Forgiveness* (Carlsbad, CA: Hay House, 2004), 113.

6. *A Course in Miracles—Text*, 367.

7. Ibid., 205.

8. Capra, *The Tao of Physics*, 27.

9. Neale Donald Walsch, *Conversations with God: An Uncommon Dialogue, Book 2* (Charlottesville, VA: Hampton Roads, 1997), 55.

10. Gregg Braden, *Beyond Zero Point: The Journey to Compassion*, DVD (Arvada, CO: Gaiam/ConsciousWave, 2001).

11. Three Initiates, *The Kybalion*, 77.

12. *The Urantia Book*, 1583, 2047.

13. Ibid., 43.

14. Walsch, *Tomorrow's God*, 73.

15. Walsch, *Conversations with God, Book 2*, 173.

16. The right brain is nonconserving in the sense that it has the left brain to take care of that task. Holistically inclined individuals are on the forefront of conservation, not because their right brain seeks conservation, but because their left brain demands conservation and their right brain, being service oriented, spurs them into action. The holistic need not be concerned with conservation because conservation is taken care of: God recycles everything (energy) automatically. The universe's abundance of unlimited resources coupled with automatic recycling frees the holistic perspective to be liberal with resources. This characteristic of holistically directed individuals can be seen in the conservative complaint that liberals, who tend to be holistic in perspective and process, are wasteful.

Chapter 5

1. Jill Bolte Taylor, "My Stroke of Insight," http://www.ted.com/speakers/jill_bolte_taylor.html (accessed February 27, 2010).

2. Drunvalo Melchizedek, *The Ancient Secret of the Flower of Life*, vol. 2 (Flagstaff, AZ: Light Technology Publishing, 2000), 375.

3. Itzhak Bentov, *Stalking the Wild Pendulum: On the Mechanics of Consciousness* (Rochester, VT: Destiny Books, 1988) 117.

4. Ohiyesa, "Native American Tradition: The Ways of the Spirit," in *One: Essential Writings on Nonduality*, ed. Jerry Katz (Boulder, CO: Sentient Publications, 2007), 84. Although Ohiyesa refers to mind here, when we read his full description of right and left mind, we see that it closely correlates with what we have learned about the left and right brain.

5. Robert Lawlor, *Sacred Geometry: Philosophy and Practice* (London: Thames & Hudson, 1982), 10.

6. Martin Gray, *Sacred Earth: Places of Peace and Power* (New York: Sterling Publishing, 2007), 8, 9.

7. This and more can be found in Melchizedek, *The Ancient Secret of the Flower of Life*, vol. 1, 29.

8. Of course, there are always exceptions. A flock of geese flying in formation exhibits, or comes very close to exhibiting, precise geometry.

9. Ornstein, *The Right Mind*, 120.

10. Ibid., 14.

11. Ibid., 68.

12. This is not to say that the left brain does not see relationships. Rather, this statement reflects the common perception of the right brain as the relationship brain. It appears that the left brain sees linear relationships, which are nested in the multidimensional relationships of the right brain.

Chapter 6

1. Terry M. Clark, "A Manifesto—I must be a conservative," Coffee with Clark, *Edmond Life & Leisure*, August 19, 2004.

2. Andrew Rice, "When liberals win conservative awards," Commentary, *Oklahoma Gazette*, December 8, 2004.

3. Wilber, *The Collected Works of Ken Wilber*, 7.

4. Ibid., 37.

5. Ibid., 38.

6. See Don Edward Beck and Christopher Cowan, *Spiral Dynamics: Mastering Values, Leadership and Change* (Malden, MA: Blackwell, 1996).

7. Peter G. Peterson, *Running on Empty: How the Democratic and Republican Parties Are Bankrupting Our Future and What Americans Can Do About It* (New York: Farrar, Straus & Giroux, 2004), 146.

8. "Democratic Sen. Zell Miller Delivers Keynote at Republican Convention," *ABC News*, September 1, 2004, http://a.abcnews.com/Politics/Vote2004/story?id=123470&page=1 (accessed June 16, 2010).

9. This is obviously a highly idealistic appraisal of a party that often fails to achieve its goals. We all know that many Democrats are self-serving—and this is especially true of the leadership—but as

a whole, reflecting their dominant brain perspective, right-brain-dominant Democrats tend to be biased toward the collective—service to others.

10. *The Urantia Book*, 1478.

Chapter 7

1. William Bonner and Addison Wiggin, *Empire of Debt: The Rise of an Epic Financial Crisis* (Hoboken, NJ: John Wiley & Sons, 2006), 14.

2. Kevin Phillips, *Wealth and Democracy: A Political History of the American Rich* (New York: Broadway Books, 2002), xviii.

3. *A Course in Miracles—Text*, 440.

4. Robert Ornstein and Paul Ehrlich, *New World New Mind: Moving Toward Conscious Evolution* (New York: Doubleday, 1989), 59, 151.

5. Bonner and Wiggin, *Empire of Debt*, 306.

6. Ernest Hemingway, "Notes on the Next War: A Serious Topical Letter," orig. published in *Esquire*, September 1935, from *By-Line Ernest Hemingway: Selected Articles and Dispatches of Four Decades* (ed. William White; New York: Scribner, 1998); reproduced at http://www.fullposter.com/snippets.php?snippet=139 (posted October 14, 2007; accessed March 9, 2010).

7. Jamie Court, *Corporateering: How Corporate Power Steals Your Personal Freedom and What You Can Do About It* (New York: Tarcher/Putnam, 2003), 44.

8. Paul Krugman, *The Great Unraveling: Losing Our Way in the New Century* (New York: W. W. Norton, 2003), 122.

9. Phillips, *Wealth and Democracy*, 418.

10. "With One Word, Bernanke Reveals Who Actually Runs the Country," Washington's Blog, March 4, 2009, http://georgewashington2.blogspot.com/2009/03/with-one-word-bernanke-reveals-who.html (accessed June 17, 2010).

11. David Sirota, "Big Money vs. Grassroots: The Fight for the Heart of the Democratic Party," *Washington Spectator*, September 1, 2006, 1–3.

12. David Cay Johnston, *Perfectly Legal: The Covert Campaign to Rig Our Tax System to Benefit the Super Rich—and Cheat Everybody Else* (New York: Portfolio, 2003), 10.

13. Ibid., 2.

14. Phillips, *Wealth and Democracy*, 326.

15. Ibid., 413–14.

16. Patrick J. Buchanan, *Where the Right Went Wrong: How Neoconservatives Subverted the Reagan Revolution and Hijacked the Bush Presidency* (New York: Thomas Dunne, 2004), 210.

17. Jack Faris, "This Monopoly Is No Game," *Alva Review Courier*, March 8, 2005.

18. *NOW with Bill Moyers*, "Big Media," January, 30, 2004—Media Regulation Timeline chart, http://www.pbs.org/now/politics/mediatimeline.html (accessed February 2, 2010).

19. Ibid.

20. Ibid.

21. *NOW with Bill Moyers*, transcript of January 30, 2004 broadcast, http://www.pbs.org/now/printable/transcript305_full_print.html (accessed June 20, 2010).

22. Buchanan, *Where the Right Went Wrong*, 7–8.

23. Ibid., 211–13.

24. Howard Buffett, "Human Freedom Rests on Gold Redeemable Money," *Commercial and Financial Chronicle*, May 6, 1948.

25. Ted Nace, *Gangs of America: The Rise of Corporate Power and the Disabling of Democracy* (San Francisco: Berrett-Koehler Publishers, 2003), 1.

26. See Beck and Cowan, *Spiral Dynamics*.

27. Lou Dobbs, *Exporting America: Why Corporate Greed Is Shipping American Jobs Overseas* (New York: Warner Business Books, 2004), 1.

28. Marjorie Kelly, *The Divine Right of Capital: Dethroning the Corporate Aristocracy* (San Francisco: Berrett-Koehler Publishers, 2003), 5.

29. Ibid., 3.

30. Ibid., 8–9.

31. Court, *Corporateering*, 4.

32. *NOW with Bill Moyers*, transcript of February 18, 2005, broadcast, http://www.pbs.org/now/transcript/transcriptNOW107_full.html (accessed February 3, 2010).

33. Court, *Corporateering*, 200.

34. Ibid., 199.

35. Ibid., 201.

36. *NOW with Bill Moyers*, transcript of December 17, 2004, broadcast, http://www.pbs.org/now/transcript/transcript351_full.html (accessed March 9, 2010).

37. John C. Bogle, "What We Must Do to Restore Owners Capitalism," Bogle Financial Markets Research Center, October 1, 2003, http://www.vanguard.com/bogle_site/sp20031001.html (accessed March 9, 2010).

38. Kelly, *The Divine Right of Capital*, xiii–xiv.

39. Nace, *Gangs of America*, 222.

40. Ibid., 241–42.

41. Ibid., 206.

42. After a letter-writing campaign, Texaco made a "good will" payment that partially covered the loss of income. BNSF initially offered $500. After this writing but prior to publication, BNSF paid $2,000 in damages after I signed an agreement in which BNSF denied any responsibility.

43. Court, *Corporateering*, 41–42.

44. Thom Hartmann, "Now Corporations Claim the 'Right to Lie,'" January 1, 2002, http://www.thomhartmann.com/2003/01/01/now-corporations-claim-the-right-to-lie/ (accessed March 9, 2010).

45. Andrew Schneider and David McCumber, *An Air That Kills: How the Asbestos Poisoning of Libby, Montana, Uncovered a National Scandal* (New York: G. P. Putnam's Sons, 2004), 23, 92–93, 166–67, 180, 383, 166, 195. May 8, 2009 update: A

federal jury acquitted the company, along with three former executives, of all charges. Defense lawyers argued that "the asbestos danger in Libby was no secret to the federal government." Update from http://www.bloomberg.com/apps/news?pid=2060108 7&sid=a2KONaswwu1Y&refer=home (accessed March 9, 2010).

46. Renard, *The Disappearance of the Universe*, 24, 337.

47. "Bechtel vs. Bolivia," the Democracy Center, http://www.democracyctr.org/bolivia/investigations/water/ (accessed June 28, 2010).

48. "Spain, the Lawless Sea," *Frontline*, http://www.pbs.org/frontlineworld/stories/spain/thestory.html (accessed March 9, 2010).

49. "Thousands of Prestige oil spill volunteers suffer health problems," *Olive Press*, June 21, 2007, http://theolivepress.es/2007/06/21/thousands-of-prestige-oil-spill-volunteers-suffer-health-problems/ (accessed October 4, 2008).

50. "Prestige Oil Spill," Wapedia article, http://wapedia.mobi/en/Prestige_oil_spill (accessed February 4, 2010).

51. Lipton, *The Biology of Belief*, 138. Lipton cites Gary Greenberg, "Is It Prozac? Or Placebo?" *Mother Jones*, November/December, 2003, 76–81.

52. Peter Russell, *Waking Up in Time: Finding Inner Peace in Times of Accelerating Change* (Novato, CA: Origin Press, 1998), 65.

53. Walsch, *Conversations with God, Book 3*, 216.

54. Buchanan, *Where the Right Went Wrong*, 15.

55. *NOW with Bill Moyers*, transcript of December 5, 2003, broadcast, http://www.pbs.org/now/transcript/transcript245_full.html (accessed March 9, 2010).

56. Catherine Austin Fitts, "Will Defense Run the 'Real' Stimulus Package?" Catherine Austin Fitts' Blog, January 9, 2009, http://solari.com/blog/?p=1983 (accessed February 4, 2010).

57. Franklin C. Spinney, "The Defense Reform Trap," *CounterPunch*, June 27, 2008, http://www.counterpunch.org/spinney06272008.html (accessed March 9, 2010).

58, Buckminster Fuller Institute, *The Buckminster Fuller Challenge* (film), http://challenge.bfi.org/movie (accessed February 5, 2010).

59. John C. Bogle, "What We Must Do to Restore Owners Capitalism," keynote speech, October 1, 2003, http://www.vanguard.com/bogle_site/sp20031001.html (accessed March 9, 2010).

60. Kelly, *The Divine Right of Capital*, xiv.

61. Ibid., 3.

62. Ibid., xiv.

63. Ibid., 15.

64. David Schweickart, *After Capitalism* (Lanham, MD: Rowan & Littlefield, 2002), quoted in Nace, *Gangs of America*, 240–41.

Chapter 8

1. *The Urantia Book*, 1220–21.

2. Walsch, *The New Revelations*, 166.

3. Ralph Metzner, *The Unfolding Self: Varieties of Transformative Experience* (Novato, CA: Origin Press, 1998), 130–31.

4. *A Course in Miracles—Text*, 155.

5. Ibid., 138.

6. Ronald K. Siegel, *Intoxication: Life in Pursuit of Artificial Paradise* (New York: Pocket Books, 1990), viii.

7. Russell, *Waking Up in Time*, 70.

8. Ibid.

9. Lester Grinspoon and James B. Bakalar, *Marihuana: The Forbidden Medicine* (New Haven: Yale University Press, 1993), ix–x, 3.

10. Jack Herer, *Hemp & The Marijuana Conspiracy: The Emperor Wears No Clothes*, ed. Chris Conrad, Lynn Osburn, and Judy Osburn (Van Nuys, CA: Hemp Publishing, 1992), 33.

11. "Deglamorising Cannabis," editorial, *Lancet* 346, no. 8985 (November 11, 1995).

12. "How Experts Rate Problem Substances," Medical Science, *New York Times*, August 2, 1994.

13. William Bonner, "A Looney Tunes United States," *Daily Reckoning*, letter, based on a story sent to him by the woman in the story, July 24, 2008, http://news.goldseek.com/DailyReckoning/1216926000.php.

14. Lynn Zimmer and John P. Morgan, *Marijuana Myths, Marijuana Facts: A Review of the Scientific Evidence* (New York: Lindesmith Center, 1997), 33.

15. Ibid., 37. For more on this subject, see Douglas A. McVay, ed., *Drug War Facts*, online edition, http://www.drugwarfacts.org/gatewayt.htm (accessed February 7, 2010).

16. *A Course in Miracles—Text*, 440.

17. Anna Kuchment, "Make That a Double," *Newsweek*, July 30, 2007, 48.

18. Daniel G. Amen, M.D., "New Study Links Coffee and Alzheimer's Disease," *Brain in the News*, January 19, 2009, http://www.mylinkupspace.com/node/486.

19. Jacob Sullum, *Saying Yes: In Defense of Drug Use* (New York, Tarcher/Putnam, 2003), 13.

20. Ibid., 27.

21. Ibid., 15. Sullum cites Jonathan Shedler and Jack Block, "Adolescent Drug Use and Psychological Health," *American Psychologist* 45, no. 5 (May 1990), 612–30.

22. Ibid., 15.

23. Ronald K. Siegel, *Intoxication: Life in Pursuit of Artificial Paradise* (New York: Pocket Books, 1990), ix–x.

24. Radley Balko, "Overkill: The Rise of Paramilitary Police Raids in America," White Paper (Executive Summary), July 17, 2006, Cato Institute, http://www.cato.org/pub_display.php?pub_id=6476 (accessed February 7, 2010).

25. Radley Balko, "Senseless Overkill," FoxNews.com, March 12, 2008, http://www.foxnews.com/story/0,2933,336850,00.html (accessed February 7, 1020).

26. "Law Enforcement: Goose Creek Agrees to Pay Up, Change Ways in Settlement of Notorious High School Drug Raid Case,"

StoptheDrugWar.org, July 14, 2006,
http://stopthedrugwar.org/chronicle/444/goose-creek-drug-raid-settlement.shtml (accessed February 7, 2010).

27. "'No-Knock' Drug Raids Challenged After Shooting of Elderly Woman," JoinTogether.org, December 1, 2006, http://www.join-together.org/news/headlines/inthenews/2006/no-knock-drug-raids.html (accessed February 7, 2010).

28. Radley Balko, "Kathryn Johnston: A Year Later," Reason.com, November 23, 2007, http://reason.com/archives/2007/11/23/kathryn-johnston-a-year-later (accessed February 7, 2010).

29. Dave Kopel and Mike Krause, "License to Kill: The (drug) war on civilians in Peru," National Review Online, August 16, 2001, http://www.nationalreview.com/kopel/kopel081601.shtml (accessed February 7, 2010).

30. Ibid.

31. Ibid.

32. Fatema Gunja, "The Social Costs of a Moral Agenda," in *The New Prohibition: Voices of Dissent Challenge the Drug War*, ed. Sheriff Bill Masters (St. Louis: Accurate Press, 2004), 103.

33. Ed Godfrey, "Drug Sentencing Questioned," *Daily Oklahoman*, December 7, 1992, http://www.newsok.com.

34. "Marijuana Arrests for Year 2006 — 829,625 Tops Record High . . . Nearly 6 Percent Increase Over 2005," NORML, September 24, 2007, http://norml.org/index.cfm?Group_ID=7370 (accessed March 11, 2010).

35. Russ Belville, NORML Stash, "872,721 marijuana arrests in 2007, up 5.2% from 2006," NORML Blog, September 15, 2008, http://blog.norml.org/2008/09/15/872721-marijuana-arrests-in-2007-up-52-from-2006/ (accessed March 11, 2010).

36. Stephen W. Dillon, "It's Not Your Parents' Prohibition," welcome address to 37th annual NORML conference, October 17–18, 2008, NORML Blog, November 10, 2008, http://blog.norml.org/2008/11/10/opening-remarks-at-norml-2008-norml-board-chair-stephen-dillon-esq/ (accessed March 11, 2010). My 21 million

figure is based on a NORML estimate that as of October 10, 2008, 20 million people had been arrested for violation of marijuana laws, combined with the 2008 Federal Bureau of Investigation arrest figure of 847,864, or 2,323 per day. There are no government statistics on the *total* number of arrests. This is a NORML estimate.

37. Walter Cronkite, "Mandated Injustice," *Alva Review-Courier*, August 8, 2004.

38. John L. Kane, "Policy Is Not a Synonym for Justice," in *The New Prohibition: Voices of Dissent Challenge the Drug War*, ed. Sheriff Bill Masters (St. Louis: Accurate Press, 2004), 49.

39. "2008 Quality of Life Index," International Living.com, http://www.il-ireland.com/il/qofl2008/ (accessed February 7, 2010).

40. David J. Brown, "Psychedelic Healing?" reproduced from *Scientific American Mind*, December 2007, http://www.sciam.com/article.cfm?id=psychedelic-healing (accessed February 8, 2010). To learn more from the mainstream press about the potential of psychedelics to heal, read "Agony and ecstasy," *Economist*, December 18, 2008. To learn more from an organization dedicated to the study of psychedelics, see the website of the Multidisciplinary Association for Psychedelic Studies, http://www.maps.org.

41. Marc Kaufman, "Worried Pain Doctors Decry Prosecutions," *Washington Post*, December 29, 2003, http://washingtonpost.com/ac2/wp-dyn/A37015-2003Dec28 (accessed February 8, 2010).

42. Zimmer and Morgan, *Marijuana Myths, Marijuana Facts*, 155. Zimmer and Morgan cite A. DiChira and J. F. Galliher, "Dissonance and Contradictions in the Origins of Marihuana Decriminalization," *Law and Society Review* 28, no. 1 (1994), 52.

43. "Albert Knew . . . ," http://deoxy.org/prohib2.htm (accessed February 8, 2010).

44. Milton Friedman and Thomas S. Szasz, *Friedman & Szasz on Liberty and Drugs: Essays on the Free Market and Prohibition*, ed. Arnold S. Trebach and Kevin B. Zeese (Washington, D.C.: Drug Policy Foundation Press, 1992), 70.

45. Jesse Ventura, "Foreword," in *The New Prohibition: Voices of Dissent Challenge the Drug War*, ed. Sheriff Bill Masters (St. Louis: Accurate Press, 2004), vii-viii.

46. Radley Balko, "Tracy Ingle: Another Drug War Outrage," May 7, 2008, "Hit & Run," Reason.com, http://www.reason.com/blog/show/126284.html (accessed February 8, 2010).

47. Associated Press (U.S.), "Jury Convicts After No-Knock Police Search," April 15, 2009, http://www.november.org/thewall/cases/ingle-t/ingle-t.html (accessed February 8, 2010).

48. "Oklahoma Re-Imprisons Paraplegic Jimmy Montgomery on Pot Charge: Family Fears for His Life," NORML Special Bulletin, April 6, 1995; Rob Stewart, "Outrage in Oklahoma: The Jim Montgomery Story," Newsbriefs, *Drug Policy Letter* 26 (Spring 1995), 17. Though this story sometimes reads like fiction, please note that I know this man and can personally verify that this is all true.

49. "Jimmy Montgomery," from Victim Stories in Marijuana Policy Project site, www.mpp.org/victims/jimmy-montgomery.html (accessed February 8, 2010); Rob Stewart, "Outrage in Oklahoma," 17.

50. "Profiles of Injustice," Families Against Mandatory Minimums Foundation, http://famm.org/ProfilesofInjustice/StateProfiles/SheilaDevereuxOklahoma.aspx? (accessed February 13, 2010).

51. Tim Talley, Associated Press, "High female incarceration rate bemoaned by state lawmakers," *Tulsa World*, September 3, 2009, http://www.tulsaworld.com/news/article.aspx?subjectid=12&articleid=20090903_12_0_OKLAHO104819&archive=yes (accessed March 11, 2010).

52. Christopher Hartney, "U.S. Rates of Incarceration: A Global Perspective" (Fact Sheet), National Council on Crime and Delinquency, November 2006, www.nccd-crc.org/nccd/pubs/2006nov_factsheet_incarceration.pdf (accessed March 10, 2010).

53. David Crary, Associated Press, "Drug-Free School Zone Laws Questioned, March 23, 2006, http://www.justicestrategies.net/?q=node/85 (accessed February 8, 2010).

54. Roger McKenzie, "Bar proprietor, bartender arrested on drug charges," *Alva Review-Courier*, February 22, 2007.

55. Alain L. Sanders, Anne Constable, and James Willwerth, "Lifting the Lid on Garbage," *Time*, May 30, 1988, http://www.time.com/time/magazine/article/0,9171,967509,00.html (accessed February 8, 2010).

56. Roger McKenzie, "Garbage leads to arrest of two Alva men on drug charges," *Alva Review-Courier*, January 20, 2008.

57. "Suspected Marijuana User Gunned Down in Home," NORML's *Active Resistance* 3, no.1 (Spring 1995), 1.

58. Pete Guither and Hypatia (guest post), "Using the Drug 'War' to Expand Government Power," April 7, 2006, Unclaimed Territory—by Glenn Greenwald (blog), http://glenngreenwald.blogspot.com/2006/04/using-drug-war-to-expand-government.html (accessed February 8, 2010).

59. "Official ATF swag inscribed: 'Always Think Forfeiture,'" June 10, 2008, http://majikthise.typepad.com/majikthise_/2008/06/official-atf-sw.html (accessed February 8, 2010).

60. Clark Duffe, "Good police work that went awry," At Random, *Oklahoma Gazette*, August 30, 1989.

61. Barbara Mikkelson, "Drug Money," February 19, 2007, Snopes.com, http://www.snopes.com/business/money/cocaine.asp (accessed February 8, 2010).

62. Eric E. Sterling, "A Businessperson's Guide to the Drug Problem," in *The New Prohibition: Voices of Dissent Challenge the Drug War*, ed. Sheriff Bill Masters (St. Louis: Accurate Press, 2004), 72.

63. Ehrenfeld, *Narco Terrorism*, xxi–xxii.

64. "The Links Between Drug Prohibition and Terrorism," Canadian Foundation for Drug Policy, http://www.cfdp.ca/terror.htm (accessed February 8, 2010).

65. Sheldon Richman, "The Drug War and Terrorism," January 2002, Freedom Daily, Future of Freedom Foundation, http://www.fff.org/freedom/fd0201d.asp (accessed February 9, 2010).

66. "Terrorism," Drug Policy Alliance, July 19, 2004, http://www.drugpolicy.org/global/terrorism/ (accessed February 9, 2010).

67. Associated Press, "Drug Agents Accused of Torture," *Daily Oklahoman*, October 26, 1992.

68. Wayne Singleterry, "Lawmen Charged in Plot to Kidnap Suspect," *Daily Oklahoman*, May 19, 1989.

69. Don Mecoy, "Love County Sheriff, Police Officer Bound Over for Trial," *Daily Oklahoman*, May 31, 1989.

70. Clark Duffe, "Some Marietta folk going too far," At Random, *Oklahoma Gazette*, June 7, 1989.

71. James P. Gray, *Why Our Drug Laws Have Failed and What We Can Do About It: A Judicial Indictment of the War on Drugs* (Philadelphia: Temple University Press, 2001), 146. Gray cites Peter Slevin and Caryle Murphy, "Results of D.C. Marijuana Vote Kept Secret Pending Court Action," *Washington Post*, November 4, 1998.

72. Gray, *Why Our Drug Laws Have Failed and What We Can Do About It*, 146. Gray cites editorial, "Marijuana Madness," *Des Moines Register*, November 9, 1998, 6A.

73. Zimmer and Morgan, *Marijuana Myths, Marijuana Facts*, 151.

74. Ron Paul, "A View of the Drug War from Capitol Hill," in *The New Prohibition: Voices of Dissent Challenge the Drug War*, ed. Sheriff Bill Masters (St. Louis: Accurate Press, 2004), 53, 52.

75. Ibid., 54.

76. Alfred Ray Lindesmith, "Traffic in Dope: Medical Problem," *Nation*, April 21, 1956, 339; "Dope: Congress Encourages the Traffic," *Nation*, March 16, 1957, 228.

77. News Makers, *Daily Oklahoman*, May 19, 1989.

78. "Bennett's Bold Suggestion," editorial, *Daily Oklahoman*, June 19, 1989.

79. Brett Zongker, Associated Press, "Police clear name of Md. Mayor after drug raid," August 8, 2008, http://www.foxnews.com

/wires/2008Aug08/0,4670,MarijuanaPackages,00.html (accessed February 9, 2010); "Police Botch Raid on Maryland Mayor's Home," *Marijuana Policy Report* 14, no. 3 (Fall 2008), 10.

80. Paul Armentano, "The Killing of Rachel Hoffman and the Tragedy That Is Pot Prohibition," July 29, 2008, *AlterNet*, http://www.alternet.org/drugreporter/93082/the_killing_of_rache l_hoffman_and_the_tragedy_that_is_pot_prohibition/ (accessed February 7, 2010).

81. Gray, *Why Our Drug Laws Have Failed and What We Can Do About It*, 20. Gray cites Chris Conrad, *Hemp: Lifeline to the Future* (Los Angeles: Creative Xpressions Publications, 1993), 23–27.

82. Ibid., 214.

83. Ibid., 20.

84. Siegel, *Intoxication*, 270.

85. Gray, *Why Our Drug Laws Have Failed and What We Can Do About It*, 23.

86. Herer, *Hemp & The Marijuana Conspiracy*, 22.

87. Ibid.

88. Walsch, *Conversations with God, Book 2*, 137.

89. Herer, *Hemp & The Marijuana Conspiracy*, 26–27.

90. Michael C. Ruppert, *Crossing the Rubicon: The Decline of the American Empire at the End of the Age of Oil* (Gabriola Island, B.C., Canada: New Society, 2004), 58.

91. Ibid., 62–68.

92. Jim Willie CB, "Gold and Currency Report," *Hat Trick Letter* no. 58, January 15, 2009, http://www.goldenjackass.com (accessed February 10, 2010).

93. "Drug War Murders," August 1993, NORML handout; November 21, 1993, conversation with Shepherd's wife.

94. *Living Bible, Revised Standard Version, Today's English Version, New International Version, Jerusalem Bible*, and *New English Bible*, among others. *Phillips* reports 20-gallon jars. The *King James* translation describes the capacity in firkins.

95. Mark 7:15, *The New English Bible with the Apocrypha, The New Testament*, 2nd ed. (New York: Oxford University Press, 1971), 52.

96. *A Course in Miracles—Text*, 29.

97. Robert Thurman, "Living Deeply: The Fate of the Earth," in Marilyn Mandala Schlitz, Cassandra Vieten, and Tina Amorok, *Living Deeply: The Art & Science of Transformation in Everyday Life* (Oakland, CA: New Harbinger, 2007), viii.

98. Ron Epstein, "Buddhist Ideas for Attaining World Peace," introduction, Lectures for the Global Peace Studies Program, San Francisco State University, November 7 and 8, 1988, http://online.sfsu.edu/~rone/Buddhism/BUDDHIST%20IDEAS%20FOR%20ATTAINING%20WORLD%20PEACE.htm (accessed June 3, 2010).

99. Gray, *Why Our Drug Laws Have Failed and What We Can Do About It*, 214.

100. Ibid., 213.

101. David C. Condliffe, "DPF Supports Sentencing Report—Where Were Others?" *Drug Policy Letter* 28 (Spring 1996), 13.

102. *Osborne v. United States*, 385 U.S. 343 (1066), http://www.supreme.justia.com/us/385/323/case.html.

103. Gray, *Why Our Drug Laws Have Failed and What We Can Do About It*, 5.

104. Owen Collins, ed., *Speeches That Changed the World* (Louisville, KY: Westminister John Knox, 1999), 386.

Chapter 9

1. "Give Peace a Number," Index, *Time*, June 18, 2007, 16–17.

2. "Global Peace Index Rankings," *Global Peace Index*, http://visionofhumanity.org/gpi/results/rankings.php (accessed February 15, 2010).

3. Julian Glover, *The Guardian*, November 3, 2006, http://www.guardian.co.uk/frontpage/story/0,,1938433,00.html.

4. Michael Berg, *The Way: Using the Wisdom of Kabbalah for Spir-*

itual Transformation and Fulfillment (Hoboken, NJ: John Wiley & Sons, 2001), 202.

5. Yogananda, *The Second Coming of Christ*, 55.

6. Paramahansa Yogananda, *Inner Peace: How to Be Calmly Active and Actively Calm* (San Rafael, CA: Self-Realization Fellowship, 1999), 3.

7. Mairead Corrigan Maguire, "Gandhi and the Ancient Wisdom of Nonviolence," *Peace Is the Way*, ed. Walter Wink (Maryknoll, NY: Orbis Books, 2000), 161.

8. Haim Harari, "A View from the Eye of the Storm," http://southerncrossreview.org/35/harari.htm (accessed July 3, 2010).

9. Yogananda, *The Second Coming of Christ*, 440.

10. Ibid., 56.

11. Wayne W. Dyer, *Change Your Thoughts—Change Your Life: Living the Wisdom of the Tao* (Carlsbad, CA: Hay House, 2007), 144–46.

12. Haskell, *Journey Beyond Words*, 247.

13. Russell, *Waking Up in Time*, 91.

14. Neale Donald Walsch, *Conversations with God: An Uncommon Dialogue, Book 1* (New York: G. P. Putnam's Sons, 1996), 36.

15. Deepak Chopra, *Peace Is the Way: Bringing War and Violence to an End* (New York: Harmony Books, 2005), 23.

16. *The Urantia Book*, 1098.

17. His Holiness the Dalai Lama, foreword to *Peace Is Every Step: The Path of Mindfulness in Everyday Life*, by Thich Nhat Hanh, ed. Arnold Kotler (New York: Bantam, 1992), vii.

18. Adi Da, *Not-Two Is Peace: The Ordinary People's Way of Global Cooperative Order*, 3rd ed. (Middletown, CA: Dawn Horse, 2009), 49, 51, 52. The Global Cooperation Project can be found at http://globalcooperationproject.org/.

19. Robert Thurman, "Living Deeply: The Fate of the Earth," foreword, in Schlitz et al., *Living Deeply*, viii.

20. Ibid., vii.

21. Ron Epstein, "Buddhist Ideas for Attaining World Peace," Lectures for the Global Peace Studies Program, San Francisco State University (1988), http://online.sfsu.edu/~rone/Buddhism/BUDDHIST%20IDEAS%20FOR%20ATTAINING%20WORLD%2 0PEACE.htm (accessed July 2, 2010).

22. Ibid.

23. Tom Kenyon and Virginia Essene, *The Hathor Material: Messages from an Ascended Civilization* (Santa Clara, CA: Spiritual Education Endeavors, 1996), 1–2.

24. Ibid., 90.

25. Thich Nhat Hanh, *Peace Is Every Step: The Path of Mindfulness in Everyday Life*, ed. Arnold Kotler (New York: Bantam, 1992), 13–14.

26. Walsch, *Conversations with God, Book 3*, 60–61.

27. Jill Bolte Taylor, "Jill Bolte Taylor's stroke of insight," TED, http://www.ted.com/talks/jill_bolte_taylor_s_powerful_stroke_of_insight.html (accessed April 30, 2010).

Selected Bibliography

Adi Da. *Not-Two Is Peace: The Ordinary People's Way of Global Co-operative Order*, 3rd ed. Middletown, CA: Dawn Horse, 2009.

The Arbinger Institute. *The Anatomy of Peace: Resolving the Heart of Conflict*. San Francisco: Berrett-Koehler Publishers, 2006.

Beck, Don Edward, and Christopher Cowan. *Spiral Dynamics: Mastering Values, Leadership and Change*. Malden, MA: Blackwell, 1996.

Bentov, Itzhak. *Stalking the Wild Pendulum: On the Mechanics of Consciousness*. Rochester, VT: Destiny Books, 1988.

Berg, Michael. *The Way: Using the Wisdom of Kabbalah for Spiritual Transformation and Fulfillment*. Hoboken, NJ: John Wiley & Sons, 2001.

Blanton, Brad. *Radical Honesty: How to Transform Your Life by Telling the Truth*. New York: Dell, 1996.

Bonner, William, and Addison Wiggin. *Empire of Debt: The Rise of an Epic Financial Crisis*. Hoboken, NJ: John Wiley & Sons, 2006.

Braden, Gregg. *Beyond Zero Point: The Journey to Compassion*. DVD. Arvada, CO: Gaiam/ConsciousWave, 2001.

Buchanan, Patrick J. *The Great Betrayal: How American Sovereignty and Social Justice Are Being Sacrificed to the Gods of the Global Economy*. Boston: Little, Brown & Co., 1998.

———. *Where the Right Went Wrong: How Neoconservatives Subverted the Reagan Revolution and Hijacked the Bush Presidency*. New York: Thomas Dunne, 2004.

Buckminster Fuller Institute. *The Buckminster Fuller Challenge.* Film. http://challenge.bfi.org/movie (accessed February 5, 2010).

Capra, Fritjof. *The Hidden Connections: Integrating the Biological, Cognitive, and Social Dimensions of Life into a Science of Sustainability.* New York: Doubleday, 2002.

— — —. *The Tao of Physics: An Exploration of the Parallels between Modern Physics and Eastern Mysticism,* 4th ed. Boston: Shambhala, 2000.

— — —. *Uncommon Wisdom: Conversations with Remarkable People.* Simon & Schuster, 1988.

Carter, Rita. *Mapping the Mind.* Berkeley: University of California Press, 1998.

Chopra, Deepak. *Peace Is the Way: Bringing War and Violence to an End.* New York: Harmony Books, 2005.

Collins, Owen, ed. *Speeches That Changed the World.* Louisville, KY: Westminister John Knox, 1999.

A Course in Miracles—Text, 2nd ed. Glen Ellen, CA: Foundation for Inner Peace, 1992.

A Course in Miracles—Workbook for Students, 2nd ed. Glen Ellen, CA: Foundation for Inner Peace, 1992.

Court, Jamie. *Corporateering: How Corporate Power Steals Your Personal Freedom and What You Can Do About It.* New York: Tarcher/Putnam, 2003.

Dobbs, Lou. *Exporting America: Why Corporate Greed Is Shipping American Jobs Overseas.* New York: Warner Business Books, 2004.

Dossey, Larry. *The Extraordinary Healing Power of Ordinary Things: Fourteen Natural Steps to Health and Happiness.* New York: Three Rivers Press, 2006.

Dyer, Wayne W. *Change Your Thoughts—Change Your Life: Living the Wisdom of the Tao.* Carlsbad, CA: Hay House, 2007.

Ehrenfeld, Rachel. *Narco Terrorism: How Governments Around the World Have Used the Drug Trade to Finance and Further Terrorist Activities.* New York: Basic Books, 1990.

Eight Translation New Testament. Wheaton, IL: Tyndale House, 1974.

Friedman, Milton, and Thomas S. Szasz. *Friedman & Szasz on Liberty and Drugs: Essays on the Free Market and Prohibition.* Edited by Arnold S. Trebach and Kevin B. Zeese. Washington, D.C.: Drug Policy Foundation Press, 1992.

Gray, James P. *Why Our Drug Laws Have Failed and What We Can Do About It: A Judicial Indictment of the War on Drugs.* Philadelphia: Temple University Press, 2001.

Gray, Martin. *Sacred Earth: Places of Peace and Power.* New York: Sterling Publishing, 2007.

Grinspoon, Lester, and James B. Bakalar. *Marihuana: The Forbidden Medicine.* New Haven, CT: Yale University Press, 1993.

Harman, Willis. *Global Mind Change: The Promise of the 21st Century,* 2nd ed. San Francisco: Berrett-Koehler Publishers, 1998.

Haskell, Brent. *Journey Beyond Words: A Companion to the Workbook of the Course.* Marina del Rey, CA: DeVorss & Co., 1994.

— — —. *The Other Voice: A Companion to the Text of the Course, Chapters 1–15.* Marina del Rey, CA: DeVorss & Company, 1997.

Hellige, Joseph B. *Hemispheric Asymmetry: What's Right and What's Left.* Cambridge, MA: Harvard University, 2001.

Herer, Jack. *Hemp & The Marijuana Conspiracy: The Emperor Wears No Clothes.* Edited by Chris Conrad, Lynn Osburn, and Judy Osburn. Van Nuys, CA: Hemp Publishing, 1992.

Herrmann, Ned. *The Whole Brain Business Book: Unlocking the Power of Whole Brain Thinking in Organizations and Individuals.* New York: McGraw-Hill, 1996.

His Holiness the Dalai Lama. Foreword to *Peace Is Every Step: The Path of Mindfulness in Everyday Life,* by Thich Nhat Hanh. Edited by Arnold Kotler. New York: Bantam, 1992.

Howard, Pierce J. *The Owner's Manual for the Brain: Everyday Applications from Mind-Brain Research,* 3rd ed. Austin, TX: Bard Press, 2006.

Huffington, Arianna. *Pigs at the Trough: How Corporate Greed and Political Corruption Are Undermining America*. New York: Crown, 2003.

Johnston, David Cay. *Perfectly Legal: The Covert Campaign to Rig Our Tax System to Benefit the Super Rich—and Cheat Everybody Else*. New York: Portfolio, 2003.

Keirsey, David. *Please Understand Me II: Temperament, Character, Intelligence*. Del Mar, CA: Prometheus Nemesis, 1998.

Kelly, Marjorie. *The Divine Right of Capital: Dethroning the Corporate Aristocracy*. San Francisco: Berrett-Koehler Publishers, 2003.

Kenyon, Tom. *Brain States*. Naples, FL: United States Publishing, 1994.

Kenyon, Tom, and Virginia Essene. *The Hathor Material: Messages from an Ascended Civilization*. Santa Clara, CA: Spiritual Education Endeavors, 1996.

King, Godfré Ray. *The "I AM" Discourses by the Ascended Master Saint Germain*. Schaumburg, IL: Saint Germain Press, 1940.

Krugman, Paul. *The Great Unraveling: Losing Our Way in the New Century*. New York: W. W. Norton, 2003.

Lawlor, Robert. *Sacred Geometry: Philosophy and Practice*. London: Thames & Hudson, 1982.

Lipton, Bruce H. *The Biology of Belief: Unleashing the Power of Consciousness, Matter & Miracles*. Santa Rosa, CA: Mountain of Love/Elite, 2005.

———. "The Biology of Perception, the Psychology of Change, Retreat." Lecture and conversation. Breckenridge, CO. August 2007. http://www.spirit2000.com/docs/2007brochure.pdf.

MacLean, Paul D. *The Triune Brain in Evolution: Role in Paleocerebral Functions*. New York: Plenum Press, 1990.

Maguire, Mairead Corrigan. "Gandhi and the Ancient Wisdom of Nonviolence." In *Peace Is the Way*. Edited by Walter Wink. Maryknoll, NY: Orbis Books, 2000.

Martineau, John. *A Little Book of Coincidence in the Solar System*. New York: Walker Publishing, 2001.

Masters, Sheriff Bill, ed. *The New Prohibition: Voices of Dissent Challenge the Drug War* (St. Louis: Accurate Press, 2004).

McTaggart, Lynne. *The Intention Experiment: Using Your Thoughts to Change Your Life and the World.* New York: Free Press, 2007.

Melchizedek, Drunvalo. *The Ancient Secret of the Flower of Life.* 2 vols. Flagstaff, AZ: Light Technology Publishing, 1998.

— — —. *Living in the Heart: How to Enter into the Sacred Space within the Heart.* Flagstaff, AZ: Light Technology Publishing, 2003.

— — —. *2012: The Prophecies from the Heart.* DVD. Santa Monica, CA: Arthouse, 2009.

Metzner, Ralph. *The Unfolding Self: Varieties of Transformative Experience.* Novato, CA: Origin Press, 1998.

Nace, Ted. *Gangs of America: The Rise of Corporate Power and the Disabling of Democracy.* San Francisco: Berrett-Koehler Publishers, 2003.

Newberg, Andrew, and Mark Robert Waldman. *Why We Believe What We Believe: Uncovering Our Biological Need for Meaning, Spirituality, and Truth.* New York: Free Press, 2006.

The New English Bible with the Apocrypha, The New Testament. 2nd ed. New York: Oxford University Press, 1971.

Nithyananda. *You Are God: Discourse on Bhagavad Gita, Chapter 2.* Bangalore: Nithyananda Foundation, 2006.

Ohiyesa. "Native American Tradition: The Ways of the Spirit." In *One: Essential Writings on Nonduality.* Edited by Jerry Katz. Boulder, CO: Sentient Publications, 2007.

Ornstein, Robert. *The Right Mind: Making Sense of the Hemispheres.* New York: Harcourt Brace, 1997.

Ornstein, Robert, and Paul Ehrlich. *New World New Mind: Moving Toward Conscious Evolution.* New York: Doubleday, 1989.

Pert, Candace B. *Molecules of Emotion: Why You Feel the Way You Feel.* New York: Scribner, 2003.

Peterson, Peter G. *Running on Empty: How the Democratic and Republican Parties Are Bankrupting Our Future and What Americans Can Do About It.* New York: Farrar, Straus & Giroux, 2004.

Phillips, Kevin. *Wealth and Democracy: A Political History of the American Rich*. New York: Broadway Books, 2002.

Pink, Daniel H. *A Whole New Mind: Why Right-Brainers Will Rule the Future*. New York: Riverhead Books, 2006.

Ratey, John J. *A User's Guide to the Brain: Perception, Attention, and the Four Theaters of the Brain*. New York: Vintage, 2002.

Renard, Gary R. *The Disappearance of the Universe: Straight Talk About Illusions, Past Lives, Religion, Sex, Politics, and the Miracles of Forgiveness*. Carlsbad, CA: Hay House, 2004.

Ruppert, Michael C. *Crossing the Rubicon: The Decline of the American Empire at the End of the Age of Oil*. Gabriola Island, BC, Canada: New Society, 2004.

Russell, Peter, *Waking Up in Time: Finding Inner Peace in Times of Accelerating Change*. Novato, CA: Origin Press, 1998.

Satinover, Jeffrey. Scene 11, Disk 1, *What the Bleep!? Down the Rabbit Hole*. Quantum ed. DVD. 2004 Captured Light & Lord of the Wind Films; Beverly Hills: Twentieth Century Fox Home Entertainment, 2006.

Schiffer, Fredric. *Of Two Minds: The Revolutionary Science of Dual-Brain Psychology*. New York: Free Press, 1998.

Schlitz, Marilyn Mandala; Vieten, Cassandra; and Amorok, Tina. *Living Deeply: The Art & Science of Transformation in Everyday Life*. Oakland, CA: New Harbinger, 2007.

Schneider, Andrew, and David McCumber. *An Air That Kills: How the Asbestos Poisoning of Libby, Montana, Uncovered a National Scandal*. New York: G. P. Putnam's Sons, 2004.

Schweickart, David. *After Capitalism*. Lanham, MD: Rowan & Littlefield, 2002.

Shultz, Jim. *The Democracy Owners' Manual: A Practical Guide to Changing the World*. New Brunswick: Rutgers University Press, 2002.

Siegel, Ronald K. *Intoxication: Life in Pursuit of Artificial Paradise*. New York: Pocket Books, 1990.

Springer, Sally P., and Georg Deutsch. *Left Brain, Right Brain: Per-*

spectives from Cognitive Neuroscience, 5th ed. New York: W. H. Freeman/Worth, 1998.

Sullum, Jacob. Saying Yes: In Defense of Drug Use. New York: Tarcher/Putnam, 2003.

Jill Bolte Taylor, "Jill Bolte Taylor's stroke of insight." TED. http://www.ted.com/talks/jill_bolte_taylor_s_powerful_stroke_of_ insight.html (accessed April 30, 2010).

— — —. "My Stroke of Insight." http://www.ted.com/speakers/jill_ boltc_taylor.html (accessed February 27, 2010).

Thich Nhat Hanh. Living Buddha, Living Christ. New York: River-head Books, 1995.

— — —. Peace Is Every Step: The Path of Mindfulness in Everyday Life. Edited by Arnold Kotler. New York: Bantam, 1992.

Thomson, Lenore. Personality Type: An Owner's Manual. Boston: Shambhala, 1998.

Three Initiates. The Kybalion, by Three Initiates: The Hermetic Philosophy. Charleston, SC: Forgotten Books, 2008.

Thurman, Robert. "Living Deeply: The Fate of the Earth." Foreword to Living Deeply: The Art & Science of Transformation in Everyday Life, by Marilyn Mandala Schlitz, Cassandra Vieten, and Tina Amorok. Oakland, CA: New Harbinger, 2007.

Tolle, Eckhart. A New Earth: Awakening to Your Life's Purpose. New York: Plume, 2006.

— — —. The Power of Now: A Guide to Spiritual Enlightenment. Novato, CA: New World Library, 1999.

The Urantia Book. Chicago: Urantia Foundation, 1955.

Vos Savant, Marilyn. The Power of Logical Thinking: Easy Lessons in the Art of Reasoning . . . and Hard Facts About Its Absence in Our Lives. New York: St. Martin's Press, 1996.

Walsch, Neale Donald. Communion with God. New York: G. P. Putnam's Sons, 2000.

— — —. Conversations with God: An Uncommon Dialogue, Book 1. New York: G. P. Putnam's Sons, 1996.

———. *Conversations with God: An Uncommon Dialogue, Book 2.* Charlottesville, VA: Hampton Roads, 1997.

———. *Conversations with God: An Uncommon Dialogue, Book 3.* Charlottesville, VA: Hampton Roads, 1998.

———. *Friendship with God: An Uncommon Dialogue.* New York: G. P. Putnam's Sons, 1999.

———. *Home with God: In a Life That Never Ends.* New York: Atria Books, 2006.

———. *The New Revelations: A Conversation with God.* New York: Atria Books, 2002.

———. *Tomorrow's God: Our Greatest Spiritual Challenge.* New York: Atria Books, 2004.

Wilber, Ken. *The Collected Works of Ken Wilber.* Vol. 7, *A Brief History of Everything.* Boston: Shambhala, 2000.

———. *The Integral Vision: A Very Short Introduction to the Revolutionary Integral Approach to Life, God, the Universe, and Everything.* Boston: Shambhala, 2007.

Wink, Walter, ed. *Peace Is the Way: Writings on Nonviolence from the Fellowship of Reconciliation.* Maryknoll, NY: Orbis Books, 2000.

Wonder, Jacquelyn, and Priscilla Donovan. *Whole-Brain Thinking: Working from Both Sides of the Brain to Achieve Peak Job Performance.* New York: William Morrow, 1984.

Yogananda, Paramahansa. *Inner Peace: How to Be Calmly Active and Actively Calm.* San Rafael, CA: Self-Realization Fellowship, 1999.

———. *The Second Coming of Christ: The Resurrection of the Christ Within You.* 2 vols. Los Angeles: Self-Realization Fellowship, 2004.

Zimmer, Lynn, and John P. Morgan. *Marijuana Myths, Marijuana Facts: A Review of the Scientific Evidence.* New York: Lindesmith Center, 1997.

Index